Best Hikes Near
Madison

MICHAEL REAM

FALCONGUIDES

GUILFORD, CONNECTICUT
HELENA, MONTANA

AN IMPRINT OF GLOBE PEQUOT PRESS

FALCONGUIDES®

Copyright © 2012 by Morris Book Publishing, LLC

FalconGuides is an imprint of Globe Pequot Press.
Falcon, FalconGuides, and Outfit Your Mind are registered trademarks of Morris Book Publishing, LLC.

TOPO! Explorer software and SuperQuad source maps courtesy of National Geographic Maps. For information about TOPO! Explorer, TOPO!, and Nat Geo Maps products, go to www.topo.com or www.natgeomaps.com.

All interior photos by Michael Ream.

Project editor: Heather Santiago
Layout artist: Maggie Peterson
Text design: Sheryl P. Kober
Maps by Mapping Specialists Ltd. © Morris Book Publishing, LLC

Library of Congress Cataloging-in-Publication Data is available on file.

ISBN 978-0-7627-7137-0

Printed in the United States of America

10 9 8 7 6 5 4 3 2 1

Contents

Overview

Map Labels

Cities and Towns:
West Bend, Waukesha, Burlington, Elkhorn, Oconomowoc, Johnson Creek, Watertown, Ft. Atkinson, Whitewater, Beaver Dam, Columbus, Janesville, Brodhead, Stoughton, Sun Prairie, DeForest, Poynette, Portage, Madison, Middleton, Waunakee, Mount Horeb, New Glarus, Monroe, Baraboo, Prairie du Sac, Sauk City, Reedsburg, Spring Green, Richland Center, Dodgeville, Belmont

Parks and Natural Areas:
KETTLE MORAINE STATE FOREST, HORICON NWR, KETTLE MORAINE STATE FOREST, Rock River, Beaver Dam Lake, Lake Koshkonong, Lake Mendota, Lake Wisconsin, Wisconsin River, Pine River, Lake Geneva

Scale:
Kilometers 0 20
Miles 0 20

N

GIFT RECEIPT

Barnes & Noble Booksellers #2944
2500 N. Mayfair Road
Wauwatosa, WI 53226
414-475-6070

TR:2944 REG:004 TRN:8176 CSHR:Charles B

est Hikes Near Madison
 9780762771370   T1
 (1 @ RL.HT)   RL.HT G

Thanks for shopping at
Barnes & Noble

)1.29B   12/18/2012 11:45AM

CUSTOMER COPY

Return Policy

<u>With a sales receipt or Barnes & Noble.com packing slip,</u> a full refund in the original form of payment will be issued from any Barnes & Noble Booksellers store for returns of undamaged NOOKs, new and unread books, and unopened and undamaged music CDs, DVDs, and audio books made within 14 days of purchase from a Barnes & Noble Booksellers store or Barnes & Noble.com with the below exceptions:

A store credit for the purchase price will be issued (i) for purchases made by check less than 7 days prior to the date of return, (ii) when a gift receipt is presented within 60 days of purchase, (iii) for textbooks, or (iv) for products purchased at Barnes & Noble College bookstores that are listed for sale in the Barnes & Noble Booksellers inventory management system.

Opened music CDs/DVDs/audio books may not be returned, and can be exchanged only for the same title and only if defective. NOOKs purchased from other retailers or sellers are returnable only to the retailer or seller from which they are purchased, pursuant to such retailer's or seller's return policy. Magazines, newspapers, eBooks, digital downloads, and used books are not returnable or exchangeable. Defective NOOKs may be exchanged at the store in accordance with the applicable warranty.

Returns or exchanges will not be permitted (i) after 14 days or without receipt or (ii) for product not carried by Barnes & Noble or Barnes & Noble.com.

Policy on receipt may appear in two sections.

Acknowledgments

Thanks are due to all those who helped me find my way to and along the many excellent hikes in this book. The staffs of the City of Madison Parks and Dane County Parks were very helpful in providing maps and information on the multitude of trails found in parks sprinkled through both city and countryside. The City of Madison Traffic Engineering Division gave me the heads-up on the miles of paved path winding through the city, some of which I would not have known about otherwise. The Wisconsin Department of Natural Resources was a treasure trove of information on what to see at state parks throughout southern Wisconsin, with park rangers at Devil's Lake, New Glarus Woods, and Governor Dodge State Parks especially helpful in pointing out sights to look for along their trails. Employees at these agencies all took time to answer questions and point me in the direction of some trails I had not initially considered, giving me the opportunity to experience some great hikes. Volunteers on many trails did the same, sharing their knowledge from cumulative years of experience.

I am indebted to Brad Herrick, ecologist at the University of Wisconsin Arboretum, for filling me in on the flora and fauna found in the diverse ecosystem that is the arboretum. Eric Sherman and the rest of the staff at the Ice Age Trail Alliance helped break down the long stretches of this national scenic trail into more manageable segments. Adam, Alexa, and the rest of the staff at Fontana Sports in Madison passed on tips about the gear and knowledge I might need for some of the trickier trails that made it into this book. Finally, thanks to all the helpful hikers I met along the trails, who shared their own personal knowledge of hikes and what to look for along the path. Their insights contributed greatly to enhancing the hikes with some hidden treasures and sights off the beaten path.

Introduction

Madison is one of the great hiking towns in one of the great hiking states. A combination of scenic geologic features and a healthy stewardship for the natural world have led to a plethora of great hiking trails.

Perched at the western edge of a landscape defined by ancient glaciers, Madison is the second largest city in Wisconsin. The state capital and home to the flagship campus of the University of Wisconsin, Madison's growing population of half a million in the city and surrounding area continues to grow, with many residents drawn to "Mad Town" by the abundant outdoor opportunities.

Numerous hiking and cycling trails offer a variety of terrain and natural features, including an assortment of trees and wildlife. Madison has a long history of conservation, reflected in an extensive system of parks and trails that snake through the city and into surrounding communities, providing an easy escape from the urban bustle. On these trails you'll feel as if you've left civilization behind, other than the occasional sighting of the dome of the state capitol.

In the center of the city, near the university, Picnic Point takes hikers onto a narrow, sylvan spit of land jutting out into one of the five lakes that define the layout of Madison and surrounding areas. The hike has excellent views of the downtown

Flowers and native grasses line a path on the Curtis Prairie trail.

skyline and a trek through a range of landscapes, including prairie and woodland. A short drive away, the university's large arboretum spreads across a wide sweep of diverse topography.

Several parks sprinkled throughout the city honor local residents notable for conservation, while the Southwest Path, popular with Madison's legions of cyclists, runs from the university football stadium to the edge of the city, where it hooks up with the Capital City State Trail, which gives hikers a choice of heading west into open countryside or east through wetlands and past old farms.

Beyond the city limits hiking options extend in all directions, with numerous parks and other hiking areas found among the vast sweep of farmland. Heading north past the high sandstone bluffs above the Wisconsin River, including a hike with breathtaking views at Gibraltar Rock State Natural Area, hikers are eventually brought to Devil's Lake State Park, perhaps the crown jewel of the Wisconsin state park system. Here a pair of 500-foot bluffs soar over a picture-perfect lake, their slopes covered with quartzite boulders dating back hundreds of millions of years. Sandy soil and hardwood oak forest ring agricultural cropland in many rural areas.

To the west of Madison are hikes running through the Driftless Area, untouched by the glaciers that ground to a halt just outside the city, and thus have a more rugged landscape of steep ridges and deep valleys. It is a landscape of rolling prairie and savanna, with streams cutting through steep ridges and deep valleys. Numerous mounds are studded across the land. Governor Dodge State Park and Blue Mound State Park are two of the showpieces of the Driftless Area, with the former featuring a cave and trail that wind along the top of a ridge.

By contrast, the landscape at Kettle Moraine State Forest, east of Madison and just west of Milwaukee, bears the mark of the glaciers, especially in the shallow depressions and long ridges that give the forest its name. Kettle Moraine is another gem of a hiking area, with a wide selection of paths that will suit everyone from novices to more experienced trail walkers.

NATURAL AND HUMAN HISTORY

Madison's topography was defined by a glacier of the last ice age, dubbed the Wisconsin Glacial Episode, which flowed across the northern United States about 25,000 years ago. The last glacier reached its southernmost extent in Wisconsin about 15,000 years ago before it receded to the north. As a result, the effects of glaciation are more pronounced and visible in Wisconsin than perhaps anywhere else.

The ice sheet rolled over a wide swath of Wisconsin, carrying huge amounts of rock and depositing it on the landscape before stopping just a few miles southwest of Madison. The line of the last glacier can be seen in the route of the Ice Age Trail, which snakes across the state in a lazy S-curve.

Reminders of the last glacier are seen in geologic features like kettles (depressions that often form small lakes), and moraines (low-lying ridges). Other remnants of glacial debris include small hills known as drumlins, including the rise the state capitol sits upon.

The glaciers laid the foundation for larger lakes as well, including the series of lakes along the Yahara River that define Madison: From north to south, they are Mendota, Monona, Waubesa, and Kegonsa, with Mendota and Monona bracketing the isthmus that is the site of downtown.

To the west of the isthmus is the university campus, while to the south is the university arboretum, which is located next to Lake Wingra, a smaller lake connected to the Yahara River chain by Wingra Creek, which flows along a city hiking trail before emptying into Lake Monona at Olin Park and Turville Park. The Yahara also flows by Cherokee Marsh and Token Creek, where hiking trails cut through the low-lying wetlands.

The other great legacy of the glaciers was the creation of rich agricultural land that allowed for the growth of human settlements after the ice age ended. Human habitation of the area actually began with the arrival of those who had migrated across the Bering Strait on the land bridge created thousands of years earlier during an earlier part of the Wisconsin Glacial Episode. Prior to developing farming techniques, these early inhabitants hunted mastodon and bison across the rugged landscape, and eventually moved to growing corn, potatoes, squash, and other crops.

Early European settlement following the exploration of southern Wisconsin by French fur traders in the 1700s marked the beginning of significant changes to the landscape with the introduction of large-scale farming. Large swaths of prairie began to vanish as settlers extinguished prairie fires and farmed the land, thus allowing trees to grow and forests to cover the land. More dramatic changes came as farmers razed landforms built by Paleo-Indians, including numerous earthen mounds used for ceremonial and other purposes. Fortunately, many reminders of early settlement have been preserved and studied by archeologists, most notably at Azatlan State Park, located about halfway between Madison and Milwaukee.

Tensions between Native Americans and the United States government over efforts to settle the frontier led to the Black Hawk War, named for a Native American chief. The war culminated in 1832 with the Battle of Wisconsin Heights, at the Wisconsin River near present-day Sauk City north of Madison. Today the site of the battle is home to a network of hiking trails as well as a historic marker that gives a short account of the war.

Madison continued to grow, becoming home to both the state capitol and the university in the mid-1800s. Beginning in the 1890s and continuing into the early years of the twentieth century, it was one of many communities across the United States where residents became interested in creating a more attractive and livable city. The city eventually hired noted landscape architect John Nolen, who worked with conservation-minded residents like Edward Owen, a professor at the university, and John Olin, a leader in creating Madison's parks, to manage and develop open spaces for aesthetics and recreation.

Today, Madison has an impressive number of conservation parks dedicated to preserving the natural environment, including one on the site of Owen's farm on the west side of the city. In addition, the University of Wisconsin Arboretum is a true treasure in this city of trails winding through well-preserved landscapes of prairie, wetland, and woods The arboretum was laid out with the assistance of legendary conservationist and ecologist Aldo Leopold, who helped create the natural landscapes based on a vision of a pre-settlement landscape. Leopold's name is also bestowed on a nature trail area on Madison's east side, adjacent to another nature area named after conservationist Edna Taylor.

A staircase leading to great views at Natural Bridge State Park.

FLORA AND FAUNA

In the countryside surrounding Madison, and even in more developed areas, you can find a rich variety of plant and animal life. City and suburban parks are home to a wealth of birds, from common varieties like robins and sparrows to a whole slew of woodpeckers that make ample use of the vast sweep of woodlands, including the red-headed and larger pileated variety. Flocks of wild turkeys may be startled by hikers along the trails; if you spot some look quickly, because they move fast.

Birds of prey soar overhead in most rural areas, with Cooper's hawk and broadwinged hawk two of the more commonly seen raptors. Turkey vultures make a stop at Devil's Lake State Park during their annual fall migration. There are huge numbers gliding lazily over the long lake and roosting in trees on the massive bluffs that define the park.

The wide network of lakes, ponds, creeks, and rivers in and around Madison is habitat for plenty of waterfowl, including egrets and herons as well as the more common ducks and Canada geese. Sandhill cranes are fairly common as well; with just a little patience you can spot whole families of the long-legged, red-capped birds alongside area wetlands.

Other wildlife include deer, which are often seen in the woods, and muskrat, mink, frogs, and snakes in the wetlands. Some areas such as Rowan Creek are known for their aquatic life, including trout and other fish.

You may spot snakes on your hikes, although most are harmless to humans. However, Wisconsin is home to two venomous rattlesnakes: the timber rattler and the eastern massasauga. These snakes have been spotted occasionally in the southern part of the state, especially on rocky bluffs. Steer clear and report any sightings to state parks employees or local trail managers.

Trees are everywhere you look, and range from majestic oaks and thick stands of pine and other evergreens in the countryside, to elms along city streets. Shagbark hickory, aspen, and birch also turn up frequently along hiking trails. Wildflowers are abundant in both spring and fall, with plenty of bluestem, coneflowers, and black-eyed susans cropping up in fields along paths. Large clumps of goldenrod are found in the many restored stretches of prairie, as are other prairie flora like joe-pye weed and golden alexander.

WEATHER

Madison can be a paradise from spring through fall, with clear skies and pleasant temperatures that make for ideal hiking conditions.

There are lots of warm sunny days in the summer months, tempered slightly by rainfall that is heaviest in June, as well as the occasional thunderstorm through August. While summer is often mild, temperatures may creep into the 90s, the heat

> *For up-to-date information on fall leaf colors statewide, check out the Fall Color Report from the state's department of tourism at: www.travelwisconsin.com/fallcolor_report.aspx.*

is mitigated somewhat by breezes blowing off the lakes. Humidity can get high in summer as well, yet another reason to have plenty of water on the trails.

Autumn brings a bit of Indian summer through October but is more typically Midwestern overall, with cooler temperatures and changing leaves through November, when they fall from the trees. There is often a tease of snow just before or around Thanksgiving and then in December, but the truly big blizzards usually don't hit until January. It's not uncommon for there to be more than a foot of snow as well as wind chills well below zero. If you hit the trails, bring your skis or snowshoes.

After the long winter, everyone is ready for the thaw, which may come as early as February. But that's often just a tempting interlude before one last punch of winter, including more snow, which is frequently over for good by mid-March. Flowers bloom in April, sometimes poking through the snow, to go with the wishy-washy weather, which can see the mercury dropping down close to freezing and then shooting up to shirtsleeve temperatures within 24 hours.

In fact, weather conditions can change rather abruptly throughout the year, with the early springlike days in February followed by snowstorms that may hit the city well into April and even May. Watch the forecast and be prepared for any possible sudden shifts before you set out on a hike.

WILDERNESS RESTRICTIONS AND REGULATIONS

The hikes in this book are on trails maintained by a variety of local and state agencies and organizations. Trail regulations vary, so take note of the details in each trail listing. Most of the urban trails and many rural trails are free, but some do charge hikers. Some trails accept donations in order to assist with the maintenance of the trail; check and see if there is a place for such donations at the trailhead.

Dogs are permitted on some trails but not others. Some trails allow only hikers whereas others are multiuse, permitting bikers, horseback riders, and other users. Some trails close at different times of the year, including unforeseen closings due to weather or other issues. Several listed trails are on land that is used for hunting for parts of the year. Contact the listed agency in charge for more details about any special considerations you should take during hunting season(s).

It's a good idea in general to contact the agency in charge ahead of time if you have any questions or concerns, as most trails do not have staff on location. Calling ahead also helps you get an idea if a trail is going to be heavily trafficked the day you plan to hike. Nothing is worse than planning for a wilderness hiking getaway, arriving at the trail, and discovering it overrun with large, noisy school groups.

SAFETY AND PREPARATION

Hiking is a great way to see a bit of nature, get some exercise, and in general have a pleasant day in the great outdoors. However, before you hit the trail it's a good idea to take the time to make sure you are prepared. Just a little preparation can mean the difference between a good hike and one that turns into a hassle, or worse.

> **Green Tip:**
> *As you take advantage of the spectacular scenery throughout southern Wisconsin, remember that our planet is very dear, very special, and very fragile. All of us should do everything we can to keep it clean, beautiful, and healthy, including following the Green Tips you'll find throughout this book, which look just like this one.*

A bridge crosses a creek near the Browntown-Cadiz Springs trail's two lakes.

Some of the biggest hazards when hiking in southern Wisconsin are sunburn, ticks, and mosquitoes. Also, poison ivy grows along many of the rural trails listed in the book. Take time to put on sunscreen and bug repellent, and learn to identify poison ivy so you can spot it on the trail. Remember: "Leaves of three, let it be." (This is also a good reason not to veer off the trail and into the woods.) Tick bites can be painful and can carry diseases. After a hike check yourself for ticks, and learn how to properly remove the little critters as well as identify the symptoms of Lyme and other diseases carried by some ticks.

Good hiking shoes are a must on wilderness trails and are recommended for urban trails as well. It's also not a bad idea to invest in some decent hiking socks; there are different kinds depending on the weather you'll be hiking in. Choose comfortable clothing appropriate for the season; loose-fitting, "breathable" clothes for summer and warmer clothes for winter. Synthetic fabrics generally provide much better water protection than cotton. In addition, you'll want a wide-brimmed hat for summer and a warm hat for winter. The sun can fry your head in minutes, and much of the body's heat escapes through an uncovered head. Sunglasses help on bright and sunny days.

Put together a small backpack of hiking essentials. You may not use all of this stuff, especially if you're not hiking in a wilderness area, but it's worth having just in case:

- **Water.** Really the most important item. Dehydration is a greater risk when hiking than many people realize. Symptoms include fatigue, headache, and general confusion. Bring plenty of water and drink it regularly. Ideally, carry your water in more than one bottle, so that if you lose one you still have some water (the water in many streams and creeks is not safe for drinking). Fill up your water bottles before you start your hike as many trailheads do not have water sources.

- **Food.** Carry at least some snack items (not junk food!), such as granola bars or trail mix. Sometimes a hike takes much longer than you anticipated and it's good to have some food for energy.

- **Trail map.** An absolute necessity. Many trails are not well-marked, and there are often other "unofficial" trails that connect with the trail you are on, but will only get you lost if you take them. It's also not a bad idea to learn how to use a compass with a map.

- **Clothes.** See above. Bring some extra clothes in case the ones you're wearing get too wet. Don't go overboard. Usually an extra shirt and pair of socks is sufficient. Rain gear is another good item to have, particularly during rainy season or if even a slight chance of rain is forecast. Get a rain jacket or pullover and rain pants you can wear over your hiking pants. Also get a rain cover for your pack if it's not waterproof.

- **Cell phone.** Phones are more common on trails these days but remember, service is often not available in remote rural areas. Use it only for genuine emergencies, and please, please turn if off or put it on vibrate. Remember, you came hiking to get into a peaceful, natural setting without annoying cell phone rings!

- **Bug repellent and sunscreen.** These prevent a lot of aggravation. Use them.

- **Watch.** You don't want to get stuck in a rural state park after it closes for the evening and they shut the gate, do you?

> *Madison has several well-equipped outdoor stores if you need to stock up on outdoor gear. Two of the largest are: REI, 7483 West Towne Way; (608) 833-6680; www.rei.com/stores/48*
>
> *Fontana Sports, 216 North Henry St. (Downtown), (608) 257-5043 or (800) 257-7666; check website for other locations: www.fontanasports.com*

The Pelishek-Tiffany Nature Trail moves through native grasses.

- **Money.** For hiking trails that require permits, including those that require a separate permit for bringing a dog onto the trail. It's best to have cash in small bills, as many trails have only self-pay kiosks for obtaining a permit.

- And of course, this book.

To make yourself the complete hiker, consider bringing the following as well. These items are not really necessities, but you may find a use for them:

- GPS
- Camera
- Pocketknife
- Walking stick
- Binoculars
- Field guides
- Journal and pen

LEAVE NO TRACE

Trails are heavily used during the warmer months. We, as trail users and advocates, must be especially vigilant to make sure our passage leaves no lasting mark. For more information about Leave No Trace principles, visit www.lnt.org.

Here are some basic guidelines for preserving trails in the region:

- Pack out all your own trash, including biodegradable items like orange peels. You might also pack out garbage left by less-considerate hikers.

- Avoid damaging trailside soils and plants by remaining on the established route. Social trails created by hikers, cyclists, and off-road vehicles are a plague on area parklands, contributing to erosion problems and creating unsightly scars on the landscape. Don't cut switchbacks, which can promote erosion.

- Don't approach or feed any wild creatures; the squirrel eyeing your snack food is best able to survive if it remains self-reliant.

- Don't pick wildflowers or gather rocks, antlers, feathers, and other treasures along the trail. Removing these items will only take away from the next hiker's experience.

- Be courteous by not making loud noises while hiking.

- Many of these trails are multiuse, which means you'll share them with other hikers, trail runners, mountain bikers, and equestrians. Familiarize yourself with the proper trail etiquette, yielding the trail when appropriate.

- Use outhouses at trailheads or along the trail.

How to Use This Guide

This guide is designed to be simple and easy to use. Each hike is described with a map and summary information that provide the trail's vital statistics including length, difficulty, fees and permits, park hours, canine compatibility, and trail contacts. Directions to the trailhead are also provided, along with a general description of what you'll see along the way. A detailed route finder (Miles and Directions) sets forth mileages between significant landmarks along the trail.

HOW THE HIKES WERE CHOSEN

This guide describes trails that are accessible to every hiker, whether visiting from out of town or a local resident. The hikes are no longer than 12 miles round-trip, and most are considerably shorter. They range in difficulty from flat excursions perfect for a family outing to more challenging treks that include moderate climbs. While these trails are among the best, keep in mind that nearby trails, sometimes in the same park or sometimes in a neighboring open space, may offer options better suited to your needs. I've selected hikes throughout southern Wisconsin, with plenty of hikes in Madison and surrounding suburbs, as well as popular parks and forests within an hour of the city, including several around the Wisconsin Dells/Baraboo area.

SELECTING A HIKE

Hike difficulty is determined this way:
- **Easy** hikes are generally short and flat, taking no longer than an hour to complete.
- **Moderate** hikes involve increased distance and relatively mild changes in elevation, and will take one to two hours to complete.
- **More challenging** hikes feature some steep stretches, greater distances, and generally take longer than two hours to complete.

Keep in mind that what you think is easy is entirely dependent on your level of fitness and the adequacy of your gear (primarily shoes). Use the trail's length as a gauge of its relative difficulty. Even if climbing is involved it won't be bad if the hike is less than 1 mile long. If you are hiking with a group, select a hike that's appropriate for the least fit and prepared in your party.

Approximate hiking times are based on the assumption that on flat ground, most walkers average 2 miles per hour. Adjust that rate by the steepness of the terrain and your level of fitness (subtract time if you're an aerobic animal and add time if you're hiking with kids), and you have a ballpark estimate of hiking duration. Be sure to add more time if you plan to picnic or take part in other activities like bird watching or photography.

Trail Finder

Hike No.	Hike Name	Best Hikes with Children	Best Hikes for Great Views	Best Hikes for Nature Lovers	Best Hikes through Urban Landscapes	Best Hikes for History Buffs	Best Hikes for Geology Lovers	Best Hikes for Lake Lovers
1	Curtis Prairie			•				
2	Gallistel Woods			•				
3	Owen Conservation Park			•				
4	Cherokee Marsh South		•	•				•
5	Cherokee Marsh North		•	•				•
6	Turville Point Conservation Park	•		•				•
7	Edna Taylor Conservation Park	•		•				
8	Southwest Commuter Path				•			
9	Capital City State Trail				•			
10	Nine Springs E-Way			•				
11	Lagoons Trail	•						
12	Wingra Creek Trail	•			•			
13	Picnic Point	•	•	•			•	•
14	Pheasant Branch Conservancy		•	•			•	
15	Token Creek Park		•					
16	Pope Farm Park	•					•	
17	Indian Lake County Park Trail						•	•
18	White Oak Nature Trail and Prairie Trail						•	•
19	Rowan Creek Trail			•				
20	Swan Lake Trail		•	•				
21	Gibraltar Rock		•				•	
22	Natural Bridge State park						•	

Trail Finder

Hike No.	Hike Name	Best Hikes with Children	Best Hikes for Great Views	Best Hikes for Nature Lovers	Best Hikes through Urban Landscapes	Best Hikes for History Buffs	Best Hikes for Geology Lovers	Best Hikes for Lake Lovers
23	Devil's Lake: West Bluff		●			●	●	●
24	Devil's Lake: East Bluff		●			●	●	●
25	Pewit's Nest						●	
26	Black Hawk Unit					●		
27	Donald Park			●				
28	Browntown–Cadiz Springs		●	●				●
29	New Glarus Woods State Park	●				●		
30	Badger State Trail		●					
31	Pine Cliff and Lakeview Trails		●					●
32	Meadow Valley and Cave Trails		●			●		
33	Stewart County Park	●	●			●		●
34	Blue Mound State Park		●					
35	Cam-Rock Park	●		●				
36	Aztalan Trail	●				●		
37	Pelishek-Tiffany Nature Trail	●		●		●		
38	Magnolia Bluff County Park		●				●	
39	Glacial Drumlin State Trail						●	
40	Emma Carlin Trail		●				●	
41	Nordic Trail		●				●	
42	Scuppernong Trail		●				●	
43	Kettle View Trail		●				●	

Map Legend

Transportation

- 90 Interstate Highway
- 18 U.S. Highway
- 19 State Highway
- ZZ Local Road
- ┣━━━━┫ Railroad Tracks

Trails

- ▬▬▬▬ Featured Trail
- ------ Trail
- ——— Paved Trail
- → Direction of Travel

Water Features

- Body of Water
- Marsh/Swamp
- River/Creek
- Spring

Land Management

- Local/State Park/Wildlife Refuge
- Wildlife Area

Symbols

- ⊨ Bench
- ≤ Boat Launch
- ▥▥▥▥ Boardwalk/Steps
- ⎵ Bridge
- ▲ Campground
- ⌒ Cave
- ⬤ Gate
- 🅿 Parking
- ⊞ Picnic Area
- ■ Point of Interest/Structure
- 👤 Ranger Station
- 🚻 Restroom
- ○ Town
- ① Trailhead
- ⊢━━┤ Tunnel
- ⊠ Viewpoint/Overlook
- ❓ Visitor/Information Center

A Capital City: Madison and Surrounding Towns

The path passes by a picturesque footbridge.

These hikes encompass a wide selection of trails in the Madison area, from paved paths cutting across the city, to suburban nature preserves and sprawling county parks, then into outlying countryside, where you'll be reminded of the prairie that once covered southern Wisconsin like a great sea of grass.

Included among the hikes is an arboretum rich with plant life, and city parks that are bucolic swaths of nature in the middle of urban development. Throughout Madison, you will also spot evidence of the glaciers that shaped the local topography. Other hikes take you through marshy landscapes that are gathering places for an array of waterfowl.

These hikes can get you really up close and personal with nature, but will never take you too far from civilization: You may be sloshing through the mud that defines a path during the day, then be enjoying modern comforts at the heart of it all near the University of Wisconsin campus that evening.

Curtis Prairie

The oldest restored prairie in the world, this is the most accessible of the five prairies and savannas in the University of Wisconsin Arboretum, which contains re-created native landscapes including prairie, savanna, forest, and wetlands spread out over 1,200 acres. Land for the arboretum was acquired by the university in the 1930s and developed by conservationists that included wildlife ecologist and longtime University of Wisconsin professor Aldo Leopold, who envisioned a reconstructed landscape of Wisconsin as it appeared pre-European settlement in the 1830s.

The Civilian Conservation Corps played a pivotal role in the early development of the arboretum. Crews from the CCC provided labor that built the initial layout of the arboretum and established the different ecological communities on its grounds.

More than 300 species of native plants are found in the arboretum, including many wildflowers. The rich tapestry of ecological communities also includes a wide spectrum of animal life, including birds, insects, amphibians, and reptiles, as well as mammals like coyote, rabbit, deer, skunk, woodchuck, vole, mole, mouse, shrew, raccoon, opossum, and mink. The arboretum has a visitor center with exhibits on the natural history of the area as well as numerous activities for visitors.

Start: From trailhead across road from Curtis parking area
Distance: 1.3-mile lollipop
Hiking time: About 1 hour
Difficulty: Moderate; short distance, but narrow path winds through tall grasses
Trail surface: Dirt, gravel
Best seasons: Spring through fall
Other trail users: None; separate trails available for bikers (strictly enforced)
Canine compatibility: No dogs permitted
Land status: University nature preserve
Fees and permits: None
Schedule: Trails and visitor center parking lot daily, 7 a.m. to 10 p.m.; other arboretum parking lots open sunrise to sunset; visitor center open weekdays, 9:30 a.m. to 4 p.m.; weekends, 12:30 to 4 p.m.
Maps: USGS Madison West, WI; trail maps available at visitor center and in wooden boxes at parking area
Trail contact: UW–Madison Arboretum, 1207 Seminole Hwy., Madison, WI 53711; (608) 263-7888; www.uwarboretum.org

Special considerations: Good sturdy hiking shoes and long pants are a must on this trail. Much of the trail is hemmed in by prairie grass and other plant life that includes sticky burrs, and there's a section that runs along boards through swampy terrain.

Be watchful of cameras and other valuables while on this hike as well; it's easy to drop and lose items in the thick plant cover.

Other: Restrooms are available in the arboretum's visitor center. Bicycles are allowed only on paved roads in the arboretum.

Finding the trailhead: From downtown Madison, follow US 151 south—be aware as it makes several twists and turns—to Beltline Highway (US 12/18), about 3 miles. Take Beltline Highway west about 2.5 miles and take exit 258A (Seminole Highway). Turn right after exiting, heading north on Seminole Highway, and drive 0.4 mile to arboretum entrance. Turn right into arboretum and drive 0.4 mile on Arboretum Drive to the parking lot for Curtis Prairie on the left. (The arboretum's visitor center is another 0.3 mile down Arboretum Drive.) Park and walk across Arboretum Drive to begin the hike.
GPS: N43 02.294' / W89 26.078'

THE HIKE

As you begin the hike, moving on the path parallel to the entrance road through the arboretum, note the thick stalks of tallgrass, including big bluestem and Indian grasses, clustered in thick bunches along the narrow path, which gets a little muddy even on clear days. Chipmunks scuttle into the surrounding thicket of grass, which is dotted with purple thistle and other wildflowers.

The grasses and sunflowers will arch over your head in some places, especially in the summer and fall, when they can reach up to 10 feet high. Dragonflies and butterflies flit through the air—over 50 species of butterflies have been observed on the prairie, or about half of all species of butterflies found in Wisconsin—while grasshoppers spring along the ground. Due to its small size the prairie is not home to grassland birds, but there are birds that nest here, especially the seed-eating goldfinch, the male species of which has a bright yellow body (which becomes dull olive in winter) with black wings. Goldfinches gather thistledown to line their nests in the summer.

Acorns from oak trees, mainly bur oak, are strewn across the path. You may also see red and white oaks. Parts of the prairie are periodically restored; you may see areas under the restoration during a hike. Researchers have also conducted numerous experiments, including controlled burns, as part of efforts to best understand the life cycle and growing conditions of a prairie.

Turning away from the road and moving into the heart of the prairie, keep an eye out for purple aster and goldenrod among the grasses, which may still be over your head. Milkweed also grows in the arboretum's prairies and is home to both the large and small milkweed bugs, which are both orange and black. From late August through September and October, you may observe large colonies of these bugs feasting on milkweed plants, using their sharp proboscis to pierce the milkweed's green seed pod and then ingesting the seeds of the plant.

The arboretum offers a variety of one-day classes on everything from Wisconsin archeology to the habits of local wildlife to outdoor and naturalist art. A fee is charged for classes. Contact the arboretum for more information.

Take in the lush scenery as you hike Curtis Prairie.

Eventually, the path moves onto boards that run alongside a wetland on your right. The grass is much lower here, with swampy water seeping up through the plant life. Moving back onto a grass path, you walk within sight of the arboretum's visitor center on the left. Near here is a section of prairie that has numerous ant mounds. Some of these mounds are over 70 years old and house nests that contain anywhere from a few hundred ants to up to 500,000 ants in larger mounds. The ant colonies are part of the teeming underground life of the prairie, which includes plant roots that may go down as far as 14 feet.

From here, you follow the path south, passing Coyote Pond at 0.7 mile and then turn right onto a track, passing the A9 marker that runs just north of the Beltline Highway. To the left are some impressive oak trees, while to the right is a sweeping view across the prairie and wetland. Note the line of goldenrod that stops at the edge of the wetland, where low-lying grasses take over.

Walking along the path between the prairie and trees, note the occasional white birch among the oaks and pines. Following the path as it curves to the right at 1.0 mile, you pass Curtis Pond, a settling pond protected by a chain-link fence, and soon after reach a junction with the path you followed earlier into the prairie. Follow it back to the arboretum road and then to the parking area.

MILES AND DIRECTIONS

0.0 Begin hike across road from Curtis parking area. Walk onto trail, turn left, and walk along a dirt and gravel path parallel to Arboretum Drive, passing the C1 marker. Walk another 425 feet and turn right onto another dirt and gravel path—marker B3 is on your right at ground level (the marker may be obscured due to overgrown grass).

0.2 Reach marker B5 on the left side of the path, just before a narrow, over-grown path, which moves directly into the prairie. Take this path, moving along through tall prairie grass. Walk 475 feet to marker B2 at a turnoff to the left and keep walking straight.

0.5 Come to a dirt and gravel track and turn right onto it, exiting the prairie.

0.7 Pass Coyote Pond and come to a junction with another track, turning right onto it and passing marker A9.

1.0 Round a bend to the right, passing alongside a chain-link fence on the left and then passing Curtis Pond.

1.1 Arrive back at the junction where you walked into the prairie earlier. Veer left to retrace your earlier route.

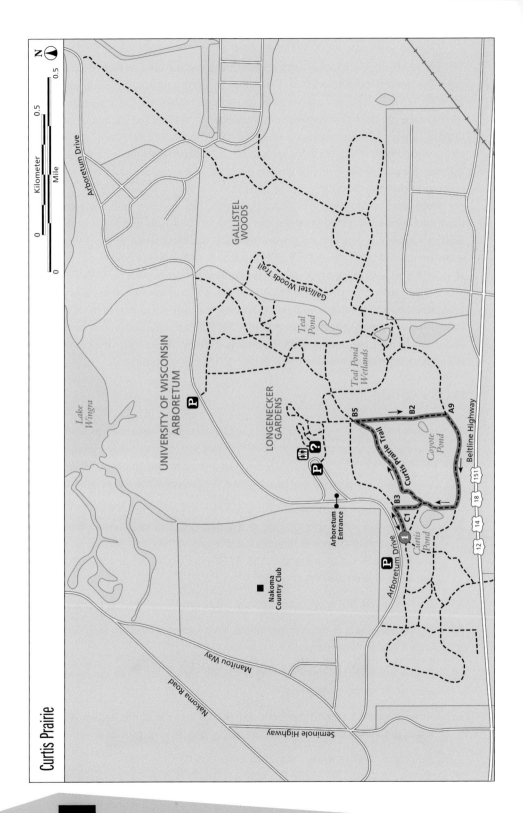

Curtis Prairie

1.2 Arrive back at track paralleling arboretum road. Turn left and walk back toward parking area.

1.3 Arrive back at parking area.

Options: Plenty of other hiking trails wind through the arboretum, with some particularly intriguing options in the oak savanna and kettle hole forest south of the Beltline Highway. These landscapes can be fun to explore, although some of the paths are overgrown and in some places nearly impassable. If a path becomes especially obscured, you may want to turn back toward the trailhead.

HIKE INFORMATION

Hike tours: Numerous guided hikes are offered at the arboretum throughout the year. These hikes are free and are often led by local naturalists and include hikes designed specifically for families. There are also night hikes that give visitors a different look at the landscapes in the arboretum.
Organizations: Friends of the Arboretum, 1207 Seminole Hwy., Madison, WI 53711; (608) 263-7760; http://uwarboretum.org/foa/

Flowers hug the boardwalk along the Curtis Prairie trail.

Gallistel Woods

On the north side of the arboretum from the visitor center, this hike through part of a 28-acre deciduous forest and wetland features wildflowers growing along the paths in both spring and fall. In the 1830s, after pioneers extinguished prairie fires that had prevented trees from taking root, oak trees began growing in the area, originally a prairie and savanna. After the University of Wisconsin acquired the land in the 1930s, scientists planted sugar maples to replace those that had been removed through logging, and today fully grown maples provide a dense canopy of shade among the oaks.

Other trees found in the woods, some planted by researchers studying plant life, include shagbark hickory, black walnut, birch, elm, ironwood, tulip poplar, and magnolia. In the center of the thick stands of trees, Teal Marsh is a wetland home for waterfowl as well as frogs, muskrat, mink, and owls. There are excellent bird watching opportunities in the woods, which are also dotted with Native American burial mounds, some dating back to cultures more than 1,000 years old.

Start: Trailhead at gravel parking area by trail

Distance: 1.4-mile lollipop

Hiking time: About 1 to 1.5 hours

Difficulty: Moderate; short distance but path goes through thick woods and some muddy terrain

Trail surface: Dirt

Best seasons: Spring through fall

Other trail users: Runners and cross-country skiers; in designated areas only

Canine compatibility: No dogs permitted

Land status: University nature preserve

Fees and permits: None

Schedule: Daily, 7 a.m. to 10 p.m.; parking area open sunrise to sunset

Maps: USGS Madison West, WI; trail maps available at visitor center

Trail contact: UW–Madison

Arboretum, 1207 Seminole Hwy., Madison, WI 53711; (608) 263-7888; www.uwarboretum.org

Special considerations: Mosquitoes can be a nuisance on this hike, especially in the marshy wetland areas; dress accordingly and consider bringing bug repellent

Other: Restrooms available in visitor center, on the other side of the arboretum

Finding the trailhead: From downtown Madison, follow US 151 south/south-west. Follow the road about 1 mile along West Washington Avenue, then turn left onto South Park Street and drive about 0.3 mile to the corner of Haywood Drive. Turn right onto Haywood Drive and drive 0.2 mile to the arboretum's Mills Street entrance, at the intersection with North Wingra Drive. Drive into the arboretum and follow Arboretum Drive with Lake Wingra on your right. After driving 1 mile, a road forks to the left. Continue driving straight for 0.8 mile to Wingra Springs parking lot on the right. Park here; the hike begins just across the road.

Alternate route: From West Beltline Highway, take exit 260/Fish Hatchery Road/County Road D, heading north. Drive 1.3 miles to Wingra Road and turn left, then drive 0.5 mile to Mills Street entrance to arboretum. Turn left, enter arboretum, and follow Arboretum Drive to Wingra Springs parking lot.
GPS: N43 02.713' / W89 25.654'

THE HIKE

The hike begins from the trailhead on the northernmost edge of Longnecker Gardens, which features long rows of evergreens and ornamental trees, which follow parallel to Arboretum Drive for about 350 yards before heading into the woods at marker G7. The maples are impressive here, with dense tree cover providing a cooling shade which is very pleasant on hot days. Logs and limbs are scattered across the path, slowly decomposing and providing food for worms, insects, and small creatures.

Descending a hill, the foliage grows even thicker as you move farther from the road. It grows noticeably quieter, and you may pick up birdcalls; many species live in the woods, including the barred owl, American woodcock, and several thrushes and warblers. You may get lucky and spot a yellow-throated warbler, Kentucky warbler, or a red crossbill. Barred owls also roost in the trees.

Massive tree trunks loom up alongside the trail as you continue along the path. The soil in the woods is not the most amenable to wildflowers, but there are still some nice spring ephemerals like Dutchman's breeches, trout lilies, toothwort, and trillium.

The duck pond in the northwestern corner of the arboretum, near the intersection of Nakoma Road and Monroe Street, features a stone staircase and entryway designed by Frank Lloyd Wright. Mallards come here even in the winter.

Gardens at the Arboretum

A 50-acre display of ornamental trees and shrubs, known for its collections of crabapples and lilacs, Longnecker Gardens has hundreds of species that burst into bloom every May. Other gardens at the arboretum include the Viburnum Garden, with numerous species of viburnums and arborvitae, and the Wisconsin Native Plant Garden, located near the visitor center and divided into over a dozen areas, including a children's garden, and featuring flowers and plants from different environments found throughout the state.

Birches line the Gallistel Woods trail.

Crossing another trail, you enter a section of woods known as the Lost City Forest, site of a failed residential development in the 1920s. There's a bench here that's a nice place to take a break. Next up are two successive small plank bridges over a marshy area, where the path gets a little muddy as well, then a longer plank walkway through more low-lying terrain. It's still very quiet, although you may be surprised by one or more of the many joggers who make use of the arboretum's trails.

A little farther along, some pine trees appear among the woods, and the ground becomes a little less marshy. The foliage is just as thick, however, and you may have to scramble over a tree stuck or several that have fallen across the path.

Soon, the path widens a bit as you follow it around a curve to the right. There are still the sounds of birds, including woodpeckers. Another 500 feet or so and the path again curves to the right. Hidden off to the left is a boardwalk that leads to a nice overlook of a small pond and surrounding wetland. The path is wider and more comfortable, and a little farther along a spur path to the right goes to an overlook of Teal Pond at 1.0 mile. Hang around to see if you can spot some duck, muskrat, or other inhabitants of the spreading wetland.

Next, you briefly skirt the edge of Juniper Knoll, a tallgrass prairie, before re-entering the forest, where some impressive white birch grow. Just as quickly you exit the woods and are back in Longnecker Gardens, not far from the hike's starting point.

Walk along the edge of the gardens with the woods just on the right, kicking aside the crabapples from nearby trees, to arrive back at the parking area.

Green Tip:
Consider the packaging of any products you bring with you. It's best to properly dispose of packaging at home before you hike. If you're on the trail, pack it out with you.

Family birding backpacks are available for checkout in the arboretum's visitor center, which also has a library open to the public and is stocked with books and other materials on local flora and fauna, natural history, and previous and ongoing restoration projects at the arboretum, as well as field guides. (The visitor center is located at the other end of the arboretum from this hike. See the previous Curtis Prairie hike for directions.)

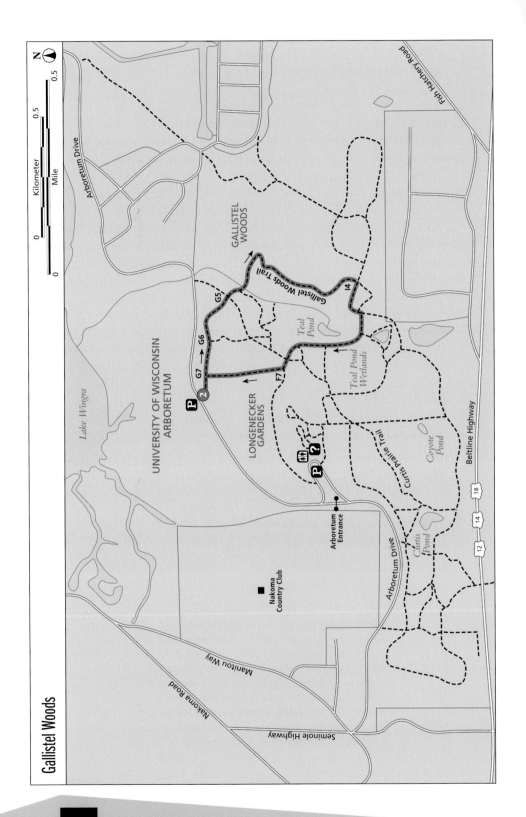

Gallistel Woods

MILES AND DIRECTIONS

0.0   From the trailhead across road from parking lot, turn left and walk toward woods with fence on your left. Follow path into woods and reach intersection marked G7. Turn left here and walk farther into woods.

0.2   Reach a fork in the road at marker G6. Go left and descend hill.

0.3   Reach another trail intersection at marker G5. Keep going straight, then take a path that forks to the left.

0.6   Path becomes a plank walkway. Follow it through woods.

0.8   At trail intersection marker I4, veer right onto wider trail and follow it to a fork in the trail. Take the path on the right.

1.0   Pass a walkway running to the left. Take it for a nice view of the wetland, then return to the path. Continuing the same way you were walking, detour down a path to the right that leads to an even better view at Teal Pond.

1.1   Back on the main path, cross an intersection of trails at marker F6, then reach a trail forking to the right at marker F7. Take this trail to an open field and walk with the woods on your right.

1.4   Arrive back at trailhead.

Options: An additional short hike can be tacked onto this one by heading north from the parking lot into Wingra Woods, a restored northern Wisconsin forest that features birch, hemlock, and sugar maple. Another trail leads through brilliant displays of wildflowers to Big Spring, which feeds into Lake Wingra.

HIKE INFORMATION

Organizations: Friends of the Arboretum, 1207 Seminole Hwy., Madison, WI 53711; (608) 263-7760; http://uwarboretum.org/foa/

Hike tours: Numerous guided hikes are offered at the arboretum throughout the year. These hikes are free and are often led by local naturalists and include hikes designed specifically for families. There are also night hikes that give visitors a different look at the landscapes in the arboretum.

3

Owen Conservation Park

A restored prairie-and-oak savanna that rises on a hilltop on the west side of Madison, this patch of nature in the city was for many years the farm and getaway of University of Wisconsin Professor Edward T. Owen. The pasture and cropland have been returned to their native state since being acquired by the City of Madison in the 1970s. Over 3 miles of trails wind through the 93-acre park, with spur trails offering access to surrounding residential neighborhoods, making this a popular spot for locals seeking a nature hike. At sunrise and sunset, golden rays paint the buildings of the university campus and Lake Mendota to the east.

Start: From the trailhead at paved parking area
Distance: 1.2-mile loop
Hiking time: About 1 hour
Difficulty: Moderate; short distance but with some climbs and narrow paths
Trail surface: Gravel, dirt
Best seasons: Spring through fall
Canine compatibility: No dogs permitted
Land status: City park
Other trail users: Cross-country skiers

Fees and permits: None
Schedule: Daily, 4 a.m. to sunset
Maps: USGS Madison West, WI; an aerial photo of the park with trails marked is posted at the parking area; trail map available from trail contact
Trail contact: Madison Parks, 210 Martin Luther King Jr. Blvd., PO Box 2987, Madison, WI 53701; (608) 266-4711; www.cityof madison.com/parks
Other: Restrooms available at parking area

Finding the trailhead: From downtown Madison, drive west on University Avenue, keeping right onto Campus Drive as you drive past the university, then back onto University Avenue. After driving a total of just over 3 miles, keep right onto Old Middleton Road, drive about 1 mile, keep left onto Old Sauk Road, and drive 0.2 mile to park entrance on the left.

Alternate route: Exit West Beltline Highway at South Gammon Road, heading north. Drive 1.5 miles on Gammon Road and turn right onto Old Sauk Road, then drive 1 mile to park entrance on the right. Park in parking area.
GPS: N43 04.383' / W89 29.247'

THE HIKE

The park is essentially divided into a woods section and a prairie and savanna section, and this hike takes in both landscapes, beginning with the woods section, which rises west of the parking lot on a recessional moraine created by a moving glacier.

Setting out from a small maintenance shed by the parking area, you climb a small hillside that has a smattering of goldenrod among thick tree cover. Just after starting, the path crosses several others set in a stone wall, then will move onto a ridge where the path narrows as it runs near the park entry road on the right.

Numerous wildflowers bloom along the path and throughout the park. Look for bluestem and purple coneflower. The path soon curves to the left as it follows the ridge as the sounds of traffic from Old Sauk Road reach through the woods.

> *Many different paths crisscross and intersect in the park, but the wide-open spaces of the prairie and savanna make it fairly easy to pinpoint your location relative to the parking area and trailhead.*

The trail winds through the woods of Owen Conservation Park.

After walking a few hundred more feet, you reach a fork in the trail at 0.4 mile. Taking the right fork, you pass another stone wall on the left while the hillside slopes down to the right; the ground is heavily carpeted with foliage, including raspberry bushes and jewelweed in the summer. Following the path uphill, you reach another junction where you veer right and immediately reach a fork within view of the parking area.

Heading away from the parking area, you pass some more impressive trees, some of which are home to cardinals and woodpeckers. Stop and listen for their tappings echoing through the woods. There are plenty of other sounds of life here as well, including chipmunks and squirrels scuttling through the underbrush and owls hooting at sunset.

The path now begins a slow descent, passing yet another intersecting trail and coming by houses just outside the park. Continuing downward on the slope, you eventually exit the woods.

The first glimpse of prairie is a memorable one, with golden stalks of tallgrass waving in the wind and stretching to the horizon. A few solitary oaks stand in the sea of grass like buoys bobbing on the water. Swaths of goldenrod wave among the tallgrass and large sunflowers dot the landscape, as does more purple coneflower.

The next turn brings you face-to-face with the prairie, and you really feel like you've left the city behind: Other than the occasional aircraft droning overhead,

Edward Owen and the Natural Landscape of Madison

The former home of Edward Owen still stands in the park at the north end of the parking area. Owen, a professor of French at the University of Wisconsin beginning in the 1870s, was interested in preserving the natural environment as Madison expanded and developed. Toward that end, he acquired real estate that was eventually used to create Owen Parkway, a "pleasure drive" dedicated to the memory of his two young daughters who died in a diphtheria epidemic in 1890. Two boulders commemorating the girls and the parkway stand on Regent Street just west of the intersection of Speedway Road and Highland Avenue, and just north of Forest Hill Cemetery, where Owen is buried. Many other prominent Madisonians are buried there as well, including US congressman and senator, and Wisconsin governor Robert "Fighting Bob" La Follette, and historian Frederick Jackson Turner, a university professor in the 1890s and early 1900s, who authored a seminal work on the American frontier. Also buried here are numerous Confederate Civil War veterans who were held prisoner at Camp Randall, a military facility and site of the future university football stadium, where they died of illness and exposure.

it's incredibly silent and still. Walking south along the path, you approach the oak savanna, which has many impressive specimens. Circling around the southern edge of the park, you walk near three ponds which serve as habitat for wildlife including herons, ducks, and shorebirds. The occasional rabbit makes a quick appearance hopping across the path before vanishing in the grass.

Along this section, benches along the path provide a nice resting spot. You soon come to the woods on the east side of the park and continue walking along the edge of the prairie. Climbing a slope, you pass the first of a series of paths that provide a shortcut through the heart of the prairie, but the hike continues its circumnavigation of the park, heading up the steepest climb yet to bring you onto the northern edge of the prairie and back to the park road near the old Owen house, before arriving back at the parking area.

> *Kettle Pond Park, located just north of Owen Conservation Park, between Old Middleton Road and University Avenue, has a short trail of its own and wildlife viewing opportunities around its kettle pond, a remnant of the glaciation that defined the landscape in southern Wisconsin.*

The trail winds through thick stands of native prairie.

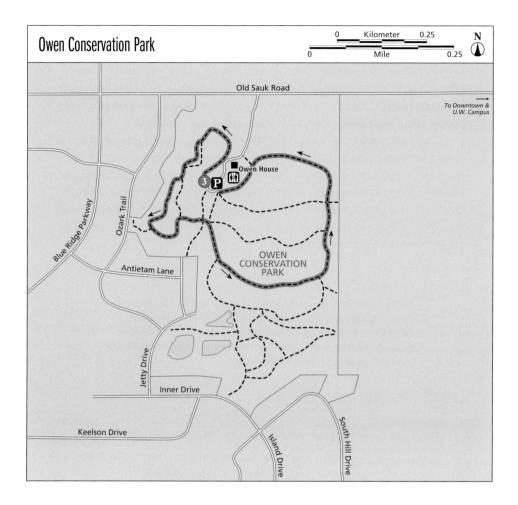

Madison's Conservation Parks: Unique Slices of Nature

Madison began its conservation parks program in 1971 with a goal of preserving natural environments in the city and re-creating native communities of flora and fauna. Today, there are over a dozen conservation parks around the city, with features that include a sand prairie, kettle lakes, and a pond utilized by migrating waterfowl. For more information on conservation parks, contact the parks department.

MILES AND DIRECTIONS

0.0 From the trailhead at the north end of the parking area, walk up the slope behind the shed and turn right onto the path.

0.2 Reach a fork in the path and take the right fork. Soon after, come to a trail junction and go right onto a path. You then reach another fork in the trail. Take the right fork, then continue onto the trail that branches off to the right.

0.4 Pass a spur trail veering off to the right and keep walking on the path that turns to the left. In another few hundred feet, you reach a fork in the trail. Keep to the right. In a short distance you reach a three-way junction. Take the middle path and walk out of the woods into the prairie, then turn right along a path with the woods on the right and the prairie on the left.

0.6 Reach a fork in the path and veer onto the path on the left.

0.8 Come to the edge of the woods. Go left and follow the path with the woods on the right. Keep walking straight as the path passes several turnoffs.

1.1 Pass a spur trail that turns off to the right, and continue walking straight on the path.

1.2 Arrive back at the trailhead.

HIKE INFORMATION

Local information: Greater Madison Convention & Visitors Bureau, 615 East Washington Ave.; (608) 255-2537 or (800) 373-6376; www.visitmadison.com

Local attraction: Sundance Cinemas, 430 North Midvale Blvd.; (608) 316-6900; http://sundancecinemas.com/madison.html, is located about 2 miles east of the park and offers an eclectic selection of foreign and independent films alongside Hollywood hits. The theater is located in Hilldale Mall, an upscale shopping center that has numerous restaurants and shops. It's worth checking out for a bite to eat after a sunset hike.

4

Cherokee Marsh South

At over 5 square miles, Cherokee Marsh is the largest wetland in Dane County and is spread out over three city conservation parks. In addition to wetland, the parks also include oak savannas, glacial drumlins (small hills), and restored prairies. This hike, a short distance as the crow flies from Dane County Regional Airport, has nice views of the Yahara River, which flows south into Lake Mendota. Nearby Cherokee Lake, a wide part of the river just north of the park, was created as a result of erosion that led chunks of the boggy soil to break free and float away.

The low-lying wetland has benefited from ongoing restoration projects, which have focused on stemming erosion along the shoreline and also included removing trees to make the area a more attractive habitat for birds like marsh hawks and short-eared owls. The marshy terrain is a breeding ground for mosquitoes, so wear long pants and have bug repellent handy, especially if you hike in the summer months.

Start: Gravel parking area by trail
Distance: 1.2-mile double lollipop
Hiking time: About 1 hour
Difficulty: Easy; a few small hills, but largely smooth terrain
Trail surface: Dirt
Best seasons: Spring through fall
Canine compatibility: No dogs permitted
Land status: City park
Other trail users: Cross-country skiers
Fees and permits: None
Schedule: Daily, 4 a.m. to sunset
Maps: USGS Waunakee, WI; trail map available at http://mad conservation.tripod.com, which also has maps of other conservation parks in Madison; Friends of Cherokee Marsh, www.cherokee marsh.org, has a wealth of information on the marsh and surrounding areas.

Trail contact: Madison Parks, 210 Martin Luther King Jr. Blvd., PO Box 2987, Madison, WI 53701; (608) 266-4711; www.cityof madison.com/parks
Other: Hiking not permitted when trails are snow covered; no restrooms available at trailhead

Finding the trailhead: From downtown Madison, drive east on East Washington Avenue/US 151 about 4 miles to the intersection with Aberg Avenue. Turn left onto Aberg Avenue, drive 1 mile, and turn right onto Packers Road/WI 113. Drive 0.8 mile and follow WI 113 as it turns left and runs congruent with Northport Drive. Follow Northport Drive for 1.5 miles and turn right onto School Road. Drive 0.8 mile to entrance of Cherokee Marsh, which is just across Wheeler Road from Northland Manor Park. From the entrance, a gravel road leads 0.4 mile to a parking area with the trail beginning on its left edge, in front of a small hill. The trailhead address is 5002 School Rd.
GPS: N43 09.196' / W89 23.018'

THE HIKE

From the trailhead the path heads up a small hill as you begin walking away from the parking area, giving a nice view of the surrounding marsh once you reach the top, with tallgrass and cattail stretching to the horizon. You can see Northport Drive in the distance. Also look here for herons and Canada geese soaring overhead.

Dipping down the other side of the hill, you are soon heading through a small wooded area, then up another hill, passing under the branches of a large oak that droop over the path. There are plenty of milkweed pods along this section as well, which provide some scenery during pollination, as the seeds spill out of the split pods and are scattered by the wind.

Exiting the woods, you pass a bench on the left, with another nice view of the marsh. There's a smattering of goldenrod blooming on the right side of the path. You then swing by a junction with a path running off to the right. Take it, walking toward the gravel road you drove in on when entering the park.

Greenish marsh water creeps toward the right edge of the path along this section, studded with tallgrass and cattail. If you wait patiently, you may see a turtle emerge from the marsh waters. Following the path, you walk between a small power station and a low brick building, which has trails on either side of it. Take either one and walk past the building to another trail junction. Here, take the right-hand path, walking toward a wooded area.

The foliage grows thicker as you move into the woods, with plenty of milkweed and thistle, as well as stands of tallgrass that in some places top 6 feet. To the right, a clump of oaks stand between the path and the marsh, providing nesting spots for birds, including blackbirds and robins. Deer are also spotted around here, moving among the oaks.

Coming out of the woods and into an open area, you should spot a large three-pronged tree trunk that pierces the sky like a giant fork. The marsh spreads out to the right, with houses visible beyond it. After walking down a small dip, follow the path as it weaves in and out of small stands of trees, then makes a loop on its way back toward the parking area.

Following the path through more stands of trees, you retrace part of the path you followed earlier and are soon back at the brick building and power station. After returning to the other side of the hill on which you started, complete the circle back to the trailhead. Along this section, you'll see a variety of butterflies ranging in size from small to very large and the occasional wildflower.

Back at the parking area, the small dock that sits on Cherokee Creek area is a nice spot to take a breather and drink in the view of the surrounding wetlands.

The path moves over soft marshland, passing the occasional tree.

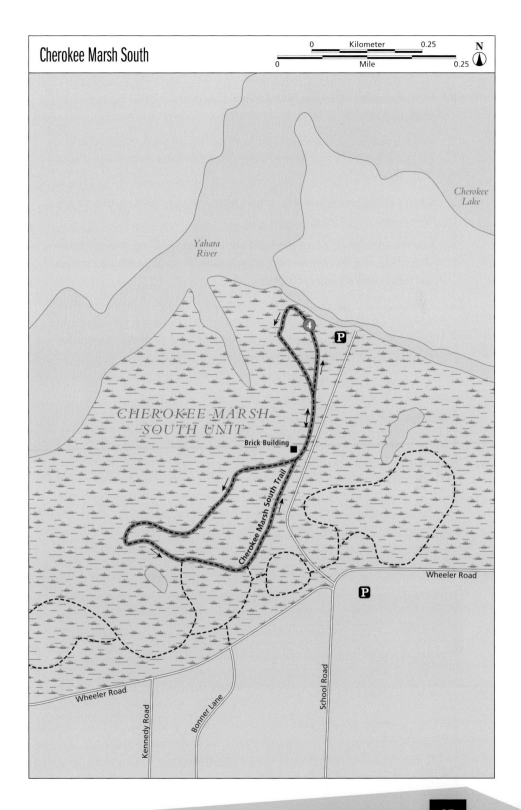

Kilometer
0   0.25

Mile
0   0.25

N

Cherokee
Lake

Yahara
River

4

P

CHEROKEE MARSH
SOUTH UNIT

Brick Building

Cherokee Marsh South Trail

Wheeler Road

P

Wheeler Road

Kennedy Road

Bonner Lane

School Road

MILES AND DIRECTIONS

0.0 From the trailhead by the parking area, step past the gate and turn right onto the path.

0.1 Reach a trail junction and go right, walking toward a gravel path and low brick building. Walk around the brick building and pick up the path on the other side.

0.3 Once past the brick building, continue on the right-hand path into the woods along the marsh.

0.6 Reach a path going off to the right and continue walking straight. Soon after, come to a junction and go left, following the path as it makes a loop and heads back the way you came.

0.8 Eventually, you return to the brick building. Continue walking on path toward parking area. Retrace path from earlier and reach path junction alongside park road, where you take the right-hand path that goes along the other side of the hill near the start of the hike.

1.2 Arrive back at the trailhead.

HIKE INFORMATION

Local information: Greater Madison Convention & Visitors Bureau, 615 East Washington Ave.; (608) 255-2537 or (800) 373-6376; www.visitmadison.com
Local attraction: Olbrich Botanical Gardens, 3330 Atwood Ave., Madison; (608) 246-4550; www.olbrich.org; located not far from the marsh on the north shore of Lake Monona, features 16 acres of gardens stretched out along the Capital City Trail. There's also a large greenhouse with a wide variety of plants and flowers, including many nice orchids, making it a nice spot to visit in colder months.

> **Green Tip:**
> *Keep to established trails as much as possible.*
> *If there aren't any, stay on surfaces that will be least affected,*
> *like rock, gravel, dry grasses, or snow.*

Cherokee Marsh North

There are more impressive views along the stretches of wetlands in this conservation park, which is a little more rugged than the section of Cherokee Marsh to the south. The wetlands were threatened with extinction in the 1840s, but expanded after a dam was built in 1849 across the Yahara River outlet to Lake Mendota. The dam raised the lake level and saturated the surrounding soil, thus spreading the marsh across the surrounding countryside and leaving extensive peat deposits.

Following the construction of another dam in 1900, hundreds of acres of wetland were lost to erosion, as large chunks of boggy soil broke away from the marsh and floated away. The floating shoreline continues to face threat of erosion, which is accelerated by the annual spring migration of carp from Lake Mendota that swim into the marsh to spawn and feed on aquatic plants and help balance the marsh's ecosystem. Conservation efforts have focused on preserving the wetlands by, among other steps, creating natural breakwaters to hold back further erosion.

Despite the threats to the marsh, this section remains an excellent spot for a hike, with boardwalks and overlooks bringing hikers through the heart of the marshy lowlands and providing opportunities to spot waterfowl and other birds, including sandhill cranes. The path also winds through long stretches of woodland on the edge of the marsh, with hills climbing high above the river.

Start: Trailhead by gravel parking area
Distance: 1.8-mile loop
Hiking time: About 1 to 1.5 hours
Difficulty: More challenging; several steep climbs
Trail surface: Dirt, gravel
Best seasons: Spring through fall
Canine compatibility: No dogs permitted
Land status: City park
Other trail users: Cross-country skiers and snowshoers
Fees and permits: None
Schedule: Daily, 4 a.m. to sunset
Maps: A trail map is available at http://madconservation.tripod .com, which also has maps of other conservation parks in Madison; Friends of Cherokee Marsh, www.cherokeemarsh.org, has a wealth of information on the marsh and surrounding areas. (These maps include a section of boardwalk trail that no longer exists; see the hike text for details.)
Trail contact: Madison Parks, 210 Martin Luther King Jr. Blvd., PO Box 2987, Madison, WI 53701; (608) 266-4711; www.cityof madison.com/parks
Special considerations: Mosquitoes are prevalent along this hike; bring bug repellent
Other: Restrooms are available at trailhead

Finding the trailhead: From downtown Madison, drive East on East Washington Avenue/US 151 about 4 miles to the intersection with Aberg Avenue. Turn left onto Aberg Avenue, drive 1 mile, and veer right onto Packers Road/WI 113. Drive 0.8 mile and follow 113 as it continues left onto Northport Drive. Follow Northport for 0.5 mile and turn right onto North Sherman Avenue. Drive along Sherman, passing the Cherokee Country Club, for 2 miles, at which point Sherman becomes a gravel road. Continue another 0.7 mile to the parking area. Trail address: 6098 North Sherman Dr.
GPS: N43 10.029' / W89 21.886'

THE HIKE

From the trailhead you enter the woods and walk past a grassy trail leading to the right. The path then swings by a stand of white birch trees and narrows as it moves through the woods. The path then becomes a wider gravel path that veers left, toward the river.

The first of a few viewing platforms on this hike soon rises on the left. It has both upper and lower levels and gives a wide view of the marsh grass and lily ponds that stretch along the edge of the river. A long boardwalk once extended south from here along the marsh and river, but it has since been removed.

Continuing down the path with the river on the left, you'll go right and head deeper into the woods. Frogs hop out of the marsh and across the path on this section. The path then heads uphill on a rather strenuous climb, past oak and hickory trees. It's not a bad idea to stop and rest partway up the hill.

Once on top, enjoy a respite as the path winds along the edge of a ridge. Before long, you reach an overlook perched above a wide open swath of prairie on the backside of the hill. There's a path running along the edge of the woods that eventually goes downhill, but go straight ahead and walk down through the prairie, eventually walking toward a small wooded area that stands at the edge of the marsh.

Planes flying overhead are a reminder that Madison's airport isn't too far away. After the descent, follow the path into the woods. Soon, you'll turn left and step onto a boardwalk, a short side trip that leads to a viewing platform at a small pond surrounded by marsh. Take a moment to survey the view, and see if you spot any herons or cranes flitting above the lowlands.

Back on the main path, you wind through more prairie and woodland, passing the path that moved along the edge of the woods from the overlook. Soon afterward, you reach a cutoff on the left that leads you on another small detour to another pond, with surrounding waters thick with cattail. A little farther down the path is a trail junction with a metal walkway leading to the left. Take this walkway, which leads to the "marshiest" part of the hike, straight through the lowlands and culminating at a viewing platform that looks out over a seemingly endless sea of marsh grasses, their tall stalks waving in the wind. This is another good bird-watching spot, but you'll probably have to be patient and wait a while for sandhill cranes or other birds to show up. (It's worth it!)

From the viewing platform, follow the hike directions through a loop that brings you back to the turnoff for the metal walkway, where you turn left and begin the homestretch. (Another option, if you'd like a slightly longer hike, is to continue walking straight on the walkway into an area of the marsh with some more ponds. This section can get very wet and muddy!) Veering right as you pass a row of sumac bushes on the left, you soon return to the hike's starting point.

MILES AND DIRECTIONS

0.0 Begin hike at the trailhead on the path behind information board. Cross road and walk into woods. Walk past a path veering off to the right as you continue walking straight.

The path moves over marshland and in and out of woods.

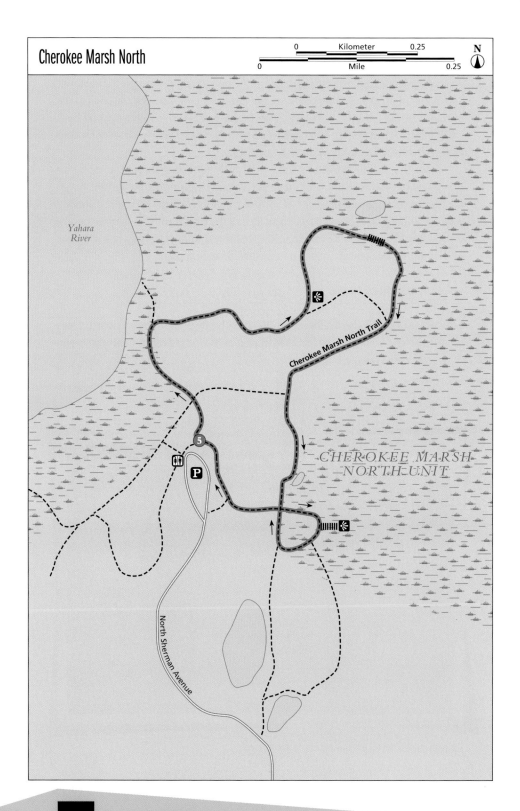

Yahara River

Cherokee Marsh North Trail

CHEROKEE MARSH
NORTH UNIT

North Sherman Avenue

0.2 Follow a short spur trail on the left to a viewing platform over the marsh and river. Return to the main path and walk with marsh and river on your left, then turn right onto path that heads uphill and into the woods.

0.5 Exit the woods to an overlook with a view of the prairie below. Walk straight downhill on the path leading through the tallgrass.

0.6 Reach an intersection with a boardwalk. Take it a short distance to the pond, then return to path and continue in the same direction you were walking before.

0.8 Pass a path that comes in from the right and continue walking straight.

0.9 Come to a junction and turn left to check out a small pond, then return to main path.

1.1 Reach a trail junction and veer left onto metal walkway, following it to a viewing platform. Just past the platform, go right and walk back to the main path, where you turn right and walk to where you first entered the metal walkway. Turn left this time and follow the path. After about 350 feet, turn right onto a different path.

1.8 Arrive back at the trailhead.

HIKE INFORMATION

Local information: Greater Madison Convention & Visitors Bureau, 615 East Washington Ave.; (608) 255-2537 or (800) 373-6376; www.visitmadison.com
Local attraction: Madison Mallards, 2920 North Sherman Ave., Madison; (608) 246-4277; www.mallardsbaseball.com. This summer collegiate team takes to the diamond at Warner Park at the corner of Northport Drive and Sherman Avenue. Known as the Duck Pond, the stadium often fills up on warm summer evenings as locals cheer on the Mallards against other teams in the Northwoods League.

Turville Point Conservation Park

Another city conservation park, with 65 acres spread out over Turville Point as it stretches into Lake Monona, within sight of downtown's modest skyline. The hike runs through thick woods that contain a plethora of trees, mainly oak, hackberry, and hickory, with green ash and black cherry being thinned out. The trees provide fine cover for spring wildflowers. Conservation efforts have included cultivating more native species while removing invasive ones, as well as restoration of a prairie near the center of the park. There is also a modest oak savanna under restoration and surrounded by the woods.

Several paths crisscross through the woods, and this hike takes you around the circumference of the park, with a stop off near the restored prairie. Turville Park is adjacent to Olin Park, one of the most popular parks in Madison. All types hang out here, from pierced and tattooed university students to downtown professionals and families with children, making this one of the best places in the city to hang out and people watch. On weekends in the spring and summer it's full of locals taking advantage of the warm weather to get outside. There are soccer and softball fields, a boat ramp, a beach, and a very nice picnic area on the shores of the lake. You might want to consider bringing your own picnic for before or after the hike.

Start: Trailhead by the parking area

Distance: 1.5-mile loop

Hiking time: About 1.5 hours

Difficulty: Moderate; a few small hills

Trail surface: Dirt

Best seasons: Spring to fall

Canine compatibility: No dogs permitted

Land status: City park

Other trail users: Cross-country skiers

Fees and permits: None

Schedule: Daily, 4 a.m. to 10 p.m.

Maps: USGS Madison East, WI; trail map available from http://madconservation.tripod.com, which also has maps for other local conservation parks

Trail contact: Madison Parks, 210 Martin Luther King Jr. Blvd., PO Box 2987, Madison, WI 53701; (608) 266-4711; www.cityofmadison.com/parks

Other: Restrooms available near trailhead, behind pavilion

Finding the trailhead: From downtown Madison, drive south on John Nolen Drive about 1 mile and turn left onto East Lakeside Drive, then immediately turn right onto Olin-Turville Court. Drive into the park, turn left into the first parking lot, drive toward the lake, then turn right, following the road past the park pavilion on your left and a playground on your right. Continue following the road behind the pavilion and park at the edge of the woods. The trail runs into the woods from there.

GPS: N43 03.216' / W89 22.502'

THE HIKE

From the trailhead you are soon walking near the lake on your left, under a cool tree cover of oak and maple. The path meanders closer to the lake and is soon right at its shore, with water lapping against fallen tree trunks.

Passing a path that comes in from the right, continue along the lakeside path. A small hill brings you away from the water, but only for a moment. After cresting the slope you are even closer to the lake. In fact, the path gets a little bit muddy here, although it's nothing to worry about.

Another hill brings you up onto a ridge overlooking the water. As you move along the ridge, look through the trees on the right for a glimpse of the prairie landscape. There are plenty of impressive oaks along this stretch with their leaf clusters particularly colorful in the fall. Also look for black walnut trees with their greenish nuts scattered across the path.

Soon, you're once again back alongside the lake, at a spot where the water is a little more clouded. Not much farther along, a spur trails runs down off the ridge, toward a nearby railroad and developed area. The dome of Veterans Memorial Coliseum is visible in the distance. Stay on the path as it heads into thicker woods, where you may spot deer grazing among the trees.

Continuing along the ridge you should now definitely be able to spot the prairie off to the right. A spur trail will take you there if you want to see it up close, and you can circle the prairie then return to the same spot in the woods to resume the

Green Tip:
When hiking in a group, walk single file on established trails to avoid widening them. If you come upon a sensitive area, spread out so you don't cut one path through the landscape. Don't create new trails where there were none before.

Turville Point Conservation Park

hike (there's also another spur trail into the prairie a little farther down the main path). There are wildflowers scattered along this part of the trail, as well as the occasional cardinal perched up in the trees. They're fairly easy to spot among the thick trunks and branches.

Coming up on the homestretch of the hike, you'll spot another parking lot in Olin Park off to the left, with a spur path running to it. Take the path that runs to the right and up a hill, walking back into the woods where the trees once again are rather large and impressive, including several dead logs strewn across the path.

The path soon becomes paved as you turn right and follow it for a short stretch to a junction of multiple paths. To the left is the oak savanna under restoration, with invasive plants being removed and native plants filling in the space. Just past the savanna, take the path farthest to the left and walk to the right of the savanna. You can spot Lake Monona off to the right. From here, it's only about 500 feet back to the turnoff you saw at the start of the hike, and then on to the trailhead and parking area. Check out the pavilion after you've completed the hike; it is over a hundred years old and is very popular for weddings and other gatherings.

The path goes deeper into the woods.

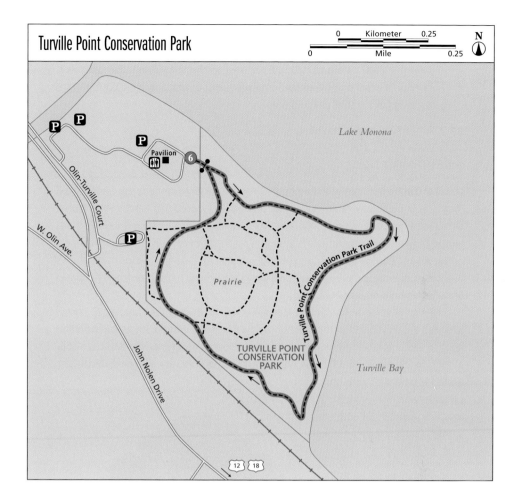

Turville Point Conservation Park

0   Kilometer   0.25

0   Mile   0.25

N

Lake Monona

Olin-Turville Court

W. Olin Ave.

Pavilion

Prairie

Turville Point Conservation Park Trail

TURVILLE POINT
CONSERVATION
PARK

Turville Bay

John Nolen Drive

12 18

MILES AND DIRECTIONS

0.0   Walk into woods, step through gate, and take the left-hand path, walking toward the lake. Come to a junction and turn left.

0.2   Follow the path as it reaches the edge of the lake, then walk along the path with the lake on your left.

0.6   Reach a path heading off to the right and continue walking straight.

0.8   Reach a path heading off to the left and continue walking straight on the same path to the left.

1.2   Come to a spur trail running to the left. Stay right as you walk up a hill.

1.4 Reach a juncture of several trails just to the right of a restored oak savanna. Take the path that branches off farthest to the left. Follow the path as it goes up a small slope and comes within sight of the lake, then continue on the way back to the parking area.

1.5 Arrive back at the trailhead.

HIKE INFORMATION

Local attractions: Veterans Memorial Coliseum, 1919 Alliant Energy Center Way; (608) 267-3976; www.alliantenergycenter.com, is located just across John Nolen Drive from the park. It's a 10,000-seat domed facility and a major entertainment venue for Madison, hosting concerts and sporting events. The coliseum is part of the Alliant Energy Center complex, which also includes space for trade shows and other events, including the Dane County Fair every summer (the Wisconsin State Fair is held near Milwaukee).

Henry Vilas Zoo, 702 South Randall Ave., Madison; (608) 266-4732; www .vilaszoo.org, is located to the west of the park by Lake Wingra. It's an outstanding spot to see animals in the heart of Madison. There's a petting zoo and train tour alongside the many animal areas, including primates, big cats, a tropical rain forest, and a herpetarium. Free admission and parking daily.

Local event: Johnsonville World's Largest Brat Fest; (608) 238-7612; www.bratfest .com

Edna Taylor Conservation Park

This 56-acre conservation park is laid out along a glacial drumlin, or small hill, not far from the eastern shore of Lake Monona. It is a wonderful spot for a quick escape from the noise and distraction of the surrounding urban environment, with paths leading through woodland, savanna, and, most notably, ponds and marshes that are home to a wide variety of waterfowl.

Edna Taylor was an actor, writer, and teacher from New York City who was quite a presence during the four decades she lived in Madison. She began raising dairy cattle on a farm in Madison in the 1940s, and eventually made plans to sell part of her farm for use as a park. The city purchased land for the park in 1972, just a few months after Taylor's death.

Start: Trailhead next to parking area
Distance: 1.7-mile lollipop with additional spur
Hiking time: About 1 to 1.5 hours
Difficulty: Easy; fairly flat terrain
Trail surface: Dirt, gravel
Best seasons: Spring through fall
Canine compatibility: No dogs permitted
Land status: City park
Other trail users: None
Fees and permits: None
Schedule: Daily, 4 a.m. to sunset
Maps: USGS Madison East; trail map available from http://madconservation.tripod.com which also has maps for other local conservation parks
Trail contact: Madison Parks, 210 Martin Luther King Jr. Blvd., PO Box 2987, Madison, WI 53701; (608) 266-4711; www.cityof madison.com/parks
Special considerations: Do not pick wildflowers or plants. No picnicking permitted. Mosquitoes can get thick; bring bug repellent, especially in summer months.
Other: No restrooms available at trailhead or in park. Restrooms available at Aldo Leopold Conservation Center, just west of park.

Finding the trailhead: Drive on East Beltline Highway toward Monona and exit at exit 265/Monona Drive, heading north. Drive 0.5 mile to Femrite Drive, turn right, and drive 0.5 mile, passing Aldo Leopold Nature Center, to parking area for park and trailhead on the left.
GPS: N43 03.109' / W89 19.010'

7

THE HIKE

From the trailhead you begin walking along a strip of prairie dominated by stands of tallgrass and speckled with goldenrod. Almost immediately, you come to a marshy area on either side of the path. Algae grows thick and green in two large ponds, and grasses and cattail sprout from the muck. Purple aster bloom alongside the path as well. Canada geese, cranes, ducks, and herons have all been spotted on the waters.

This is a nice spot to pause and reflect. The park is circled by housing and a water tower looms in the distance, but it feels removed from the bustle on nearby Monona Drive, US 51, and the Beltline Highway, just as Edna Taylor surely intended. Day hikers frequent the park, making good use of the winding paths.

Passing some sumac plants, you walk out of the marshy area and into the woods, where you soon reach a path junction and veer to the right. The path narrows here as you head into thick stands of oak trees.

After circling a short distance through the woods, you reach a boardwalk that leads into more marshy terrain alongside another pond. Cattails here soar over the head, and you may feel as if you're on a raft floating over the greenish water, where frogs and turtles skitter on and off rocks hidden just below the surface.

Once off the boardwalk, you're soon back in the woods. After passing a spur path running up a hill through the woods on your right, you'll come to a T-junction

A lagoon popular with waterfowl.

where the left-hand path goes to a school. Go right and climb the hill. As you reach the top of the hill, the path turns right again and runs along a ridge. The sound of traffic is more noticeable here, but it's still a nice walk through the woods.

As you walk along the ridge, you pass the site of effigy and linear mounds, ceremonial burial spots that date from AD 650 to 1100. Continue along the ridge, passing again the spur path on your right, then another spur path to the left that leads to a nearby housing development.

Looming on the right is an oak savanna with some especially impressive trees. A large, lone hickory is next, to the right, then a smattering of black walnut trees just as the path levels out and you return to the junction you took earlier into the woods.

Keep walking straight then follow the path as it bends right, becomes gravel, and comes into another marshy area near some ponds. Arriving at a junction, take the path farthest on the left, walking past a thicket in a pond where goldfinches roost. Stop for a little bit to see how many of the birds you can spot.

More houses loom just outside the park boundary as you walk along this section past the marsh, eventually following the narrowing path between ponds on either side. There are viewing platforms stretching into both ponds, and this is an excellent spot to view ducks and other waterfowl.

A little farther down the path, you leave the park and enter the Aldo Leopold Nature Center (watch for the signs). It's worth sampling a small bit of the nature center on this hike: Stay on the path and follow it as it curves left and comes to another pond with a bridge leading out to a small island and wooden viewing platforms. Canada geese are prevalent here and you may spot a great blue heron picking its way through the thick clumps of grass on the edge of the pond.

From here, retrace your steps back into the park, passing again between the two ponds, then reaching the junction where you veer right, then right again, and walk through the prairie and marsh landscapes back to the trailhead and parking area.

Aldo Leopold: Father of American Conservation

Aldo Leopold (1887–1948), whose name graces the adjacent nature center, was a pioneering American ecologist and conservationist. A professor at the University of Wisconsin, he was an expert on wildlife and wilderness conservation, and advocated ways for people to live in greater harmony with nature and restore landscapes to their natural state. His best-known book, *A Sand County Almanac,* first published in 1949 and focused on observations around his Wisconsin farm as well as other spots in North America, renewed interest in ecology and was a huge influence on the development of the modern environmentalist movement.

Edna Taylor Conservation Park

MILES AND DIRECTIONS

0.0 From the trailhead, step onto path and walk through prairie and then between two ponds.

0.3 Reach a junction of two paths. Take the right-hand path, walk a short distance into the woods, then take the path that splits off to the left.

0.4 Come to a boardwalk and follow it about 250 feet through a marshy landscape with tall cattails. Step off boardwalk and follow path through more woods, passing a spur path that runs off to the left toward a school. Turn right and walk up a hill. Follow path as it bends right again and runs along a ridge.

0.9 Complete the loop through the woods, walk briefly on the path you took earlier into the woods, and arrive back at the path junction you passed by near the start of the hike. Veer right, walk a short distance, then reach a junction. Turn left, then immediately turn left again and walk into the marshy area surrounded by water.

1.1 Arrive at viewing platforms extending into ponds on both sides of the trail. After taking in the view, continue along the path, passing a small path off to the right.

1.2 Arrive at border between park and Aldo Leopold Nature Center. Continue on path into nature center and follow it as it bends left and arrives at pond with viewing platforms. From here, retrace your route, following the path back between the ponds and then through the prairie along the marsh.

1.7 Arrive back at the trailhead.

Option: You may want to continue along the path into the Aldo Leopold Nature Center, which has numerous landscapes to explore, including a prairie, meadow, oak savanna, and wetland. Numerous birds and insects can be seen among the tall grasses and oaks, hickories, and other trees. Literature describing the different habitats is available at the center's headquarters. This is a popular spot for local school groups that come to the center to learn more about the flora and fauna native to Wisconsin. The center also has numerous events throughout the year; go to www.naturenet.com/alnc for more details. Pick up a brochure explaining the landscapes in more detail at the center's headquarters, which is located west of Edna Taylor Conservation Park on Femrite Drive.

HIKE INFORMATION

Local information: Greater Madison Convention & Visitors Bureau, 615 East Washington Ave.; (608) 255-2537 or (800) 373-6376; www.visitmadison.com
Local attraction: Madison Children's Museum, 100 State St., Madison; (608) 256-6445; www.madisonchildrensmuseum.org

🐛 Green Tip:
If you see someone else littering, muster up the courage to ask them not to.

8

Southwest Commuter Path

This hike heads northeast across Madison, eventually reaching Camp Randall Stadium, just west of the University of Wisconsin campus. Beginning alongside Dunn's Marsh in the suburb of Fitchburg, the hike along a rails-to-trails conversion takes you from a bucolic setting on the outskirts of the city right into the bustling center. Plenty of cyclists use the path, including, of course, commuters whizzing to jobs downtown from the suburbs. At lunchtime, both cyclists and joggers crowd onto the path for a quick workout.

The hike begins along a short section of the Capital City State Trail (small fee required) before turning onto the Southwest Commuter Path, and also provides access to the Military Ridge Trail, which runs for many miles into the countryside to the west of Madison and is also popular with cyclists.

Start: Trailhead at Dawley Conservancy parking lot
Distance: 9.8 miles out and back
Hiking time: About 3.5 to 4 hours
Difficulty: Moderate; paved path, but long distance with some tricky street crossings
Trail surface: Paved path
Best seasons: Spring through fall
Canine compatibility: Leashed dogs permitted
Land status: City bicycling trail
Other trail users: Cyclists and runners
Fees and permits: State trail pass required on first part of hike, which goes along a section of the Capital City State Trail; information on obtaining a state trail pass is available from the Wisconsin Department of Natural Resources; http://dnr.wi.gov/org/land/parks/fees/trailpass.html

Schedule: Daily, 4 a.m. to 10 p.m.
Maps: USGS Madison West, WI; a map of city trails is available through Madison Traffic Engineering, which maintains city bike paths; www.cityofmadison.com/trafficengineering/bicyclingmaps.cfm. A more basic map of city trails is available through the homepage for the Capital City State Trail; http://dnr.wi.gov/org/land/parks/specific/capcity.

8

Trail contact: Madison Traffic Engineering, 210 Martin Luther King Jr. Blvd., Suite 100, Madison, WI 53703; (608) 266-4761; www.cityofmadison.com/traffic engineering. Information on state trail passes available from Wisconsin Department of Natural Resources; http://dnr.wi.gov/org/land/parks/fees/trailpass.html.

Special considerations: There are a lot of cyclists who use this trail. Stay alert while hiking.

Other: No restrooms at trailhead

Finding the trailhead: From downtown or I-39/90, take Beltline Highway to exit 259/Seminole Highway, heading south, and drive 0.6 mile, passing Dunn's Marsh on the right, to the parking lot for Dawley Conservancy on the right. Be watchful. It's a small, almost hidden turnoff to the parking area. From the west side, take Beltline Highway to exit 258 (Verona Road/US 18/151), heading south, drive 1.9 miles, and turn left onto County Road PD/McKee Road, then drive 0.8 mile, turn left onto Seminole Highway, and drive 0.4 mile to Dawley Conservancy parking area on your left.
GPS: N43 01.221' / W89 27.190'

THE HIKE

From the trailhead, you descend toward the pond and marsh, which serve as a storm water retention basin, and pass fields of goldenrod, purple aster, and other wildflowers. Birds chirp in the trees, and a few houses on the farther side of the pond, along with the sound of traffic on Seminole Highway, are the only signs of civilization.

The noise soon fades as you turn left onto the Capital City Trail, cross over a rocky creek bed, and move through a low marshy area and then into the woods. Water sloshes over the path, especially after heavy rains. Fall leaf colors are especially impressive here. Look for brilliant golds, oranges, and yellows.

After crossing under an old railroad bridge, you go right and step onto the Southwest Commuter Path and abruptly re-enter civilization, with apartment complexes sprouting on both sides of the path. The appeal of the path to Madison's legions of cyclists is apparent here as well, as they zip like a laser to the horizon.

After passing under Raymond Road, you enter a gritty industrial area, with concrete all around and a workingman's tavern off to the left. Still, a few sparrows flit across the path. After crossing the Beltline Highway on an elevated walkway, you are back in arboreal territory, with sumac mixed in with the wildflowers blooming along the path. Boneset and black-eyed susan are especially prevalent here, as is the yellow stick-tight flower. Goldfinches hide in the thick tree cover while black-capped chickadees dart quickly across the path. Blink and you'll miss them!

A few houses soon appear on the right, then you pass a spur trail heading off to the left. After the spur, the ground on the left sinks into a depression, while there are some nice aspens and oaks on the right.

Crossing Midvale Boulevard can be a bit tricky. It's a major traffic artery and there is no stop sign or traffic signal. Before you cross, check out the buffalo sculptures welcoming you to the Midvale Heights neighborhood, which you leave behind after you cross the road and enter the Westmoreland neighborhood.

The path now takes you onto a bridge over a small creek, then through a stretch marked with thicker tree cover. Next up are some hills that were used by the Ho-Chunk native people for campsites overlooking Lake Wingra, which is a little to the southeast. A stand of tall pine trees rises to the left above power lines.

The paved path curves through a belt of forest alongside Madison's residential neighborhoods.

After crossing Odana Road (another tricky crossing) you reach Dudgeon Monroe prairie on the right. This is a perfect spot to stop and catch your breath. The small triangular swath is thick with tallgrass and wildflowers. The path then swings close by houses on both sides. Many have backyard gardens and the benefit of large pines and maples that define this section of the path. There's also Glenwood Children's Park, which sits serenely in a glen to the right as you approach Glenway Street.

Another impressive prairie is next, on the left, with a riot of color, including pink joe-pye weed and golden alexander. A little farther down is a large willow tree. A ravine then stretches from one side of the path to the other, with the right side developed with homes.

An overpass with sandstone bleachers beneath it is another nice spot for a rest. After walking under a few more overpasses, you get your first look at the capitol dome, rising off to the right. There's one last stand of maple and pine trees, and cardinals hop in the branches before you suddenly exit the path and come face to face with the massive edifice of Camp Randall Stadium. Stroll around the outside of the stadium and adjacent field house, and check out the large sculpture of footballs on the corner. Also see if you can spot the short street dubbed Crazylegs Lane, the nickname of former Badger football great and longtime university athletic director Elroy Hirsch.

Once you've seen enough around the stadium, step back onto the path and retrace your route back to the parking area.

Camp Randall Stadium

Built on the former grounds of an army training facility that held Confederate prisoners during the Civil War, Camp Randall Stadium has been home to the University of Wisconsin football team since 1895. The oldest stadium in the Big Ten conference, it is perhaps more revered that the state capitol. The towering coliseum holds up to 80,000 of the Badger faithful on autumn Saturdays. In front of the stadium stands the beloved old Wisconsin Field House, known for years as the Barn, which served as home to the Badger basketball teams until 1998, when they moved into the new Kohl Center. The field house still hosts university wrestling and volleyball, and was also home for many years to Wisconsin's top-ranked boxing team.

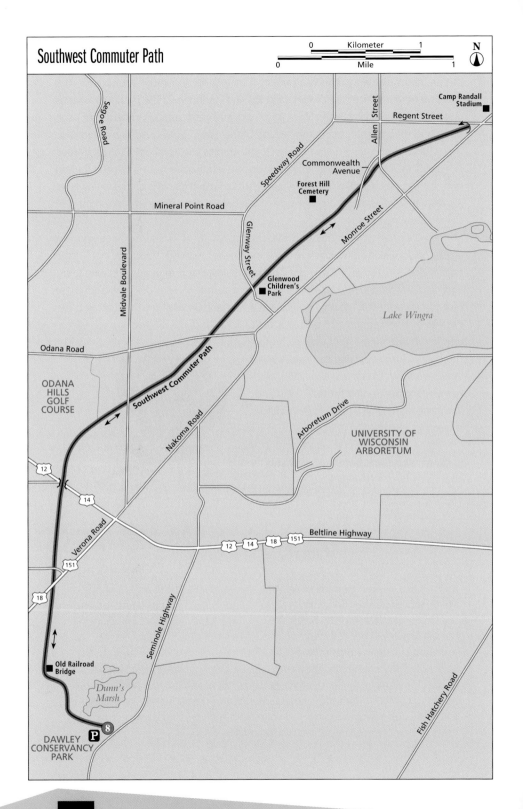

Southwest Commuter Path

0 Kilometer 1
0 Mile 1

N

Camp Randall
Stadium

Allen Street

Regent Street

Segoe Road

Speedway Road

Commonwealth
Avenue

Forest Hill
Cemetery

Mineral Point Road

Monroe Street

Glenway Street

Midvale Boulevard

Glenwood
Children's
Park

Lake Wingra

Odana Road

Southwest Commuter Path

Nakoma Road

ODANA
HILLS
GOLF
COURSE

Arboretum Drive

UNIVERSITY OF
WISCONSIN
ARBORETUM

12

14

Verona Road

Beltline Highway

12 14 18 151

151

18

Seminole Highway

Fish Hatchery Road

Old Railroad
Bridge

Dunn's
Marsh

P 8

DAWLEY
CONSERVANCY
PARK

0.0 From the trailhead walk on the paved path toward the pond and reach a T-junction. Turn left onto path. You are now walking on the Capital City State Trail.

0.5 Pass under an old railroad bridge, then walk past an old, unused set of railroad tracks on the left and come to a path branching off to the right. Turn onto this path You are now on the Southwest Commuter Path.

1.0 Cross under Verona Road/US 18/151 and then Raymond Road, continuing to walk straight on the path. Next you cross Verona Frontage Road, continuing on the path.

1.5 Cross Hammersley Road, then follow an elevated walkway over the Beltline Highway. After crossing the highway, a spur path goes to the right. Keep walking straight on the path.

2.2 Pass Vale Circle and cross Midvale Boulevard. This brings you from the Midvale Heights neighborhood into the Westmoreland neighborhood.

2.6 Reach an intersection with paved paths leading off to Parman Terrace and Council Crest. Continue walking straight on the path and cross Odana Road.

3.2 Walk past Glenwood Children's Park on the right and a small generating station on the left as you follow the path and cross Glenway Street.

3.9 Pass a spur path leading off to Sheldon Street and Virginia Terrace as you continue walking straight along the main path.

4.3 Cross Commonwealth Avenue and, shortly afterward, pass under an arched overpass at Edgewood Avenue. Several ramps and overpasses follow as you move along the path, beginning with South Prospect Avenue, then Harrison Street, and finally Spooner Street. Continue walking straight on path.

4.9 Reach Camp Randall Stadium, by the intersection of Regent and Monroe Streets. This is the turnaround point for the hike, so look around the neighborhood surrounding the stadium before you retrace your route back along the path.

9.8 Arrive back at parking area (remember when you reach the final turn by the old railroad bridge to go left onto the Capital City State Trail that takes you through the woods and back to the trailhead at Dunn's Marsh).

Options: You may want to continue on the Capital City State Trail, which takes you onto the hike listed for that trail. You could turn right at the railroad bridge on the way to the Military Ridge Trail. For more on this trail, see the honorable mentions section of the book.

You may also keep walking on Monroe to the northeast as it cuts diagonally toward the heart of campus, turning left on Randall Avenue and then right on Johnson Street to walk toward the State Street Pedestrian Mall, a walk of about 1 mile. This is a nice option if you want to do a one-way hike only, ending at downtown, and can have someone drop you off at the trailhead.

HIKE INFORMATION

Local attractions: Dawley Conservancy, opposite the starting point for this hike, is a public conservation area owned by the City of Fitchburg. The conservancy abuts the southern fringe of the University of Wisconsin Arboretum and has a short walking trail that loops through the woods. It begins right across Seminole Highway from the parking area.

Mickie's Dairy Bar, 1511 Monroe St., Madison; (608) 256-3811. Right across the street from the stadium and field house, this is a great, old-fashioned diner and a nice spot for a mid-hike break. It's renowned in Madison for milk shakes, and there are good burgers and other short-order delights as well.

Eplegaarden, 2227 Fitchburg Rd., Fitchburg; (608) 845-5966; www.eplegaarden .com. A pick-your-own orchard with delicious apples and other fruit, as well as Halloween-related attractions and events every September and October.

> **Green Tip:**
> *Don't take souvenirs home with you. This means natural materials such as plants, rocks, shells, and driftwood as well as historic artifacts such as fossils and arrowheads.*

Beginning at the trailhead by Dunn's Marsh, at the same starting point as the South-west Commuter Path hike, this is a pleasant stroll along a cycling trail that runs along the outskirts of Madison, passing the edges of housing developments and flitting through prairie and woods before coming to a historic fish hatchery near a busy road intersection.

The hike begins just south of the University of Wisconsin Arboretum, and lies entirely along the Nine Springs E-Way, a continuous network of greenbelt with lots of open countryside that is a showcase of native ecology. Some cyclists like to ride the entire trail. Several miles past the hike's turnaround point, the trail comes to the Nine Springs E-Way Trail, as well as a county park and state recreation area, with numer-ous facilities for visitors. From there, the trail turns north and runs along the shore of Lake Monona and across the Isthmus to Olbrich Botanical Gardens.

Start: Trailhead at Dawley Conservancy parking area

Distance: 4.6 miles out and back

Hiking time: About 2 to 2.5 hours

Difficulty: Moderate; a few hills along the path

Trail surface: Paved path

Best seasons: Spring through fall

Canine compatibility: Leashed dogs permitted

Land status: State trail

Other trail users: Cyclists and runners

Fees and permits: State trail pass required; passes are available for purchase at a kiosk at the Verona Road Trailhead, located just past the Verona Road turnoff; information on obtaining a state trail pass is available from the Wisconsin Department of Natural Resources at http://dnr.wi.gov/org/land/parks/fees/trailpass.html

Schedule: Daily, 6 a.m. to 11 p.m.

Maps: USGS Madison West, WI; trail map available from trail contact listed below

Trail contact: Capital Springs State Park, 3101 Lake Farm Rd., Madison, WI 53711; (608) 224-3606; http://dnr.wi.gov/org/land/parks/specific/capcity/

Other: No restrooms at trailhead

9

Finding the trailhead: From downtown or I-39/90, take Beltline Highway to exit 259/Seminole Highway, heading south, and drive 0.6 mile, passing Dunn's Marsh on the right, to the parking lot for Dawley Conservancy on the right. Be watchful. It's a small, almost hidden turnoff to the parking area. From the west side, take Beltline Highway to exit 258 (Verona Road/US 18/151), heading south, drive 1.9 miles, and turn left onto County Road PD/McKee Road, then drive 0.8 mile, turn left onto Seminole Highway, and drive 0.4 mile to Dawley Conservancy parking area on your left.
GPS: N43 01.221' / W89 27.190'

THE HIKE

The hike begins at the trailhead by Dawley Conservancy, just north of the pond in Dunn's Marsh. Walking down the slope from the parking area, you may spot ducks and geese lolling on the pond in the marsh. Butterflies and dragonflies zip among the tall grasses on the edge of the marsh to the left, as traffic passes on Seminole Highway to the right.

Crossing the highway, you soon pass under the limbs of some majestic oaks, then pass very close to some large, upscale homes on both sides of the path. Past the houses to the north, you should be able to spot the treetops of the University of Wisconsin Arboretum.

The terrain here is rolling hills covered with trees. Check out some of the backyard gardens and flower plantings as you move past more houses. A cluster of pine trees on your right soon opens up onto a large grassy field with a playground and gazebo.

Coming around a bend, the next open space is more reminiscent of prairie, with thick stands of tallgrass stretching to the horizon. Passing a basketball and tennis court on the left, you cross a small residential street, then follow the path into another stretch of woods. There are some nice hickory trees hanging over the path as it dips and runs downhill. Crane your neck to see how many birds' nests you can spot up in the branches.

Continuing along the path, you walk across a small bridge and pass a spur path on the right, while a brook bubbles pleasantly on the left. The brook runs under another bridge that you cross, then swoop around on the path and through a long concrete tunnel. Moving through the tunnel, you follow the path as it winds past a small, picturesque pond, then comes alongside another brook. Here you pick up the sound of traffic in the distance, the first intrusion of civilization on this sylvan walk.

To the left is a hillside with a variety of trees growing tall and drooping their branches over the path. After you ascend the hill, follow the path out of the woods, where you face the busy intersection of Fish Hatchery Road and McKee Road.

Crossing Fish Hatchery Road on a green metal overpass, you are now just a short distance from Nevin State Fish Hatchery at a Wisconsin Department of Natural Resources Service Center. From here, turn around and head back to the trailhead. It's a lot easier going down the hill just past the overpass than it was coming up. Just keep an eye out for cyclists zipping around blind curves and zooming downhill! It's nice to stop for a breather along the brook that flows near the path, where wildflowers bloom including yellow stick-tight and purple joe-pye weed.

MILES AND DIRECTIONS

0.0 Walk from the trailhead toward the pond in the marsh. Reach a T-junction with a paved path and turn right, walking with the pond on your left.

0.3 Cross Seminole Highway and continue walking on the paved path. Come to a fork and follow the left-hand path.

The path goes past wildflowers and impressive trees as it skirts the edge of the city.

Capital City State Trail

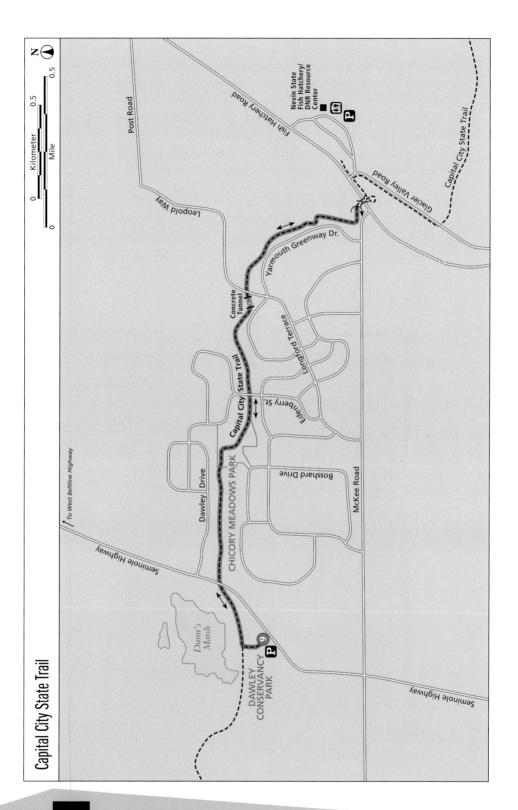

0.7 Walk past an open field on the right side of the trail. Immediately after the field, you pass a spur trail running to the left. Continue walking on the main path.

1.0 Reach Edenberry Street. Follow the path across the street and continue walking on the path into the woods.

1.4 Reach a concrete tunnel, walk through it, and continue walking on the path.

1.9 Walk across a succession of three bridges over a creek and continue walking on the path.

2.3 Walk onto a green overpass and cross Fish Hatchery Road by McKee Road. Just off the path at 3911 Fish Hatchery Rd. is the Nevin State Fish Hatchery, located in the Wisconsin Department of Natural Resources Service Center. This is the turnaround point for the hike. Head back along the path, retracing your route.

4.6 Arrive back at the trailhead.

Option: For an all-day hike, you may continue walking east on the path, another 6 miles, to reach Capital Springs State Park and Dane County's Lake Farm Park, which include campgrounds, picnic areas, a wildlife pond, and an archeological area with interpretive signs about the area's native plant life and Native American inhabitants.

From here, you may continue on the Capital City State Trail north into Madison, then switch onto the John Nolen Path. Follow it to Olin Park and step onto the Wingra Creek Path (see hike 12: Wingra Creek Trail). Once you reach Lake Wingra, another 4 miles, you may take city streets to the Southwest Commuter Path and follow it for a final 5-mile stretch that completes a loop back to the hike's starting point. Try this only if you are very ambitious and have plenty of time, and make sure you have a good city map as well to find your way from the Wingra Creek Path to the Southwest Commuter Path. You may also continue on the John Nolen Path, heading north into downtown Madison, where you will eventually reach Monona Terrace Community and Convention Center, on the northwest shore of Lake Monona.

HIKE INFORMATION

Local information: Greater Madison Convention & Visitors Bureau, 615 East Washington Ave.; (608) 255-2537 or (800) 373-6376; www.visitmadison.com
Local attraction: Nevin State Fish Hatchery, 3911 Fish Hatchery Rd., Fitchburg; (608) 275-3246. The oldest DNR-managed property, it raises over half a million rainbow, brook, and brown trout a year. Visitors are welcome at the fish hatchery and guided tours are available.

Nine Springs E-Way

This hike takes in a trail that is part of a longer e-way (environmental way), a corridor of parks and green space stretching across the southern edge of Madison, including nearby Lake Farm Park and Capital Springs State Park. This hike definitely takes in some rugged terrain, but also includes a very peaceful stretch along Nine Springs Creek and takes in a section of the Capital City State Trail before returning to its starting point.

Start: Trailhead by parking area

Distance: 3.2-mile double lollipop

Hiking time: About 2 to 2.5 hours

Difficulty: More challenging; rugged terrain including a lengthy marsh crossing with a poorly marked trail

Trail surface: Dirt, grass

Best seasons: Spring through fall

Other trail users: Cross-country skiers; permit required; available for purchase at trailhead

Canine compatibility: Leashed dogs permitted; permit required, and is available for purchase at a self-pay kiosk at the trailhead or from Dane County Parks; www .reservedane.com/permits/

Land status: State and county land

Fees and permits: None for hikers

Schedule: Daily, 5 a.m. to 10 p.m.

Maps: USGS Madison East, WI; trail maps available at Lussier Family Heritage Center; 0.7 mile down Moorland/Lake Farm Road from parking area

Trail contacts: Capital Springs State Recreation Area, 3101 Lake Farm Rd., Madison, WI 53711; (608) 224-3606; http://dnr.wi .gov/org/land/parks/specific/cap-springs/; Dane County Parks, 1 Fen Oak Court, Room 234, Madison, WI 53718; (608) 246-3896; www .countyofdane.com/lwrd/parks/ nine_springs.aspx

Other: Restrooms available at trailhead. Good shoes and long pants are a must on this hike. You will get muddy on the marsh crossing segment!

Finding the trailhead: From the Beltline Highway, take exit 264/South Towne Drive, heading south. Follow South Towne Drive for 0.8 mile, passing through a roundabout along the way, then turn left onto Moorland Road and drive 0.2 mile to the parking area for the trail on the right. The parking area has information boards and a restroom but no water supply (water is available at the Lussier Family Heritage Center, 0.7 mile farther down the road).

GPS: N43 01.854' / W89 20.942'

THE HIKE

As you start off on the shorter loop to your left, note the smattering of cattail along the path. Cross a wooden bridge and continue along the path. The trail can get muddy here as you take a left, passing numerous wildflowers, including the ubiquitous purple aster and joe-pye weed. As you head up a small hill along the well-groomed path, keep your ears open for the honking of Canada geese as they flap overhead, heading for the lagoons just to the north.

Once atop the hill, you have a great view of the surrounding landscape, including the nearby lagoons, as well as traffic moving on the Beltline Highway in the distance. At a junction alongside Moorland Road, a small path runs over to the Capital City Trail, which in turn runs off toward the Lussier Family Heritage Center, a clearinghouse of information on local trails and outdoor recreation opportunities.

Climbing another hill, there is a viewing platform dedicated to a local parks commissioner who was one of the first to envision an e-way through Madison. Arriving back at a junction by the trailhead, turn left to move onto the longer portion of the hike. Soon, you are in a wetland landscape, and plenty of tiny frogs hop across the path. Birds are plentiful as well, with sparrows and cardinals two of the more common species you'll spot. Walking along the somewhat muddy trail, keep an eye on the bottomlands to your left. You may catch sight of a heron rising up and flying over the nearby marsh.

The next landmark along the trail is a wooden bridge that crosses Nine Springs Creek. Ducks frequently congregate here. Turning right, you follow the path along

The rugged trail moves past wildflowers.

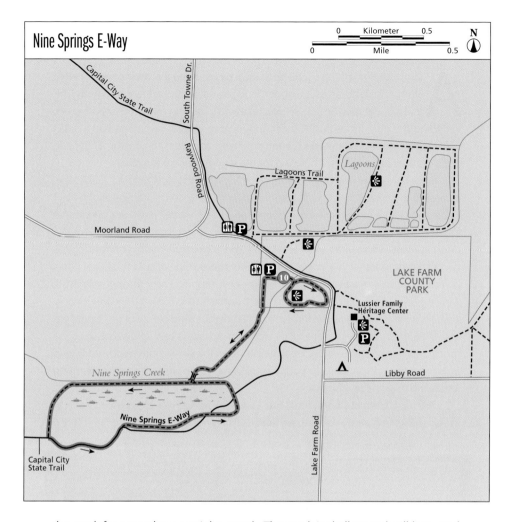

the creek for a very long, straight stretch. The creek is shallow and still here, and there are few trees along its banks. It's incredibly quiet in general, save the occasional jet passing overhead.

Eventually, you come to a cluster of trees growing out of the opposite bank of the creek, then another wooden bridge. Keep walking straight, following the path as it becomes a boardwalk. After walking to the end of the boardwalk, you'll pass a brick building on your right. Here you'll turn left and walk down a gravel road, with a cornfield on your right. **Note:** This area may be closed to hikers, in which case you'll need to turn around and retrace the route back to the trailhead. After a short distance, the gravel road intersects with a paved road, with a paved path running between them. This paved path is the Capital City State Trail. Turn left and follow it.

Civilization soon reappears in the form of a few houses, and you may have to dodge some cyclists along this section. After about 0.5 mile, you'll spot the bridge you crossed over the creek off to the left. Shortly after, you'll enter a wooded area and pass a bench on your left and a small cutout into the woods on your right. This is the starting point for crossing the marsh on your left, and it's the trickiest part of the hike. After entering the marsh, there's virtually no path, and the ground is very muddy and soggy. Watch out for the pools of water hidden in the tall grass. Just keep the bridge in sight. You want to exit the marsh just to the right of the bridge, at the creek. Once you reach the bridge, cross over and follow the path back to the trailhead. If you don't want to brave the marsh crossing, simply turn around and retrace the route you just took back to the bridge. Yet another option is to continue on the paved path (Capital City State Trail) and follow it as it moves out of the marsh area and then turns to the left along Lake Farm Road. After a short distance, the path turns left and follows Moorland Road, heading back to the parking area.

MILES AND DIRECTIONS

0.0 Begin hike at trailhead. Take the left-hand path, walking uphill through a prairie landscape, then take another left onto a small loop trail.

0.2 Reach a trail junction where a path runs off to the left and crosses a road. Turn right and head uphill.

0.5 Arrive back at trail junction and go left onto path.

1.0 Cross a wooden bridge over Nine Springs Creek. Turn right and walk along a path with the creek on your right.

1.4 Reach a wooden bridge on your right. Keep going straight as the path becomes a boardwalk. Follow it past a brick building and merge onto a gravel road. *Note:* This section may be closed to hikers.

1.7 Walk down the gravel road to an intersection with a paved path and take a left onto the path.

2.3 Catch sight of the bridge over the creek off to the left, across the marsh.

2.6 Cross the marsh and walk alongside the creek back to the bridge. Cross the bridge and head along the path back toward the trailhead.

3.2 Arrive back at the trailhead.

HIKE INFORMATION

Local information: Greater Madison Convention & Visitors Bureau, 615 East Washington Ave.; (608) 255-2537 or (800) 373-6376; www.visitmadison.com
Local event: World Dairy Expo, 3310 Latham Dr., Madison; (608) 224-6455; www .world-dairy-expo.com

11

Lagoons Trail

Part of Capital Springs State Park and Recreation Area and located along the Nine Springs E-Way, this hike goes on paths that run past former wastewater ponds near the city wastewater treatment plant. Part of the Madison Metropolitan Sewerage District, the lagoons were restored as native marshland and dedicated in 2001.

Since they were discontinued as a wastewater disposal site, the lagoons have become an ideal spot for viewing birds: The nearly 200-acre site includes opportunities to see sandhill cranes, great blue herons, and red-winged blackbirds. From late spring to early summer, keep an eye out for golden and black-bellied plover and other shorebirds. A nearby wildlife viewing platform overlooks the intersection of two creeks, where you can often spot ducks diving for food. Deer, fox, muskrat, and turtles live in the marshy terrain.

Start: Trailhead across road from parking area for the Nine Springs E-Way (hike 10)
Distance: 1.4-mile loop
Hiking time: About 1 hour
Difficulty: Easy; flat, smooth trail surface
Trail surface: Dirt, gravel
Best seasons: Spring through fall
Other trail users: None
Canine compatibility: Leashed dogs permitted
Land status: Part of Capital Springs State Park
Fees and permits: None
Schedule: Daily, 5 a.m. to 10 p.m.
Maps: USGS Madison East, WI; trail map available at Lussier Family Heritage Center, in Lake Farm Park/Capital Springs State Park; entrance just east of the parking area near the trailhead, down Moorland Road, after it goes right and becomes Lake Farm Road

Trail contacts: Capital Springs State Park, 3101 Lake Farm Rd., Madison, WI 53711; (608) 224-3606; http://dnr.wi.gov/org/land/parks/specific/capsprings/; Dane County Parks, 1 Fen Oak Court, Room 234, Madison, WI 53718; (608) 246-3896; www.countyofdane.com/lwrd/parks/nine_springs.aspx
Other: No restrooms at trailhead; restrooms available at the parking area as well as at the nearby Lake Farm Park/Capital Springs Centennial State Park and Recreation Area

THE HIKE

Heading onto the path alongside the lagoons, you're almost certain to spot ducks and other waterfowl splashing in the waters. With patience, you'll see an entire flock at once. Take the time to wait, especially if you have a camera. It's an impressive sight. The terrain around the lagoons is marshy, with thick grasses atop lowlands extending past the edge of the waters.

Off to the right, you may see the wildlife viewing platform over Nine Springs Creek, which you'll come even closer to near the end of the hike. Walk along a dike between two lagoons. It can be a challenge to fully appreciate the natural surroundings with busy roads and modern development just to the north and west, but stop and watch the birds. Before long you won't even notice those distractions.

The path is a bit overgrown and there are still some old rusty pipes hidden among the marshy grasses from the lagoons' previous life as sewage disposal sites. Turning right onto a gravel track, you walk with the lagoons on your right and a placid canal on the left lined with trees and tallgrass.

Passing a turnoff on the right that goes back to the other side of the lagoons, keep walking straight, coming soon to an impressive willow tree, its branches dipping into the canal. Eventually, you reach a T-junction where you will head left. This stretch brings you even closer to a marsh just to the left. Keep following the path as it turns to the right. If you look to the left, you'll spot the Beltline Highway in the distance, traffic moving along at a steady clip. There are some railroad tracks to the left as well. Look for the crows perched atop an old signal box.

The marsh spreads all around as you turn right and begin crossing atop a dike between lagoons back to the other side. The path here is grassy and somewhat overgrown. Soon, you come to a four-way intersection and take the path farthest on the right. A short walk brings you to a gravel path running east-west along Nine Springs Creek, heading back to the starting point of the hike.

The observation path is just a short distance up ahead on the left. Stop here to catch your breath and do some bird watching, with or without binoculars. You should have an especially good chance of spotting shorebirds during southward migration from July through October, while springtime brings a variety of ducks, gulls, terns, and herons. Sandhill cranes are also seen during spring migration.

From here, it's just a short walk back to the trailhead. Check out the large mud-flat on the right, where plenty of birds alight. After finishing the hike, head back to the parking area and check out the viewing platform; even if you walked out to it earlier it's definitely worth a return visit.

MILES AND DIRECTIONS

0.0 From the trailhead walk up to the path and turn right, walking with the lagoons on your left. Then come to a junction of paths, go left, and walk along a dike between the lagoons.

0.2 Reach the opposite side of the lagoons. Turn right onto path and walk along a gravel track with the lagoons on the right.

0.5 Reach a T-junction and veer left, keeping the lagoons on the right.

0.7 Go right onto a grassy path, moving in between lagoons. Reach a four-way intersection and take the path farthest on the right, continuing to move along the lagoons.

The path reaches the confluence of two creeks punctuated by a wildlife observation platform.

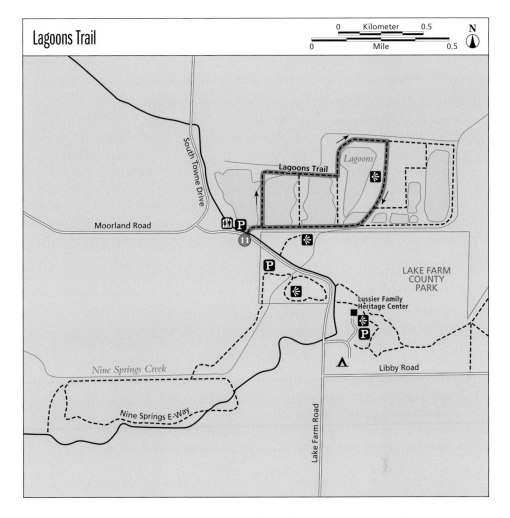

1.0 Pass a path coming in from the left, then reach another gravel track. Turn right onto this track and walk toward the observation platform standing over the water on the left.

1.4 Arrive back at the trailhead.

Option: In addition to the hike listed here, there is a short boardwalk that goes out to a nice viewing platform overlooking Nine Springs Creek.

HIKE INFORMATION

Local information: Greater Madison Convention & Visitors Bureau, 615 East Washington Ave.; (608) 255-2537 or (800) 373-6376; www.visitmadison.com
Local attraction: Chazen Museum of Art, 800 University Ave., Madison; (608) 263-2246; www.chazen.wisc.edu

Wingra Creek Trail

Beginning at one of Madison's smaller lakes, this hike follows a bicycle path along a winding creek just beyond some older commercial development. It reaches its half-way point at one of Madison's most popular parks just outside of downtown on the shores of Lake Monona.

This hike, which runs along the north bank of the creek for both its out and back segments, also runs near some of the other hikes in this book, passing by the Arboretum entrance that leads to the Gallistel Woods Trail (hike 2), and reaching its turnaround point at Olin Park, making it a nice hike to combine with others if you're interested in a full day of hiking.

Start: Parking area by path
Distance: 3.8 miles out and back
Hiking time: 1.5 to 2 hours
Difficulty: Easy; flat and straight terrain
Trail surface: Paved path
Best seasons: Spring through fall
Canine compatibility: Leashed dogs permitted
Land status: City bicycling trail
Other trail users: Cyclists and runners
Fees and permits: None
Schedule: Daily, 4 a.m. to 10 p.m.
Land status: City bicycling path
Maps: USGS Madison West, WI; a map of city trails is available through Madison Traffic Engineering, which maintains the city's bike paths, at www.cityofmadison.com/trafficengineering/bicyclingmaps.cfm. A more basic map of city trails is available through the homepage for the Capital City State Trail at http://dnr.wi.gov/org/land/parks/specific/capcity.
Trail contact: Madison Traffic Engineering, 210 Martin Luther King Jr. Blvd., Suite 100, Madison, WI 53703; (608) 266-4761; www.cityofmadison.com/trafficengineering/
Other: No restrooms at trailhead

Finding the trailhead: From downtown Madison, drive on West Washington Street/US 151, traveling about 1 mile, then follow 151 as it turns left onto Park Street. Get in the right lane after turning onto Park and after 3 blocks turn right onto Erin Street. Drive 3 blocks and turn left onto Orchard Street, then drive downhill to the edge of the lake, at the eastern edge of Vilas Park. Find parking on the street or in an open parking lot. The path runs alongside the lake. From Beltline Highway, take exit 261/US 151, drive about 3.8 miles to Erin Street, turn left, and follow directions above.
GPS: N43 03.495' / W89 24.425'

THE HIKE

From the trailhead green lily pads stud pools of water on the edge of Lake Wingra off to the right of the paved path as you begin the hike. Water actually flows out of Lake Wingra and into Wingra Creek, which is a drainage ditch that flows into Lake Monona to the east. Canada geese prowl the banks of the creek and fishermen cast their lines from small piers projecting over the water.

As you continue walking along the creek, you pass a picturesque bridge which marks an entrance to the University of Wisconsin Arboretum. There are more fishermen along the surrounding banks, and canoeists float by on the creek. The creek is wide and placid here, and marked with the occasional cove where ducks and geese paddle across the surface before suddenly diving down to search for food.

After crossing busy Fish Hatchery Road, move back into the bucolic scene along the banks of Wingra Creek, with some very nice pine trees and wildflowers, as well as an attractive footbridge across the creek. Clearly, a good deal of effort has gone into making this a nice trail for local residents. Keep walking on the path with the creek on the right.

Another busy crossing at US 151/South Park Street brings more long lines of traffic, but once again it grows quiet on the other side of the road. The path runs past an old railroad trestle and another nice footbridge. There are plenty of wildflowers along this section, and if you walk in the late afternoon you'll hear crickets chirping all around.

The path passes by a section of the creek popular with canoeists.

Wingra Creek Trail

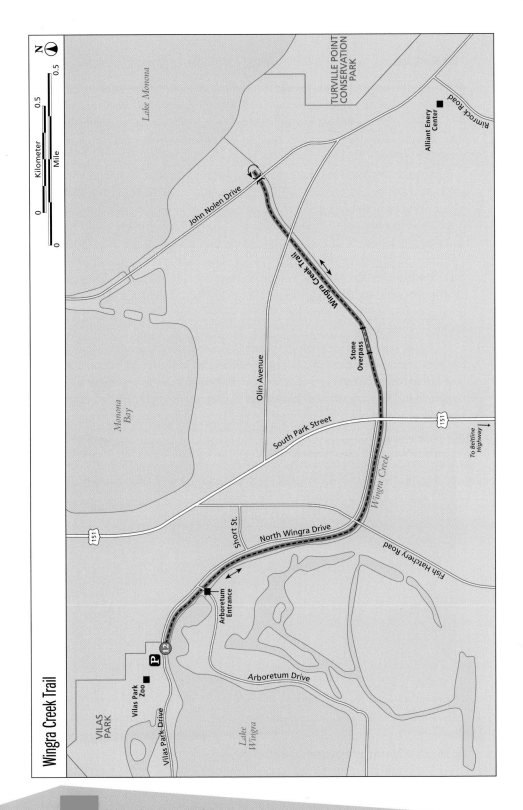

Moving along the path, you continue through older neighborhoods and eventually come to a stone archway. After passing under the archway, you'll notice that the creek grows even more wild and natural, with tree trunks drooping toward the water and grass and other vegetation growing even thicker on the banks. There's a small exercise area tucked away on the opposite bank, then some nice maples standing near the path. A few bridges span the creek, making this section almost like walking through a cavelike landscape, then a spur path merges in from the left.

At this point, you are following the path as it moves very close to the creek. Crossing under one final bridge at John Nolen Drive, you soon enter Olin Park, adjacent to Turville Point Park and another nice hike. This is also the turnaround point, where you retrace your route back to Lake Wingra.

MILES AND DIRECTIONS

0.0 Begin from the trailhead, walking along path with lake on your right. A creek flows over a small spillway, then under a bridge at South Mills Street, the entrance to the University of Wisconsin Arboretum.

0.4 Pass the intersection with Short Street on the left and continue walking along the path with the creek still on the right. You then pass intersections with Midland and Spruce Streets in succession.

The path passes by a footbridge over the creek.

0.7 Reach Fish Hatchery Road. Cross the street and continue on the path on the other side. Pass South Street running to the left.

1.0 Reach South Park Street/US 151. Cross the street and continue walking on the path, passing Beld Street.

1.3 Pass under stone overpass and continue walking on path.

1.7 Pass under bridge at Olin Avenue and continue walking on path.

1.9 Walk under a railroad bridge and then under John Nolen Drive to reach Olin-Turville Court. Turn right to enter Olin Park. This is the turnaround point. Head back on the path, retracing your route toward the trailhead.

3.8 Arrive back at the trailhead.

Options: Pick up Turville Point Conservation Park Trail (hike 6) near the turnaround point by walking to the far end of Olin Park and passing the pavilion to reach the edge of the woods.

Another option is to follow Arboretum Drive at the Mills Street entrance, near the beginning of the hike, into the University of Wisconsin Arboretum to reach the trailheads for hikes through Gallistel Woods and Wingra Woods. *Note:* You may want to drive if you choose to add these hikes. It's close to 2 miles from the entrance to the parking area near the trailheads.

HIKE INFORMATION

Local information: Greater Madison Convention & Visitors Bureau, 615 East Washington Ave.; (608) 255-2537 or (800) 373-6376; www.visitmadison.com
Local attraction: Henry Vilas Zoo, 702 South Randall Ave., Madison; (608) 266-4732; www.vilaszoo.org

Picnic Point

A 300-acre nature preserve that stretches along the shore of Lake Mendota from just past the University of Wisconsin Hospital to a residential area surrounded by woods, this pocket of wilderness just a few minutes from Madison's urban bustle also includes landscapes of prairie and marsh, as well as two points on the lake with breathtaking views across the open water.

Over 200 species of birds have been spotted here and the area is known for being a stop on both the fall sparrow migration and the spring and fall waterfowl migration, which sees Canada geese and other birds come through until the lake freezes over. Bring a pair of binoculars, find a nice isolated spot along the trail, and wait for the birds to alight in the trees.

Start: Trailhead across road from parking area, behind stone wall
Distance: 3.7-mile loop
Hiking time: About 2 to 2.5 hours
Difficulty: Moderate; some rough terrain and small hills
Trail surface: Dirt, gravel
Best seasons: Spring through fall
Canine compatibility: Leashed dogs permitted
Land status: University nature preserve
Other trail users: Cyclists; allowed only on some parts of trail
Fees and permits: None
Schedule: Daily, 4 a.m. to 10 p.m.
Maps: USGS Madison West, WI; trail map available from contact website listed below
Trail contact: Lakeshore Nature Preserve, 610 Walnut St., WARF Building, Madison, WI 53726; (608) 265-9275; www.lakeshorepreserve.wisc.edu

Other: Good hiking or walking shoes are a must on this hike; there are some muddy sections. Do not walk on Indian burial mounds. No restrooms available at trailhead; there are restrooms located along the path, just over a mile into the hike.

Finding the trailhead: From downtown Madison or the university campus, follow University Drive to the west. Stay on University Drive as it splits off to the left, with Campus Drive forking to the right. At Walnut Street, roughly 1 mile west of State Street and the capitol, turn right and follow Walnut as it goes around a roundabout and then veers left as it runs between parking lots. Reach the junction with University Bay Drive, turn right, and drive 0.2 mile to Parking Area 129, on the right, and Parking Area 130, on the left. Park in either of these lots (both lots have three-hour limits and close at 10 p.m.), then walk past the stone wall just past Parking Area 129 and pick up the trail next to the marsh.
GPS: N43 05.067' / W89 25.722'

THE HIKE

Beginning just past the stone walls, formerly the estate of a wealthy lumberman who sold the surrounding land to the university, follow the path along a marshy area. The capitol dome looms in the distance. Grab a quick look, as you are soon in the woods.

At the base of the large cottonwoods occasional wildflowers are scattered, including clusters of white boneset. This area has been cleared of invasive buckthorn and honeysuckle by volunteers who tend to the nature preserve. The waters of University Bay, an arm of Lake Mendota, peek through the tree cover on the right. You may catch a glimpse of a loon or great blue heron skimming over the surface. Passing a path that leads off toward Frautschi Point, which you'll follow later, keep going straight to Picnic Point. As the spit of land narrows, the algae-choked waters come right up to the edge of the path.

To the left, a chained-off area protects five ancient burial mounds. Passing another mound on the right, you are soon surrounded by water, as you come to a sandy spot on the left known as Picnic Point Beach. Look out over the water to see if any boaters are out on the lake. Other trails wind through the thin strip of woods on either side of the path, leading down to the water. At the point itself there's a large fire ring. Stop to take in the view, then turn around and follow the trail that leads off to the left.

After passing by an open area with a bench and a great view of the capitol dome, rejoin the main trail you walked on before. Walk a short distance and stay to the right at Picnic Point Beach, so you are walking with the water on your right. Stop for a moment and listen to the water lapping on the shore. Just ahead is a massive cottonwood. It really is awe-inspiring.

This stretch of the trail is very peaceful, perhaps because it sees less use than the path out to Picnic Point itself. Consequently, it's a lot easier to spot birds in the low and marshy terrain just beyond the tree line on the left. Species seen in the area include the black-capped chickadee, redstart golden wing, blue warbler, and rusty blackbird, as well as Canada geese and great blue herons. Frogs hop across the path, which gets muddy in places. The path then grows sandy and the marsh becomes a full-blown bog, with tree trunks sticking up out of the stagnant, greenish waters.

After passing a path veering off to the left, you re-enter the woods. Hop over some fallen trees at the water's edge and climb a small rise, dodging the falling acorns from the numerous oaks. A few more small rises take you gradually away from the lake, eventually culminating in a steep climb that brings you to a wide swath of prairie landscape, with another path joining from the left. This is Biocore Prairie where, beginning in 1997, university students began restoring this area to its native tallgrass prairie.

Just ahead, a trail branches off to the left. Keep going straight as you head toward Frautschi Point, which is another 0.2 mile down the trail. It's the spot with a large stone fireplace on the water, to the right of the path. After checking out Frautschi Point, head back toward the prairie, but go right onto another path after going about 500 yards. This is the Big Oak Trail. Reaching a T-junction, turn right, then look to your right as you pass a giant oak. At the next junction, go left, then left again onto a gravel path. Soon, you exit the woods. Turn left and walk along Lake Mendota Drive 0.25 mile, passing the Eagle Heights Apartments on your left, until you reach the intersection with Eagle Heights Drive. Take the bike trail on your

A bench provides a chance to rest and take in the view.

Picnic Point

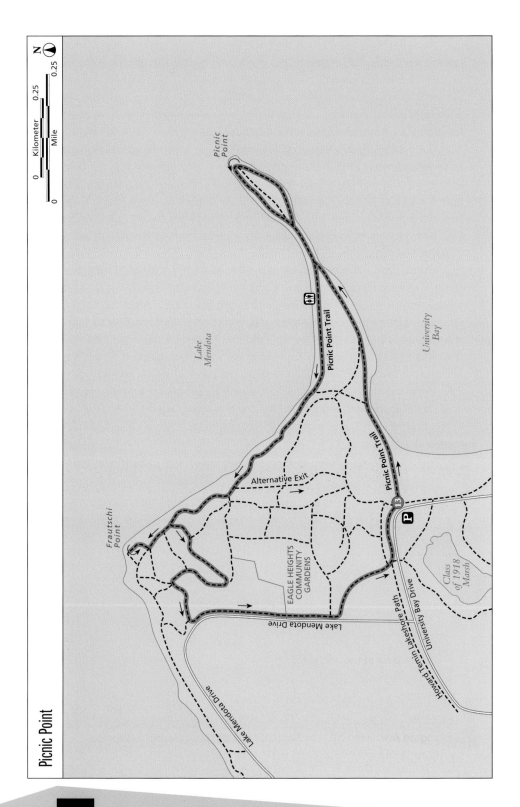

N

Kilometer
0   0.25
Mile
0   0.25

Lake Mendota

Picnic Point

Picnic Point Trail

University Bay

Frautschi Point

Alternative Exit

Picnic Point Trail

EAGLE HEIGHTS COMMUNITY GARDENS

Lake Mendota Drive

Lake Mendota Drive

Howard Temin Lakeshore Path

University Bay Drive

Class of 1918 Marsh

13

P

left as it winds downhill, ending up just north of the parking lots where you began the hike. A well-preserved marsh sits just off the road.

MILES AND DIRECTIONS

0.0 Begin at the trailhead by parking area. Walk onto gravel path past stone wall with marsh on your right.

0.2 Reach a junction/turnoff for Picnic Point Beach and Frautschi Point on your left. Keep walking straight along path.

0.5 The path joins a wider path, with water on either side. Keep walking straight, toward Picnic Point.

0.8 Reach Picnic Point. As you turn around, take the trail that goes to the left, leading into the woods with the water on the left.

1.3 Go right at Picnic Point Beach and pass restrooms on the left.

1.6 Reach a path running to the left. Keep walking straight, with the water on your right.

1.8 A path joins from the left. *Note:* This path leads back to the parking area if you're interested in a shorter hike. Continue straight on the path and pass another path that veers to the left as you move into the woods, with the water on your right.

2.1 Reach Frautschi Point, which features a stone fireplace. Turn around and head back toward the prairie, but turn to the right after you've gone about 500 yards onto the Big Oak Trail.

2.4 Reach a junction with a giant oak tree on your right. Take the path on the right, then a left onto another path, then left again onto a gravel track.

2.7 Exit the woods, turn left, and walk along Lake Mendota Drive with Eagle Heights Apartments on your right.

3.3 Reach Eagle Heights Drive. Veer onto the bike path that heads into the woods on your left.

3.7 Arrive back at the trailhead.

HIKE INFORMATION

Local information: Greater Madison Convention & Visitors Bureau, 615 East Washington Ave.; (608) 255-2537 or (800) 373-6376; www.visitmadison.com
Local attraction: Wisconsin Union, 800 Langdon St., Madison; (608) 262-2263; www.union.wisc.edu

Pheasant Branch Conservancy

Pheasant Branch Conservancy is a gem of a nature preserve tucked away in the Madison suburb of Middleton. This hike runs through a wealth of habitats, including oak savanna, prairie, sedge meadow, marsh, and lowland forest. It also takes in a very high hill right at the start of the hike and has numerous footbridges crossing Pheasant Branch Creek, which flows just south into Lake Mendota. The conservancy is a great spot for bird watching, with hundreds of species documented, both year-round residents and migratory birds.

The trail and conservancy have both seen extended volunteer efforts, ever since a community group formed in the 1960s to hold off further development of the area. Today volunteers, including many local high school students, have been instrumental in restoring habitats and keeping sections of the conservancy well maintained.

Start: Parking area in city park
Distance: 3.1-mile loop
Hiking time: About 2 hours
Difficulty: Easy; fairly flat with some small hills
Trail surface: Gravel
Best seasons: Spring through fall
Other trail users: Cyclists
Canine compatibility: Leashed dogs permitted; permit required; available for purchase at trailhead
Land status: Parts of the conservancy are owned by the City of Middleton, Dane County, and the Wisconsin Department of Natural Resources
Fees and permits: None for hikers
Schedule: Daily, 5 a.m. to 10 p.m.
Maps: USGS Madison West, WI; trail map available from Friends of Pheasant Branch, www.pheasant branch.org/aboutFOPB.html, which also has additional trail information

Trail contacts: City of Middleton Public Lands Department, 7426 Hubbard Ave., Middleton, WI 53567; (608) 827-1044 or (608) 821-8360; www.ci.middleton.wi .us/; Dane County Parks Division, 1 Fen Oak Court, Room 208, Madison, WI 53718; (608) 224-3730; www.countyofdane.com/lwrd/ parks
Other: Restrooms available at trailhead

Finding the trailhead: Take the Beltline Highway to the west, staying on US 12/14 as it splits off from US 18/151 and heads north toward Baraboo. Exit the highway at exit 150/County Road M/Century Avenue, heading east. Drive 1.7 miles to the merge with County Road Q, and stay on the road another 1 mile, then follow County Road Q as it goes left. Drive 0.4 mile and turn left onto Rolling Hill Drive. Take the next right onto Larkspur Drive, then drive 0.2 mile and turn right onto Valley Ridge Road. Take the next left onto Sedge Meadow Road, then a left into the parking area at Orchid Heights Park. The paved path runs toward the conservancy from in front of the picnic shelter, by a map board.
GPS: N43 07.121' / W89 28.640'

THE HIKE

Facing the map board and picnic shelter, go right at the trailhead and walk along the paved path, toward the backs of some houses just outside the park. Alongside the pond to the left, you may spot sandhill cranes, just one of the over 200 species of birds that have been observed in the park, including a large number of rare species like the Carolina wren and varied thrush. More common are waterfowl like duck, goose, and teal, as well as barred owls. Plenty of crows and cardinals hop around in the trees in the woods farther down the path.

Reaching the edge of the park, turn left onto a gravel path, walking past a sunken rain garden that soaks up runoff water and helps prevent erosion and flooding. Wildflowers in this area include purple coneflower and boneset. The surrounding terrain is sedge meadow, or wetland, and includes cattail, horsetail, duckweed, and wild rice.

The explosion of plant life doesn't let up as you continue the hike, with milkweed pods sprouting up along the path. Moving up a hill, one of the highest in Dane County, you turn left and start to leave behind the houses that stand along the edge of the park. From here on out it's just wild nature, save for the large power lines that cut across the center of the conservancy. The meadow is joined by prairie to the north. Both are thick with grasses, with the meadow stretching out toward the woodland to the west.

A small overlook to the left gives you a view of Pheasant Branch Springs, the headwaters of Pheasant Branch Creek, first used as a water source by Native Americans over 10,000 years ago. The setting is very bucolic and peaceful, and fossils and ceremonial mounds have been excavated nearby.

Just past the overlook, a path winds down to a platform right by the springs. It is definitely worth checking out to see the sandy soil bubbling up with springwater.

Note: Pheasant Branch Springs produces over 2.6 million gallons of water a day.

Returning uphill to the gravel path, you walk a short distance then descend from the ridgeline toward ground level. Birds of prey soar overhead, including turkey vultures and red-tailed hawks.

A few twists and turns bring you alongside Pheasant Branch Road on the western edge of the conservancy. The path here goes through the middle of fields thick with tallgrass and cattail. Veering to the left, the path passes a small parking area and then continues leftward, moving away from the road. A paved path here turns to the right, but stay on the gravel path as it moves into the woods.

Shortly after walking into the woods, you pass a small valley on the left studded with birdhouses. There's also a particularly impressive large oak tree on this stretch.

Reaching a small gate intended to keep cyclists out of part of the conservancy, you'll turn to the left onto a boardwalk, then go right, walking deeper into the

The path runs through numerous habitats, passing many native plants.

*A separate path moves south to Century Avenue/
County Road M, where it crosses the road and
continues along the west leg of Pheasant Branch
Creek. This section adds a few miles to the hike,
but it goes through some nice scenery as well.*

woods. Next, cross a bridge over Pleasant Creek and keep walking straight. Soaring oaks and cottonwoods create a cool forest canopy here.

Moving from forest to marsh, you walk along another boardwalk, this one running a fairly long distance through the lowland soil. Watch for frogs and garter snakes slithering across the path. Right after the boardwalk ends, you cross the creek on another footbridge. The next section of the hike has houses perched on a bluff above the path as the landscape shifts from woodland to savanna.

Just past a stand of white birch trees, you exit the woods and pass a large open field with a water tower. A short walk through a stand of prairie tallgrass brings you within sight of the park where you began. Hang out by the pond long enough to spot some more sandhill cranes. You'll probably see a whole family of them.

A hike on the Pheasant Branch trail will treat you with various terrains and stunning landscapes.

Pheasant Branch Conservancy

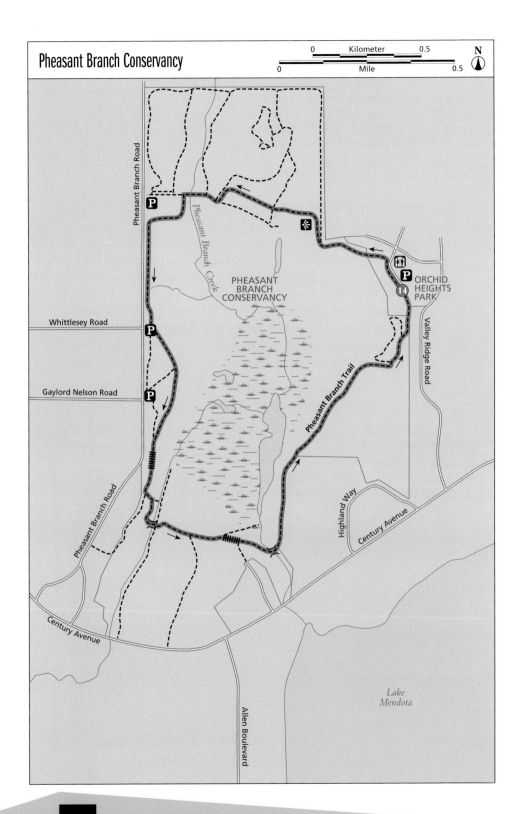

0   Kilometer   0.5

0   Mile   0.5

N

Pheasant Branch Road

Pheasant Branch Creek

PHEASANT
BRANCH
CONSERVANCY

Whittlesey Road

Gaylord Nelson Road

Pheasant Branch Road

Century Avenue

Allen Boulevard

Pheasant Branch Trail

ORCHID
HEIGHTS
PARK

14

Valley Ridge Road

Highland Way

Century Avenue

Lake
Mendota

MILES AND DIRECTIONS

0.0 From the trailhead begin heading north on the path with the pond on the left. Reach a fork in the path and veer left, onto the gravel path.

0.2 Pass a grassy loop running off to the left. Stay on the main gravel path and continue walking straight.

0.7 Descend a hill and turn left, following gravel path. Surrounding terrain changes from meadow to woodland.

1.1 Follow the path as it veers left and moves away from Pheasant Branch Road on your right, then passes a small parking area at the intersection with Whittlesey Road. Keep walking on the gravel path, with the woods to the left.

1.5 Reach a bench at a spot where the path goes right, but keep walking straight, reaching a small gate. Walk past gate, follow path, and turn onto boardwalk on the left, then onto another boardwalk to the right just before you reach a bridge.

1.8 Cross a bridge over a creek and reach a crossroads of paths, where you continue to walk straight.

2.2 Reach another bridge and cross over a creek, continuing to walk on the path.

2.7 Exit the woods, walking alongside a grassy field on the right, marked by a water tower. Reach a trail junction and go left, following the gravel path as it moves through tallgrass.

3.1 Arrive back at the trailhead.

HIKE INFORMATION

Local attractions: Branch Street Retreat, 2644 Branch St., Middleton; (608) 836-7750. This restaurant lies alongside Century Avenue/County Highway M, west of the turnoff for the conservancy, and is a fun little bar and grill that makes for a nice post-hike snack or beverage. Bogey's Family Fun Park, 3110 Laura Lane, Middleton; (608) 831-5559; www.bogeysfamilyfunpark.com.

Organization: Friends of Pheasant Branch Conservancy, PO Box 628242, Middleton, WI 53562; www.pheasantbranch.org/aboutFOPB.html

Token Creek Park

This hike circumnavigates a county park featuring landscapes of prairie and sedge meadow, with rugged sections near the park's namesake creek that are a bit more challenging than the typical day hike. It's a nice opportunity to see a restored prairie up close, as well as wetland plants and birds along a boardwalk near the end of the hike.

Located north of Madison's airport and east of Cherokee Marsh in rolling countryside along a major interstate highway, Token Creek is popular for camping and horseback riding, as well as cross-country skiing in the winter. There's even a horseshoe pit right by the trailhead. See if you can rustle up some shoes from the park office.

Start: Trailhead by parking area

Distance: 3-mile loop

Hiking time: About 1 to 1.5 hours

Difficulty: Easy; a few small rough spots, but overall very flat and smooth terrain

Trail surface: Dirt

Best seasons: Spring through fall

Other trail users: Cross-country skiers and horseback riders

Canine compatibility: Leashed dogs permitted; a dog permit is required, and is available for purchase at a self-pay kiosk in the park or from Dane County Parks; www.reservedane.com/permits.

Land status: County park

Fees and permits: None for hikers

Schedule: Daily, 5 a.m. to 10 p.m.

Maps: USGS DeForest, WI; trail map available from trail contact; a trail map is also posted on a map board near the trailhead.

Trail contact: Dane County Parks Division, 1 Fen Oak Court, Room 208, Madison, WI 53718; (608) 224-3730; www.countyofdane .com/lwrd/parks

Special considerations: The path can get very muddy on some stretches of the hike; good hiking shoes and long pants are recommended.

Other: Restrooms available by trailhead

Finding the trailhead: Follow I-90/94 north of Madison toward Wisconsin Dells. Take exit 132/US 51 north, heading north, and take the first right turn at the park entrance, entering the park. Follow park entry road 0.4 mile, passing the park office and restroom, to the parking area by a trailhead on the right, across the road from park shelter No. 2. The grass and dirt path runs south into the park from here.

GPS: N43 10.951' / W89 19.159'

THE HIKE

From the trailhead you walk past a smattering of milkweed plants along the path. Next is a large field of purple aster as the path winds southward, then swings to the right and runs literally right by the interstate highway, separated only by a thin line of pine trees. Along this section the path goes through thick woods dominated by oak and shagbark hickory.

You'll hear the roar of traffic on the highway as you continue down the path through the woods, with a large open field in the center of the park on the left. You should be able to spot some of the holes on the park's disc golf course.

The path moves gradually to the left as you reach the southern end of the park, crossing the park road and coming by a small prairie restoration, then passes by the park's dog exercise area.

The trail passes through a wide array of terrain, including woods, prairie and wetlands that are crossed via a wooden walkway.

The path now goes through another stretch of restored prairie on the left, with tallgrass coming up to the edge. There are asters, goldenrod, and sunflowers in the park prairies, which sprouted after the area was dredged in the 1930s, thus lowering the water level. Stop for a moment to see if you can spot butterflies in the thick cover, as well as squirrels and chipmunks. Next, you head back into another stretch of woods with some more nice oaks and shagbark hickories.

Exiting the woods, you find yourself in a wide-open field with a mound rising on the left. It's just a short walk through the field before you head back into woods, with a picturesque red barns hidden off beyond the trees on the right. There are some aspens among the oaks and hickories, as the path narrows and runs along a small creek on the left.

Stepping out of the woods, you're in a prairie landscape. This is a nice spot to take a breather and watch for some of the birds and wildlife that call the park home. Squirrels and chipmunks skitter through the tallgrass as it waves in the wind, while swallows swoop down from overhead. You may also spot deer among the trees you just walked through.

The path next curves left around a small pond, then plunges into even thicker grass and shrubs as you move into a wetland. The terrain here is the most rugged of the hike, and it can get quite muddy along this section, with water seeping up through the soggy ground and along the edges of the overgrown path.

Towering trees thickly line portions of the trail.

Soon, you're back in the woods, where the path runs through another low-lying section of the wetlands also susceptible to mud. This is another good bird-watching section. Dodge the muddy slough as you look for cranes and herons in the surrounding wetlands.

After crossing a bridge look for Token Creek winding lazily off to the right. Soon, another bridge brings you out of the wetland and into a small clearing alongside a road that loops through the northeast section of the park. Turn right and walk along the road, passing a small campground, until you reach a boardwalk.

The boardwalk immediately splits at a T-junction. Go left and follow the board-walk with Token Creek on the right as it moves past thick wetland vegetation. The wide variety of plants is supported by thick alkaline peat deposits, which likely formed when river drainage was blocked during the melting of glaciers between 10,000 and 20,000 years ago.

If you're visiting on a spring evening, this is a good spot to see the sky dance of woodcocks among the pussy willows in wetland open area. The birds make a loud noise, almost a beeping sound, from their beaks, before spiraling upward into the sky and, just as suddenly, dropping to the ground. It's definitely one of the more unique things you'll ever see while out hiking!

Following the park road, it's just a short walk back to the parking area by the trailhead, where you can relax at the nearby picnic shelter and perhaps scrape some of the mud off your boots before enjoying a picnic lunch.

> *For a vivid description of the sky dance, check out Aldo Leopold's essay in his classic work, A Sand County Almanac.*

MILES AND DIRECTIONS

0.0 From the trailhead walk along the path with the park road on your left, then cross over a creek to the right.

0.3 Follow the path as it moves close to the park road on the left, then follow it as it turns right and heads into the woods.

0.5 Reach an intersection with a spur trail running off to the right. Keep walking straight on the path past another spur trail on the left.

1.2 Come around the south end of the park to an intersection with the park road, where you turn left, cross the road, and pick up the path again on the other side of the road. Walk past a small prairie landscape and past two spur trails on the right, continuing on the path. Next, follow the path across

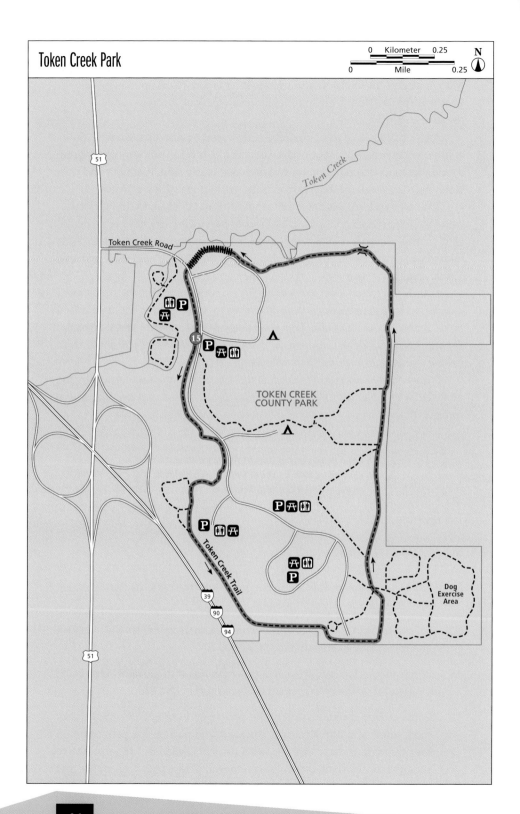

Token Creek Park

0   Kilometer   0.25
0   Mile   0.25
N

Token Creek

51

Token Creek Road

15

P

P

TOKEN CREEK
COUNTY PARK

P

P

P

Token Creek Trail

39

90

94

51

Dog
Exercise
Area

a gravel road leading to the park's dog exercise area and continue on the path as it moves north along the east edge of the park.

1.4 At the fork bear right. Walk straight, passing a path that goes off to the left, then reach a four-way junction and keep going straight.

1.6 Come to another trail junction. Turn right on path and follow it as it curves left, then right. Soon, the path enters an open field and picks up another path from the left. Keep going straight.

1.9 Reach a junction with a trail that goes to the left. Keep straight, following the path as it moves into the woods.

2.3 Exit the woods and follow the path through a field of low-lying grass and wildflowers. Soon after, cross a bridge over a creek.

2.5 Reach a park road and turn right.

2.7 Come to a boardwalk on your right and step onto it. Walk until you reach a T-junction, where you go left and walk with the creek on your right. After reaching the end of the boardwalk, you come to the park entrance road near the park entrance. Turn left at the road and walk back toward the park office and trailhead.

3.0 Arrive back at the trailhead.

HIKE INFORMATION

Local information: Greater Madison Convention & Visitors Bureau, 615 East Washington Ave.; (608) 255-2537 or (800) 373-6376; www.visitmadison.com; Gander Mountain Outdoor Store, 6199 Metro Dr., De Forest; (608) 242-9532

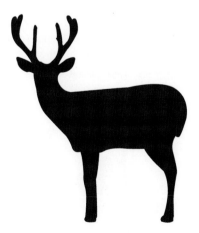

Pope Farm Park

This former farm in a suburban belt west of Madison is a place where houses are filling in the remaining fields. Yet at the same time, it is a living museum of Wisconsin's geologic history, with restored prairie, oak savanna, and native agriculture. There's a large cornfield sprawled over a pair of recessional moraines, which were created by retreating glaciers thousands of years ago.

Numerous interpretive signs fill in the details of natural history and Native American settlement. The wide open fields that surround the paths through the park make you feel like you're in the middle of wide open country, and there are some nice views of surrounding hills and the distant skyline, including the dome of the Wisconsin State Capitol.

Start: Trailhead by parking area

Distance: 1.8-mile loop

Hiking time: About 1 hour

Difficulty: Easy; a well-marked path goes through wide-open spaces

Trail surface: Gravel

Best seasons: Spring through fall

Other trail users: Cross-country skiers

Canine compatibility: No dogs allowed

Land status: City park

Fees and permits: None

Schedule: Daily, 7 a.m. to 30 minutes after sunset, Apr 1 to Oct 31; 7 a.m. to 9 p.m., Nov 1 to Mar 31

Maps: USGS Middleton, WI; a trail map is posted at the trailhead

Trail contact: Town of Middleton, 7555 Old Sauk Rd., Verona, WI 53593; (608) 833-5887; www.town.middleton.wi.us/recreation/index.htm

Other: Restrooms available at parking area along trail

Finding the trailhead: Follow Beltline Highway to the west, exiting at exit 253/Old Sauk Road, heading west. Drive 2.2 miles to park entrance and parking area on the left.

GPS: N43 04.512' / W89 33.971'

THE HIKE

tarting out from the trailhead, you will probably notice a display of native agriculture off to the left. You'll come back closer to this display later in the hike; for now, focus on moving uphill, passing a stone wall made of rocks carried along by glaciers and deposited in the countryside. Farmers cleared the rocks from their fields and used them to build walls like this one.

You'll notice a restored prairie dotted with wildflowers like purple aster and goldenrod marching up the slope of the recessional moraine you are climbing. Glaciers formed recessional moraines as they moved across the landscape and deposited boulders and other debris that remained when the glaciers receded. There are actually two recessional moraines in the park. Once you reach the top, see if you can find the second one. The summit also served as a spot where native hunters could keep watch over surrounding countryside, with a clear view all the way to the shore of Lake Mendota to the east.

Atop the moraine is a small circle of rocks, which makes a nice spot to take in the view yourself. You should be able to spot the capitol on a clear day. A wide valley unfolds to the north. This is the Black Earth Creek Valley, which has produced a wealth of sand and gravel mined from its bottoms. The sand and gravel was deposited by the glaciers as well. Look to the right to spot a ski jump standing over the valley. There's another parking area atop the hill, with restrooms nearby.

Wide-open fields are interspersed with native grasses and cornfields.

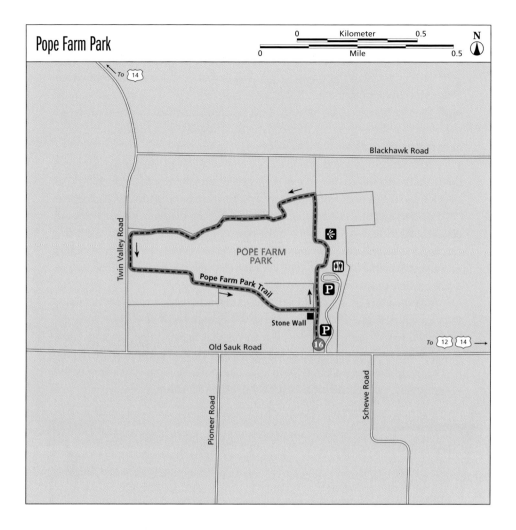

Pope Farm Park

To 14

Blackhawk Road

POPE FARM
PARK

Twin Valley Road

Pope Farm Park Trail

P

Stone Wall

P

16

To 12 14

Old Sauk Road

Pioneer Road

Schewe Road

After moving along the path past the stone wall, you find yourself walking into a wide open field, with paths laid out like a grid. There's a lone tree to the right and a soybean field to the left. Veering toward the right, you eventually reach a concrete spillway standing over a ravine, built by the Civilian Conservation Corps in 1938 and designed to prevent a gully from cutting further into the hillside. It is one of many projects worked on by the CCC during the Great Depression. Cottonwood and oak grow along the ravine, which has a path leading down into it, making for an interesting although somewhat challenging side trip. Make sure your footing is steady if you take this path.

Next up you see a grove of pine trees, as well as a few oaks, as you head toward the western edge of the park at Twin Valley Road, passing by woods then turning away from the road to walk past a large cornfield. Sun dapples on the stalks as you reach the edge of the field then hit a hilly stretch of path, dipping down a ridge then up one of the recessional moraines. As you pass oak savanna, you see some impressive trees along the path and on the slope. There's another stone wall on the moraine here.

After circling around the moraine, you move onto the final stretch of the hike, which brings you onto a path leading back toward the trailhead. Just before you reach the parking area, you pass closer to the reconstructed gardens, with a Native American garden that has corn, squash, and beans typical of a native settlement from AD 1000 and a garden modeled after one used by pioneer settlers in the nineteenth century, which has potatoes, melons, and herbs mixed in with corn and other native crops. These gardens are maintained by volunteers, including local schoolchildren.

MILES AND DIRECTIONS

0.0 Begin at the trailhead by the parking area. Walk along the gravel path, a stone wall on your left, heading toward the rise in front of you.

0.3 Come to a gap in the stone wall atop the recessional moraine. Follow the path as it turns right, then follow the path a short distance to a junction, where you go left and continue on a path.

0.5 Walk past a path on your right and continue going straight. Reach a fork in the path and go left.

0.8 Reach a junction and follow the path to the right.

1.1 Arrive at a fence at the edge of the park. Turn left and walk parallel to Twin Valley Road. Go left at the next turn and walk along the path with a cornfield on your right.

1.4 Reach a junction at the corner of the cornfield. Veer right and follow the path down a ridge. Come to an open field and stay on the path as it moves uphill and away from the cornfield.

1.6 Come to a fork in the path and continue right, heading in the direction toward the parking area.

1.8 Arrive back at the trailhead.

HIKE INFORMATION

Local information: Greater Madison Convention & Visitors Bureau, 615 East Washington Ave.; (608) 255-2537 or (800) 373-6376; www.visitmadison.com
Local attraction: Capital Brewery Company, 7734 Terrace Ave., Middleton; (608) 8316-7100; www.capital-brewery.com

Indian Lake County Park

One of the largest parks in Dane County, Indian Lake has nearly 500 acres of rugged countryside with trails winding up steep hills to give impressive views over the park's small lake, a kettle lake, with water filling in a depression created by a receding glacier.

The hike is a hodgepodge of the five trails that run through the park, including the Ice Age Trail, which passes through as it makes its way across the state. The first leg of the hike follows a path up to a modest chapel, built in 1857 by a German settler, then moves through the woods. Farther on, there's a popular pet exercise area at the west end of the park. Dogs romp through the fields just past the park's boat ramp. Along this section of the hike the path comes right alongside the lake, providing an opportunity to see waterfowl.

Start: Trailhead by parking area
Distance: 4-mile loop
Hiking time: About 2 hours
Difficulty: More challenging; numerous steep hills
Trail surface: Dirt, gravel
Best seasons: Spring through fall
Other trail users: Cross-country skiers, horseback riders, and snow-mobilers
Canine compatibility: Leashed dogs permitted; permit required; available for purchase at trailhead
Land status: County park
Fees and permits: None for hikers

Schedule: Daily, 5 a.m. to 10 p.m.
Maps: USGS Springfield Corners, WI; USGS Black Earth, WI; trail map available from trail contact
Trail contact: Dane County Parks, 1 Fen Oak Court, Room 234, Madison, WI 53718; (608) 246-3896; www.countyofdane.com/lwrd/parks/indian_lake.aspx
Special considerations: Dogs are prohibited on designated ski trails when snow is present.
Other: Restrooms available at parking area

Finding the trailhead: Follow the Beltline Highway west of Madison. From the point where US 12 splits off from US 14, follow US 12 north about 8.3 miles to WI 19. Take WI 19 west about 2 miles to park 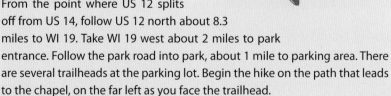 entrance. Follow the park road into park, about 1 mile to parking area. There are several trailheads at the parking lot. Begin the hike on the path that leads to the chapel, on the far left as you face the trailhead.
GPS: N43 11.368' / W89 37.219'

THE HIKE

From the trailhead the hike starts with a vigorous climb as the path winds uphill to the St. Mary of the Oaks chapel, built in 1857 by John Endres as a tribute to his faith after his family survived a diphtheria epidemic. Endres and his son hauled two tons of stone up the hill, using an oxcart.

The path winds up a steep hill, passing by a wild apple tree and then a stretch where sumac sprouts among the trees. Climbing a long wooden staircase, you pass a juneberry bush, then swing past some gnarled oaks. The tiny stone chapel sits among towering trees, including birch, oak, and aspen. The 18-inch-thick stone walls are covered with mortar scored in a block pattern.

It's cool inside the chapel, with a handsome wooden altar and small, simple windows allowing in beams of sunlight. There are also a few religious icons as well as a guest book. It's very peaceful in and around the chapel, with birds chirping in nearby treetops.

Just down the path from the chapel is a scenic overlook with great views over the lake and surrounding countryside. The park lies on the boundary between areas shaped by the glaciers and those that were not. For example, the surrounding valley has steep slopes of exposed rock, obviously untouched by a glacier, yet large boulders found in this area were deposited by a finger of ice that broke off a glacier.

The view at the edge of the hilltop trail is worth the climb.

Indian Lake County Park

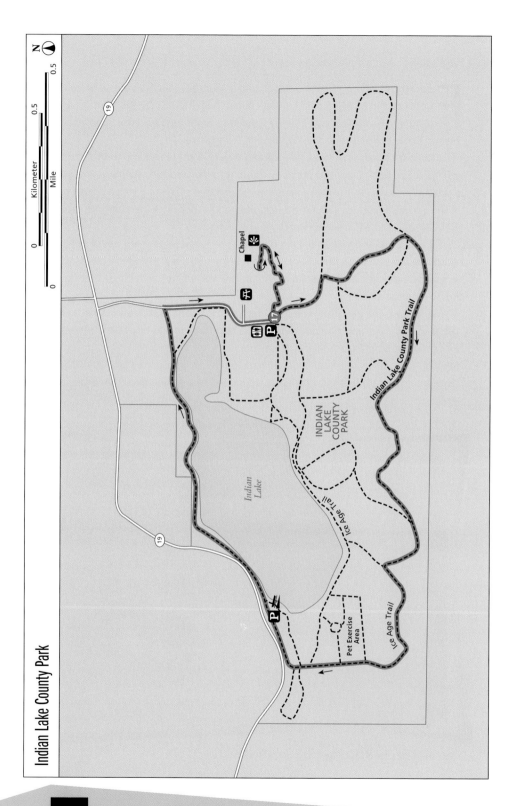

The walk back downhill gives you more chances to listen for robins, cardinals, and other birds. The hills in the park and surrounding areas were once covered with prairie, but trees grew after settlers moved in and began extinguishing prairie fires that once swept across the terrain.

Once you get back to ground level, you want to walk along the path next to the chapel path, which is marked with yellow blazes as a stretch of the Ice Age Trail. You'll walk through an open field where you crest a small rise, passing a striking lone oak tree. You then follow the path as it runs through alternating stretches of woods and open field, until you reach a trail junction just inside the woods. Don't worry about the many Wrong Way signs you'll encounter on this stretch of the hike. They're posted to prevent cross-country skiers from colliding into each other.

You next move past some tall maples as the path skirts the southern edge of the park. Climbing a hill you pass more maples as well as some cottonwoods. Another hill takes you up and along a wooded ridge, where the path gets a little sandy and soft. You then drop down a steep descent, exit the woods, and circle a bald spot of grass on the right, coming within sight of the lake.

At this point you may walk toward the lake and follow a path along the south shore back to the parking area, but this hike takes you to the left, onto another stretch of the Ice Age Trail and down into the flatlands to the west of the lake.

As you walk past the west end of the lake, you descend through a wide-open field where numerous paths crisscross the land. Soon you come to a small bridge over a creek that flows into the lake. Just past the bridge is more open space that is set aside as a pet exercise area and usually has at least a couple dogs scampering quickly over the ground. There are some nice willow trees just past here by a boat ramp on the lake.

Moving along the lake, the path becomes very narrow and hemmed in by trees. *Caution:* The path comes very close to the water and the ground becomes very soggy. Walk this section carefully, especially after a rainstorm. The last stretch of path runs past fields of wildflower and cattail along the water until you reach the park road, which you follow back to the trailhead and parking area.

As you hike, look for the signs with poems on them along the paths. There are odes to flora and fauna and the annual rebirth of the natural world.

MILES AND DIRECTIONS

0.0   From the trailhead follow the path as it enters the woods on the way to the chapel. Just inside the woods, you reach a three-way junction. Follow the middle path as it winds uphill. Walk about 300 yards, reach a fork in the trail, and go left. Go up the steps to the chapel.

0.3   Follow path past the chapel to a scenic overlook. Turn around and retrace your route down the hill.

0.7 Arrive back at parking area and take the path right next to the chapel path as it moves toward the woods. Reach a trail junction with a gate. Walk past the gate and down a gravel road. Reach an open field and turn right. You want to stay on the yellow loop trail here.

1.2 Reach a junction just inside the woods. Go straight, following the yellow blazes.

1.5 Reach another junction and go left, staying on the red loop trail.

1.9 Come to another trail junction and turn left, continuing on the red loop trail.

2.2 Reach a trail junction and turn left. This is the Ice Age Trail. Soon after turning left, you will pass a path running off to the right. Keep walking straight and follow the path as it bends to the right, running between an open field and a cornfield. Follow the path all the way across the field, heading toward WI 19.

2.7 Cross a bridge over a creek and veer right onto path as it runs parallel to WI 19. Pass a parking area by a boat ramp, as you follow a path into a wooded area running slightly above the lake, then dipping down to lake level.

3.8 Reach park entrance road. Turn right onto road and walk toward trailhead at parking area.

4.0 Arrive back at the trailhead.

HIKE INFORMATION

Local information: Greater Madison Convention & Visitors Bureau, 615 East Washington Ave.; (608) 255-2537 or (800) 373-6376; www.visitmadison.com
Local attraction: On the Creek Fishing Shop, 2120 Main St., Cross Plains; (608) 798-1137; www .onthecreekflyshop.com

White Oak Nature Trail and Prairie Trail

Located just south of Madison, Lake Kegonsa is one of Madison's four lakes, created when the Wisconsin Glacier slid over the landscape during the last ice age. Lake Kegonsa State Park is a popular, well-tended park and a nice escape from the urban grind, with several miles of hiking and skiing trails and a small beach area that includes a spot for pets to swim. Anglers cast for panfish and bass on the waters.

Trails run through woods and past prairie, and there's a short boardwalk to a small wetland with ducks, geese, and muskrat. In addition to the White Oak Nature Trail, also known as the green loop trail, and Prairie, or blue loop trail, this hike also includes the Bluebird, or yellow loop trail. Trails wind through the woods and past a swath of prairie before heading down to the lakeside.

Start: Trailhead by parking area
Distance: 3.7-mile triple loop
Hiking time: About 1.5 to 2 hours
Difficulty: Easy; largely flat surfaces
Trail surface: Dirt, gravel
Best seasons: Spring through fall
Canine compatibility: Leashed dogs permitted; but not on the White Oak Nature Trail
Land status: State park
Other trail users: Cross-country skiers
Fees and permits: Permit required; available for purchase at park entrance

Schedule: Daily, 6 a.m. to 11 p.m.
Maps: USGS Stoughton, WI; trail map available from trail contact
Trail contact: Lake Kegonsa State Park, 2405 Door Creek Rd., Stoughton, WI 53589; (608) 873-9695; http://dnr.wi.gov/org/land/parks/specific/lakekegonsa/
Special considerations: Hiking and dogs are not allowed on most trails in the park when they are snow covered and groomed for skiing
Other: Restrooms available by parking area for trail

Finding the trailhead: From Madison, exit the Beltline Highway/US 12/18 at exit 267/142 and take I-39/90 south. Drive 5 miles to exit 142/County Road N and exit, turning right. Drive 0.7 mile on County Road N and turn right onto Koshkonong Road. Drive 1.8 miles to where the road ends at a T-junction with Door Creek Road. Turn left and drive 0.9 mile to the turnoff for the park entrance on the right. Drive 0.2 mile to the park entrance, where you can obtain a permit. Just past the entrance, turn right and drive to a parking area by a restroom building and playground. The trailhead for the White Oak NatureTrail is to the right of the playground. There is a post numbered 14 on the left side of the path.
GPS: N42 58.824' / W89 14.178'

18

THE HIKE

A
t the trailhead there is a wooden box that has nature guides to the White Oak Nature Trail inside. There are numbered posts along the path that correspond to points in the guide. From the beginning of the hike, there is plenty of wildlife to see with possums, squirrels, chipmunks, and rabbits making their homes among the trees.

The wide path cuts through towering oaks. After about 0.3 mile, it passes a restroom off to the right, then swings to the left, coming alongside a bench within sight of farm fields off to the right.

The path then goes over a small hill as it passes an Indian mound to the right, with a small power station in the distance. Stay off the mound as you continue walking on the path. You then come even closer to the adjacent farm field. It's a long view to the horizon and particularly impressive if you're hiking at sunset.

You then veer away from the field and pass another bench, as well as some nice cottonwoods, then an impressive sight on the right, a large pine plantation, or tight cluster of pine trees. There are plenty of birds along this section as well, especially sparrows and crows.

Passing yet another bench, you follow the path up and over a small rise and then to the left. It then goes up a longer, more gradual rise, giving a good view of the trees all around, as you head back to the trailhead.

From here you go right and hop onto the blue loop, walking past a fire pit, then exiting the woods. Here the path begins circling the prairie. Boxed in by trees in the distance, the prairie is a wide sweep of grass as well as prairie plants like coneflower, goldenrod, milkweed, clover, and bluestem, one variety that turns from blue-green in summer to deep red in the fall.

The path hugs the edge of the figure-eight-shaped prairie. Turning right, you pass a long stretch of aspen followed by evergreens. In the distance through the trees you'll spot houses along the shore of the lake, where you'll be heading shortly.

You soon step off the prairie trail and pass a picnic area near a grove off aspen. Next you head under an overpass, then cut across a park road and swing into the woods. Moving uphill, you pass more aspen and sumac then eventually go left and pass another picnic area as you descend a steep hill to the shore of the lake.

Along the lake's modest beach are a boat ramp and playground. Continuing the hike, you come to a short boardwalk leading to an observation point over the wetland. Look here for ducks, frogs, and muskrat. Canada geese often soar overhead and you may spot some sandhill cranes as well.

Returning to the path, you come to another park road crossing, then re-loop the stretch you hiked earlier before coming back to the prairie. Now you finally complete the loop around the prairie as you head back to the trailhead and parking area.

White Oak Nature Trail and Prairie Trail

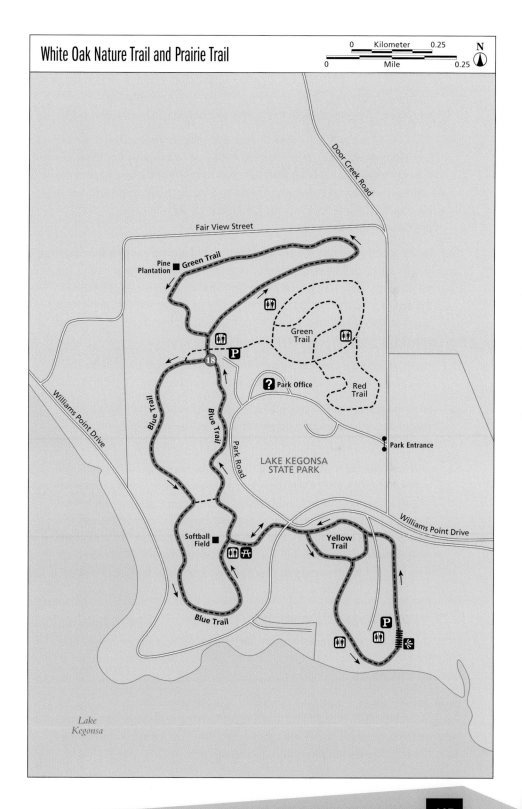

0 — Kilometer — 0.25

0 — Mile — 0.25

N

Door Creek Road

Fair View Street

Pine Plantation

Green Trail

Green Trail

Red Trail

Park Office

18

Blue Trail

Blue Trail

Park Road

P

Park Entrance

LAKE KEGONSA STATE PARK

Williams Point Drive

Softball Field

Williams Point Drive

Yellow Trail

Blue Trail

P

Lake Kegonsa

18

MILES AND DIRECTIONS

0.0 Begin on the White Oak Nature Trail, or green loop, turn onto the right fork and follow the path through the woods and past several numbered posts.

0.4 Follow the path as it goes to the left and loops back toward the direction you just walked. Pass a bench on the right side of the path. Continue following the path as it passes pine plantation on the right. Arrive back at the trailhead where you swing right, walking past the playground and heading toward the prairie. At a path junction, go right and begin circling the prairie on the blue loop trail.

1.4 Reach a path junction surrounded by prairie. Turn right and follow path as it passes a ball field to the left. Circle around the southern end of the prairie and pass a picnic area to the right. Reach a turnoff on the right for the yellow loop trail and proceed onto it. Pass a gate on the left and a restroom on the right. Cross under an overpass, then veer right, cross a road and follow the path into the woods.

2.1 Reach a fork in the trail and head left onto a path leading through the woods. Walk along the path and reach a junction where you veer right, heading uphill.

2.3 Near the top of the hill, reach a fork in the path and go left. Pass a picnic area and toilet building as you descend toward the lake. Walk with the lake to the right.

2.6 Reach a boardwalk and walk on it to a small observation platform. Return to the path and follow it past a parking area on the left. Reach a park road, to the left of the intersection of Williams Point Drive and Door Creek Road. Cross the road, turn left on path, and re-hike the hill you climbed earlier. This time at the top of the hill go right. You then come back to cross the road and walk under the overpass and past the restrooms before returning to the path by the prairie, where you veer right, back onto the blue loop trail.

3.3 Reach a junction and go right as you begin the last stretch of path to circle around the prairie on the blue loop trail.

3.7 Reach a junction, turn right, and walk the final 0.2 mile to the trailhead.

HIKE INFORMATION

Local information: Stoughton Chamber of Commerce, 532 East Main St., Stoughton, WI 53589; (608) 873-7912 or (888) 873-7912; www.stoughtonwi.com
Local attraction: Stoughton Historical Museum, 324 South Page St., Stoughton; (608) 873-4797; www.stoughtonhistoricalsociety.com

Resort and Vacation Mecca: Wisconsin Dells and Baraboo Area

Devil's Doorway atop the bluff at Devil's Lake: East Bluff.

Although Wisconsin Dells is overwhelmed with tourists who flock to its many honky-tonk attractions every summer, it's still possible to find peaceful and quiet hikes in the surrounding countryside. The area is home to one of Wisconsin's hiking meccas in Devil's Lake State Park, as well as plenty of more low-key trails squirreled away off country roads. There are stunning views on hikes that head up cliffs overlooking the Wisconsin River Valley, and opportunities to spot birds and wildlife along smaller rivers and creeks.

Plenty of history is found on these trails as well, from the site of one of the last great skirmishes in the Indian Wars that raged east of the Mississippi between the warrior Black Hawk and federal troops, to the site of an earlier thriving indigenous community centered on an impressive natural sandstone bridge.

Also in the area is the woodland farm of pioneering conservationist Aldo Leopold, which is worth a side trip, both for the pristine sylvan surroundings and to learn about his philosophy and efforts to preserve the natural landscape.

Rowan Creek Trail

This is one of the more bucolic and pleasant hikes in southern Wisconsin, with paths looping through the woods and along Rowan Creek just outside the town of Poynette. The hike takes in diverse habitats over its short length, including wetlands, a coldwater stream, prairie, and both upland and lowland forest, with a variety of trees and wildlife to spot along the paths.

Rowan Creek is one of the more highly regarded trout streams in the state, with brown trout and numerous other fish darting through the clear waters. The creek flows from the fishery area into Lake Wisconsin and the Wisconsin River.

Start: Trailhead by parking area

Distance: 2.9 miles double-looped lollipop

Hiking time: About 1 to 1.5 hours

Difficulty: Moderate; path goes over a few hills

Trail surface: Dirt, sand

Best seasons: Spring through fall

Other trail users: Cross-country skiers

Canine compatibility: Leashed dogs permitted

Fees and permits: None

Schedule: Open daily

Land status: State fishery area

Maps: USGS Poynette, WI; trail map posted at trailhead; a map of the area is available through the trail contact

Trail contact: Fisheries manager, DNR State Game Farm, N3344 Stebbins Rd., Poynette, WI 53955; (608) 635-4989; http://dnr.wi.gov/org/land/wildlife/wildlife_areas/rowancreek.htm; DNR Service Center, W7303 County Hwy. CS, Poynette, WI 53955; (608) 635-8110

Special considerations: Parts of the trail are open to hunters; check with the trail contact for details.

Other: No restrooms or water at trailhead. Make sure you have good, sturdy shoes for this hike.

Finding the trailhead: From Madison, take I-39/90/94 about 20 miles north of the airport to exit 115; exit the highway and head east on County Road CS. Drive about 2.5 miles to parking area and trailhead on your left (slow down and keep an eye out for the turnoff; it doesn't have good signage).

GPS: N43 22.868' / W89 24.895'

THE HIKE

You begin from the trailhead, walking along the path through soft, sandy soil. The surrounding landscape is upland forest, with some very nice oak, hickory, and cedar trees, which are later joined on the trail by maples and aspens.

Following the path down a modest slope, you pass a large pine tree on the left and soon reach a boardwalk that gives you your first look at the marshes and wetlands that predominate along this section of the creek. Take your time walking along the boardwalk through the marsh. You may hear and even see any number of birds and wildlife, including mallards and wood ducks, great blue herons, and ruffled grouse, as well as deer, frogs, and turtles. Cattail rise up from the swampy bottomland and there are numerous spring wildflowers, including marsh marigolds.

Crossing a second boardwalk brings you out of the marsh and into the area known as Pine Island, which definitely earned its name. The path is carpeted with needles and a cathedral of treetops soars overhead. A pine forest was planted here

Sunlight filters through the cathedral of pines.

in the 1930s and then devastated by a tornado in 1988. With careful management the forest regenerated and today is more impressive than ever. Ferns, wildflowers, and aspens fill in the area under the tree cover, providing additional habitat for deer and other wildlife.

After circling around Pine Island, you retrace your way back along the boardwalks then come back to the trail junction in the woods. Turn left and walk along a ridge at the edge of the woods, just above the wetland. As you pass some nice cedar and pine trees keep your ears open for the birds, then reach a wetland overlook where there's one of several benches placed along the path, all of which were crafted by local high school students. Take a rest on the bench and watch the wetland for ducks, geese, and sandhill cranes.

Back on the path, you move onto another ridge that gives you an even better look at the wetland, with more birds flying overhead. Soon after moving onto the ridge, the path swings past a pool thick with algae just a few feet away on the right. Another pine forest rises up on the right, and after a short distance along the ridge you follow the path downhill to another boardwalk, springwaters flowing underneath it.

A little farther on you reach Rowan Creek, flowing peacefully to the left of the path. This is also the boundary where you cross from upland to lowland forest, with the latter featuring ash, box elder, elm, and willow trees, and serving as a habitat for barred owls, woodcocks, and woodpeckers, among other birds.

Follow the path along the slow, clear creek, spotting the occasional robin or blue jay in the trees. Farther upstream faster water flow keeps the gravel bottom of the creek clear of silt, making it an excellent site for trout reproduction, but stocking is required along this stretch of the creek where the streambed is sand and a more moderate slope makes for slower water flow.

The surrounding wetlands, in addition to absorbing runoff, also keep the groundwater around 52°F, thus keeping the creek waters warm enough for trout eggs to hatch every February. The water is also ideal for trout to spawn in November.

Looping past Poynette's wastewater treatment facility, you soon reach a small parking area at Mill Street as you come to the outskirts of town. Follow the paved path to your left along the creek to the site of an old dam. A mill produced flour here until 1911. When part of the dam was removed in 1940, the stream subsequently cooled down, while more removal in 1987 created better water flow, washing away silt and allowing trout to spawn freely and feed on insect larvae, thus strengthening and expanding the trout population. (Note as you walk

The wetland plays an important role in making Rowan Creek a first-class trout stream by absorbing both floodwaters and soil runoff from nearby farms, thus keeping the trout stream clear and more habitable to fish.

along the creek how much faster the waters are moving than they were earlier along the path through the woods.)

After walking a little farther along the paved path, within sight of a recreation complex across the creek, you'll start to retrace your route back along the creek and through the woods. This time, you'll turn left before you reach the boardwalk and take a very short loop through the area known as Oak Island, which has plenty of nice trees. Past the boardwalk, you'll go left at the top of a hill and again walk along a ridge through the forest, passing some more nice wetland views. Look for a tranquil pond, and listen for woodpeckers in the oaks and cedars on the home-stretch that brings you back to the trailhead.

MILES AND DIRECTIONS

0.0   Starting at the trailhead walk into the woods and bear left at a fork in the trail.

0.1   Continue walking straight as a path veers off to the right. Move from the path onto a boardwalk, then walk along another boardwalk and turn left onto a path, moving into the forest on Pine Island.

0.7   Complete the circuit around Pine Island, then turn left and return through the wetland on the boardwalk. Exiting the wetland, turn left onto a path at the foot of a hill, and head into the woods.

A marsh along the trail.

Rowan Creek Trail

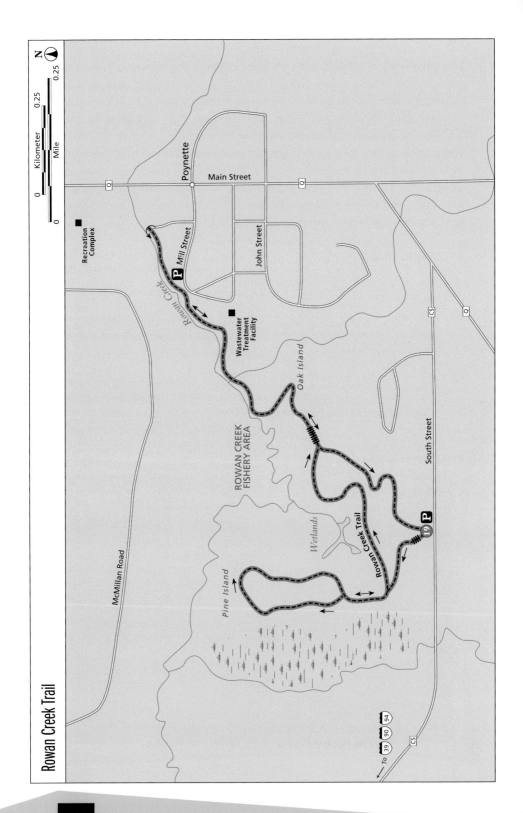

N

Kilometer
0.25

0   0.25

Mile
0

Recreation
Complex

Poynette

Main Street

Mill Street

John Street

Rowan Creek

Wastewater
Treatment
Facility

Oak Island

ROWAN CREEK
FISHERY AREA

Wetlands

Rowan Creek Trail

Pine Island

McMillan Road

South Street

CS

Q

P

19

To 39 90 94

CS

0.8   Reach a point overlooking a stretch of wetland. Continue following the path as it goes right and heads uphill and then veer left on path.

1.1   Reach a junction, turn left, and walk along a boardwalk, then follow the path as it veers to the left, passing two spur paths on the right, which make a loop out to Oak Island (you'll take this loop later). Continue to follow the main path as it moves along the creek.

1.4   Walk past a wastewater treatment facility and soon after reach a parking area just off a city street. Follow a paved path to your left along the creek, passing the site of an old dam, and continue on the paved path.

1.9   Reach a footbridge leading to a ball field to the left. Turn around here and retrace your route, heading back past the parking lot and wastewater treatment facility and then along the creek.

2.4   As you retrace your route, turn left onto the path to Oak Island. Follow the loop through the woods, then turn left back onto the main path. Follow the boardwalk you took earlier, then climb a hill. At the top of the hill, your original route goes to the right. Go left here instead.

2.7   Reach a trail junction and turn left, then walk past another path on your left.

2.9   Arrive back at parking area and trailhead.

HIKE INFORMATION

Local information: Columbia County Visitor's Bureau, 711 East Cook St., Suite 202, Portage; (608) 742-6161; www.travelcolumbiacounty.net

Local attractions: The MacKenzie Environmental Education Center, W7303 County Hwy. CS, Poynette, WI 53955; (608) 635-8110; http://dnr.wi.gov/education/mackenzie and www.mackenziecenter.com, is located past the other side of Poynette from Rowan Creek and operated by the Wisconsin Department of Natural Resources. It is a wonderful nature and wildlife preserve, featuring native animals like deer, wolves, and eagles, as well as several short trails winding past habitats including prairie and woodland and a conservation museum.

Lapacek's Orchard, N1959 Kroncke Rd., just off County Road CS outside of Poynette, has a wide variety of apples for sale, as well as orchard tours and other fresh produce; (608) 635-4780; www.lapaceksorchard.com.

> *Trout up to 20 inches long have been caught in Rowan Creek. The creek mainly holds brown trout, but also has brook trout and bass, pike, and walleye.*

This hike goes through rugged terrain, including some stretches of standing water on the path that may leave quite a bit of mud on the cuffs of your hiking pants. (Be sure to wear them!) However, those who brave this path in a state wildlife area are in for a treat. At the halfway point the path snakes through thick grass to the banks of the Fox River, an isolated and wild spot that is perfect for spotting any number of waterfowl. Snakes and frogs are also common in the wetlands that dominate along this hike. It's possible to stop and sit for an hour or more just watching the different wildlife along the low pools thick with vegetation. Pack a lunch and make a morning or afternoon of it.

Start: At trailhead 0.1 mile past parking area, along County Road P
Distance: 3.9 miles out and back
Hiking time: About 2 hours
Difficulty: Moderate; fairly flat, but some rough terrain along the trail
Trail surface: Dirt, gravel
Best seasons: Spring through fall
Other trail users: None
Canine compatibility: Leashed dogs permitted
Fees and permits: None
Schedule: Daily, 5 a.m. to 10 p.m.
Land status: State wildlife area
Maps: USGS Portage, WI; area map available online from trail contact
Trail contact: DNR Service Center, W7303 County Hwy. CS, Poynette, WI 53955; (608) 635-8110; http://dnr.wi.gov/org/land/wildlife/wildlife_areas/swanlake.htm
Special considerations: The area right around the parking area is used as a shooting range, and there is hunting allowed in areas along the trail as well; check with trail contact for details. The terrain on this hike is rather rugged in some places. It's a good idea to wear long pants and good hiking footwear.
Other: No restrooms or water at trailhead

Finding the trailhead: From Madison, take I-39/90/94 north, driving about 24 miles, and then follow I-39 about 3 miles and take exit 87 onto WI 33, heading toward Portage. Drive just over 2 miles and turn right onto West Wisconsin Street/US 51. Drive just under 3 miles and turn left onto County Road P. Drive 0.5 mile, passing over the railroad tracks, to the parking area on the left. The trail begins a little farther down County Road P. You'll have to walk up to the road from the parking area, turn left, and walk about 0.1 mile on the left side of the road. Look to the left for a metal gate. The trail begins behind it.
GPS: N43 31.144' / W89 24.267'

THE HIKE

he path actually begins 0.1 mile to the east of the parking area, and you know from the beginning this will be an adventurous hike. As you walk along the county road facing the wildlife area, you need to keep your eyes peeled for an old metal gate that marks the trailhead.

Once you've made your way up the small rise that leads to the gate, you find yourself on a rutted dirt track through a wide open field of tallgrass. There's the occasional pine or oak tree and clusters of milkweed pods, as well as the backside of a residential development on the right.

Soon enough, you're in completely natural surroundings, as you pass the last house and move farther into the field, with a view of the Fox River off in the distance. Garter snakes slither across the path and frogs hop out of the thick grasses as you begin to move into the wetland. The ground is noticeably softer here and tree cover has grown extremely sparse. You are walking on a dike through the wildlife area at this point, and soon there's a pond on the left where you may spot ducks or other waterfowl.

You really have to keep an eye out for the boardwalk you need to take on the right, as it is practically swallowed up by tallgrass. If you watch the horizon, you should be able to spot the path cutting through some trees in the distance, which will give you some idea of where the boardwalk lies.

Fall foliage paints the trail.

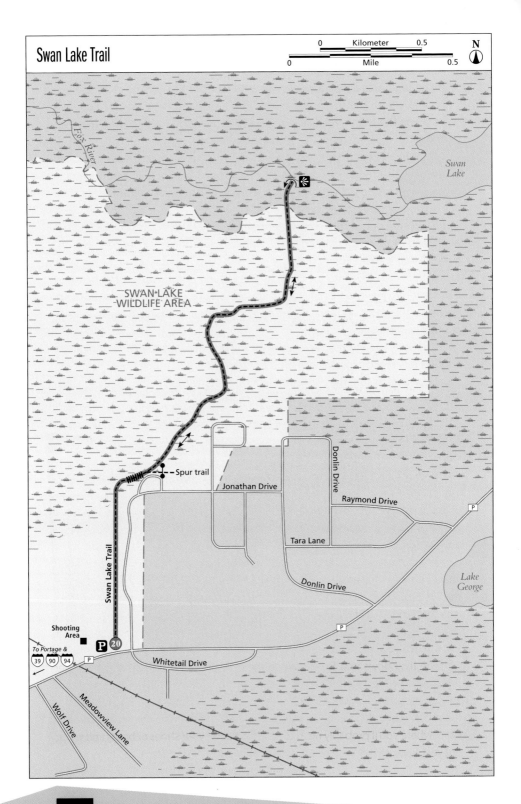

Swan Lake Trail

Kilometer
0   0.5
0   0.5
Mile

N

Fox River

Swan Lake

SWAN LAKE
WILDLIFE AREA

Donlin Drive

Spur trail

Jonathan Drive

Raymond Drive

Tara Lane

Swan Lake Trail

Donlin Drive

Lake George

Shooting Area

To Portage &
39 90 94

P 20

Whitetail Drive

Meadowview Lane

Wolf Drive

Taking the boardwalk across the wetland, you walk about 500 feet before you are ready to re-enter the woods. Note the large white birch on the right as you step off the boardwalk. It's a good landmark for your return when you'll need to find the boardwalk again.

Veer left onto the path, passing a security gate on the right, and follow the track past a smattering of homes. Stay on the main path as you pass a few spur trails, then once again leave the signs of civilization behind, moving into more rugged countryside. Soon you come to an oak savanna that opens up through a gap in the woods on the right. There are plenty of blue jays hopping in the treetops.

Up next is some more marshy landscape close to the trail, beginning with marsh grasses which then fade to a large stretch of open water on the right. This is one of the best places on this hike—or any hike—to stop and watch for waterfowl. You may even want to find cover behind a nearby tree in the wooded area just down the path. It's well worth the wait, as you may spot a heron, crane, or even the blazing white form of the great egret.

Oak savanna stretches off to the left, heading toward the railroad tracks section you crossed earlier just before arriving at the parking area. Train whistles occasionally mingle with birdcalls. Moving along, you'll have to navigate a small channel that crosses the path. If it's low enough you can jump over or skip across on larger rocks, otherwise you'll have to either ford it or find your way around it.

Leaving the wetlands behind, you pass a cluster of pine saplings, then an impressively large, dead stump surrounded by milkweed. After passing a thicket of aspen, you'll come alongside a wide open field on the right. This is an ideal spot to watch for hawks and other raptors who often soar over the field, silhouetted against the sun.

The path soon grows sandy and then a little soggy with standing water. It finally comes to a dead end as it loops around a patch of tallgrass. This is definitely the turnaround point to head back to the trailhead, but don't leave yet! Instead, look for a small trail that cuts through the surrounding grass on the right as you face the turnaround. Take it and walk the short distance to the banks of the Fox River, which you can see from the turnaround point.

The river flows into Swan Lake to the east, and the riverbank is yet another prime viewing spot for birds and other wildlife. Keep very quiet and you may spot an egret or some sandhill cranes, as well as turtles and frogs slipping in and out of the murky water. Stay here as long as you'd like before heading back to the trailhead, where you'll probably need to scrape mud off your shoes or boots and wring out your socks, to the background noise of shooters taking target practice.

20

MILES AND DIRECTIONS

0.0   Walk 0.1 mile from the parking area to the trailhead, behind the gate on the left side of the road

0.1   Walk behind the gate and begin walking down a dirt track. Walk along the track and past several spur trails leading to the residential neighborhood on the right.

0.6   Reach wetland territory, with some open water on the left. About 450 feet later, spot the entrance to a boardwalk on the right. Follow the boardwalk across the wetland, then follow the path as it turns to the left, passing a spur trail on the right.

1.2   Come alongside more wetland on your right and continue walking straight along the path.

1.6   Come to a fork in the path and take the left-hand path.

1.9   Path ends at a dead end. Look for a narrower path running through the thick grass and take it to the banks of the Fox River, then begin retracing your route back to the trailhead and parking area.

3.9   Arrive back at the trailhead, then follow road the final 0.1 mile to the parking area.

HIKE INFORMATION

Local information: Portage Chamber of Commerce, 104 West Cook St., Portage; (608) 742-6242; www.portagewi.com

Local attractions: In nearby Portage, you may want to visit the Old Fort Winnebago Surgeon's Quarters; (608) 742-2949; www.forttours.com/pages/fort winnebago.asp, which is the fort's last remaining building, or the Historic Indian Agency House; (608) 742-6362; http://agencyhouse.org, which sits next to the Ice Age Trail and historic Portage canal.

Gibraltar Rock

Like its namesake, the site of this hike is a stunning large rock set amidst breathtaking scenery views, although here it's open countryside stretching to the horizon rather than Mediterranean waters. Don't be fooled by the hike's relatively short length. It is a workout for your legs and lungs, with a very steep climb that follows a path to the top of a high butte, then a winding walk along the edge of a sheer rock face, and provides striking views of the Wisconsin River Valley.

One route to the trailhead is just as adventurous as the hike, with a short car ferry ride at the town of Merrimac, across Lake Wisconsin, a wide spot in the Wisconsin River, which has several waterside dining options. The drive from Madison takes you through the town of Lodi, on the same side of the river as the hike, and a good base for canoe and kayak trips.

Start: Trailhead by parking area
Distance: 1.4-mile lollipop
Hiking time: About 1 hour
Difficulty: More challenging; steep climb and rugged terrain
Trail surface: Paved path, dirt
Best seasons: Spring through fall
Other trail users: None
Canine compatibility: Leashed dogs permitted
Fees and permits: None
Schedule: Open daily
Land status: State natural area
Maps: USGS Lodi, WI; basic map available from Wisconsin Department of Natural Resources at http://dnr.wi.gov/org/land/er/sna/index.asp?SNA=73
Trail contact: Devil's Lake State Park, S5975 Park Rd., Baraboo, WI 53913; (608) 356-8301; www.devilslakewisconsin.com/information-center/other-natural-areas/gibraltar-rock/
Other: Rock climbing is not permitted; no restrooms or water available at trailhead; area is open during hunting seasons; check with the trail contact for more details

Finding the trailhead: From Madison, take I-39/90/94 north to exit 119/WI 60, turn left and drive west 4 miles to WI 113, turn right (Lodi is to the left). Drive 5 miles to County Road V, turn left and drive 1 mile, and turn left onto Gibraltar Rock Road, with a parking area just past the turnoff. The trailhead is a short walk from the parking area, with the path beginning behind a metal gate.

> **Alternate route:** Coming from the north at Baraboo and Devil's Lake State Park, follow WI 113 to Merrimac, where you take the free car ferry across the river, then drive to County Road V and drive the final mile to the turnoff to the parking area. (The ferry runs 24 hours a day when the lake is not frozen. Total trip time across is 10 minutes.)
>
> **GPS:** N43 20.901' / W89 35.951'

THE HIKE

Even if you come to the trailhead from Madison, you might want to loop around and take the free car ferry at Merrimac in order to get a good look at the wide spot in the Wisconsin River known as Lake Wisconsin. The water here is very dark, due to the dark roots of the tamarack trees, which bleed dye into the river farther to the north. Lake Wisconsin covers 9,500 acres and has over 57 miles of shoreline, and gets as deep as 40 feet. Numerous sandbars provide spots to tie up boats, as well as nice swimming and picnicking opportunities.

You might want to do some stretches to get ready for this hike. The strain on your legs begins almost right away from the trailhead as you walk uphill at a very steep angle, following an old paved road. The road goes past some soaring, magnificent oaks and maples. Try to come here in the fall when the leaf colors are absolutely breathtaking. If you really want to see some stunning scenery, wake up early and get out to the trail as the sun is rising. The golden rays cutting through gaps in the thick tree cover are quite a sight.

Following the cracked pavement up the hill, you traverse some switchbacks as it keeps up its steep and steady climb. Take it easy and stop and catch your breath if you need to. Clumps of ferns grow at ground level while the occasional birch tree stands out among the more prevalent oaks and maples, their white trunks arching over the road. The road levels out for a short stretch, giving you a short breather before it picks up the climb again.

Birdcalls echo through the trees as you continue to move uphill, finally catching sight of the blue sky poking through the treetops, signaling the top of the flat-topped butte. Reaching the top, you follow a narrow spur trail to the right which comes close to the edge of the cliff atop the butte. *Caution:* There are no safety railings here. Before you walk out to the edge, stop to look at a plaque honoring pioneer settlers, the Richmonds, early homesteaders for whom this area was originally named before it became a state natural area in 1969.

There are actually two paths here: The wider path, which you'll eventually take back down to the trailhead, runs parallel to the spur trail that comes closer to the cliff's edge. This smaller path runs past lots of gnarled tree trunks sprouting from the gray rock face.

Breezes blow off the cliff edge and the ground grows soft and sandy. Walk carefully as you move along the path. Pines, red oaks, and cedars provide a canopy of shade overhead, while farmland unfolds down below. Keep an eye out for hawks and other raptors riding the thermals above the valley. This is a great spot to stop and use binoculars, as there is nothing but open space above the butte and across the river valley below. The occasional small plane zips by as well, contrails fading into the air behind it.

Jumbles of rock are piled up below the jagged cliff face. Take a moment to check out the impressive formations as you continue along the path and come alongside a small field of wildflowers growing in a gap between the thick trees atop the butte.

Coming to the far edge of the cliff, you begin a descent through the woods. Almost immediately you are in rugged terrain with its own challenges that are just as much a hurdle as the steep climb that brought you to the top. The path is heavily overgrown, so stay alert to make sure you don't wander off into an unmarked area of the woods. You'll also have to go over or around numerous fallen trees. Again, make sure you don't lose the path. The vegetation and tree cover are so thick they blot out the sun in many spots.

The trail ascends through forest on the steep climb to the top.

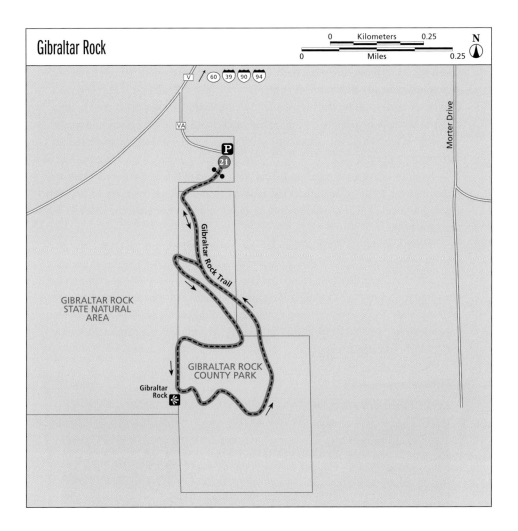

Stay alert as you move through the woods and come toward the road you hiked up earlier. After exiting through the trees, you turn right and walk down the road back toward the trailhead. It's definitely easier heading down than going up!

The nearby town of Lodi is known for its mascot, Susie the Duck, named for a mallard who laid her eggs and hatched her brood right in the middle of downtown. Since then other ducks have come to the same spot to hatch their ducklings as well. Every summer, Lodi hosts Susie the Duck Day, with events that include a parade, carnival midway, and duck derby on nearby Spring Creek.

MILES AND DIRECTIONS

0.0 Begin the hike at the trailhead, following the wide paved road as it winds uphill.

0.3 Follow the paved road as it turns right and the incline grows even steeper.

0.5 Reach a small spur trail near the top of the butte and veer right onto it, following the narrow path just above the edge of the sheer rock face. *Caution:* There are no safety railings.

0.7 Move away from the edge as you begin a gradual descent, following the path through thick woods.

1.0 Exit the woods and step onto the paved road, veering right onto the track and following it downhill.

1.4 Arrive back at gate and trailhead.

HIKE INFORMATION

Local information: Lodi Chamber of Commerce, Lodi; (608) 592-4412; www .lodiwisconsin.com

Local attraction: Treinen Farm, W12420 State Rd. 60, Lodi; (608) 592-3481; www .trienenfarm.com. Stop by in the fall for a hayride and to pick up a pumpkin in the pumpkin patch as well as trying your luck in the corn maze. It's trickier than it looks!

Gnarled trees grow along the edge of the summit.

Natural Bridge State Park

This double loop hike takes in an impressive sandstone arch, or natural bridge, along a hilly, rugged path that also leads to an impressive scenic overlook. A variety of trees and plants line the path as it winds back to the parking area, where you pick up a second path that goes past an old cabin and smokehouse.

Getting to this trail requires a drive of over 10 miles west of Baraboo through completely empty countryside. Upon arriving, it's incredibly silent, a nice contrast to the nearby Devil's Lake State Park, which draws in a steady stream of visitors.

This hike focuses on the section of the park north of County Road C, the road that leads to the turnoff for the parking area. The paths along this section have numerous signs explaining the surrounding flora and fauna. While trail maps may indicate additional paths south of the road, they are not well marked and go through very damp, soggy terrain that does not make for a very enjoyable hike. Stick to the trail hike listed here.

Start: Trailhead by parking area
Distance: 1.3-mile double loop
Hiking time: 1 hour
Difficulty: Moderate; some steep climbs, including up a woodland staircase
Trail surface: Dirt, gravel
Best seasons: Spring through fall
Other trail users: None
Canine compatibility: Dogs not permitted
Land status: State park and natural area
Fees and permits: Permit required; self-pay permit available at parking area
Schedule: Daily, 6 a.m. to 8 p.m.
Maps: USGS Black Hawk, WI; trail map available through trail contact
Trail contact: Devil's Lake State Park, S5975 Park Rd., Baraboo, WI 53913; (608) 356-8301; map also available through Wisconsin Department of Natural Resources at http://dnr.wi.gov/org/land/parks/specific/naturalbridge/
Other: Restrooms available at parking area

Finding the trailhead: From Baraboo drive south on US 12 about 7 miles and turn left onto County Road C, heading west. Drive 11 miles and turn right at park entrance, following entrance road as it winds into parking area. The trailhead is past the far end of the parking area, where two paths begin right at the edge of the woods. You want to take the left-hand path.
GPS: N43 20.787' / W89 55.818'

THE HIKE

The natural bridge is fairly early on in the hike, arching across the path after you have hiked uphill through the woods and past a field on the left. Tucked into the oak forest, it's the largest natural bridge in Wisconsin, standing 25 feet high by 35 feet wide, with the weathered sandstone sculpted by wind erosion.

Archeologists have discovered evidence of human settlement by Paleo-Indians some 10,000 to 12,000 years ago, at the same time the Wisconsin Glacier was melting at nearby Devil's Lake. Since then hundreds of generations of Native Americans, including the local Sauk and Fox tribes, passed through this area also. Beginning in the 1920s it became a popular spot for picnics as well as a tourist destination.

The wooden stairs climb upwards and eventually present a view of the surrounding hills.

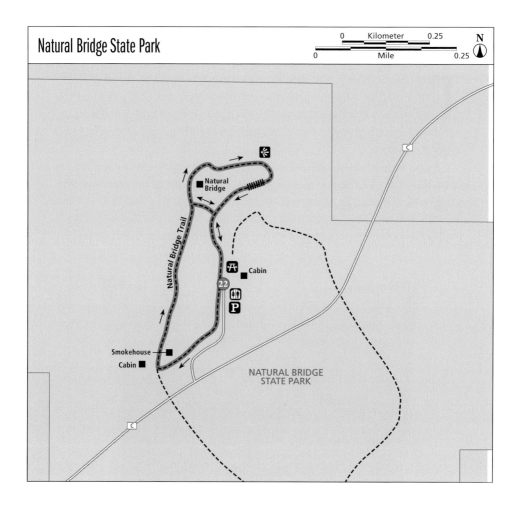

Today it's rather quiet in the park, which sits amidst farmland and woods in a rural area, giving you plenty of time to admire the bridge as it soars overhead in the rays of sunlight that pierce the tree canopy. There are other interesting rock formations standing in the nearby woods, and you may also catch sight of pileated woodpeckers in the trees. Turkey vultures and the occasional bald eagle soar overhead, and woodchucks play in the shadows of the bridge. (You have to be very patient—and quiet—to see them.)

Also in the shadow of the bridge are the remains of a rock shelter used by the Paleo-Indians. The remains of numerous animals, some fifteen species of mollusks and fifty species of vertebrates, with finds including turkey, bobcat, elk, and wolf, have been discovered here as well.

After taking in your fill of the natural bridge, move along the path as it continues to ascend a ridge. The foliage grows even more interesting along this stretch, with a small witch hazel tree on the left and numerous types of wildflowers.

The path then swings higher up the ridge and goes past a thick stand of aspen. Scan the ground for signs of gooseberries, but be careful that you don't brush up against any poison ivy!

The climb now grows steeper as you mount a wooden staircase and then reach a scenic overlook with a great view of the valley below. Geometric farmers' plots intermingle with open countryside and thick woods. The overlook extends along the edge of the ridge, where you reach another staircase that takes a long descent. The steps are so steep it feels almost vertigo inducing. Take it slow here if you have to. The staircase is squeezed between prickly ash on one side and some interesting rock formations on the other.

After leaving the staircase, you walk through the woods back to the parking lot. Take a break if you want before heading onto the next path, which is a little tricky to find. It cuts away from the parking area, running roughly parallel to County Road C, the road you drove on to reach the park. Look for some clusters of sumac right about where it starts.

The path follows a low rise, cutting through forest with thick ground cover. After a short distance you come to a small clearing fronting on County Road C. Here stands an old cabin and a shed-like building that was used as a smokehouse. Both structures are a bit rundown. Turning right and walking away from the road, you soon find yourself in a field of tallgrass and goldenrod, which stands out against the thick forest off to the right.

Coming back into the woods, you pass by the junction with the path you took earlier to reach the natural bridge. Go on back for a return visit if you're so inclined. You probably won't see a natural bridge this large or impressive in many other places. Then find your way back to the trailhead and parking area.

MILES AND DIRECTIONS

0.0 Begin at the trailhead by walking past a wooden boot scraper and into the woods on the path. Turn left after you enter the woods, pass two spur trails, then come to a fork in the trail, where you'll bear right.

0.2 Reach the park's sandstone natural bridge. Follow the path as it passes the bridge and continues to move uphill.

0.4 Come to a scenic overlook. Continue walking on the path, eventually descending a wooden staircase, then taking the left fork of the path. You next come to a path junction and continue walking straight, heading downhill, until you reach a T-junction and go right onto a path.

0.6 Arrive back at the parking area, walk to the opposite end, and pick up the path on the right that leads into the woods, parallel to the road that runs past the park entrance.

0.9 Come to a path junction and turn right, passing between the old cabin and smokehouse and heading uphill.

1.2 Walk through a field and reach a trail junction, turning right and cutting diagonally across the field before you enter the woods and begin to walk downhill toward the trailhead.

1.3 Arrive back at the trailhead.

HIKE INFORMATION

Local information: Baraboo Area Chamber of Commerce, 600 West Chestnut St., Baraboo; (800)-BARABOO (227-2266) or (608) 356-8333; www.baraboo.com
Local attraction: Wollersheim Winery, 7876 Hwy. 188, Sauk City; (608) 643-6515; www.wollersheim.com. This is the oldest winery in the state. Established in the 1850s, the winery's ivy-covered château and extensive cellars produce and store a variety of whites and reds. Guided tours and tastings are popular, and there are special events focused on wine throughout the year. Open daily, year-round.

Badger Army Ammunition Plant

Though there is little sign of life there today, the intersection of US 12 and County Road C, which is the turnoff to the park, faces the site of the Badger Army Ammunition Plant, which was the largest munitions works in the world when it opened during World War II. The plant employed tens of thousands and was a virtual city, with a school and medical and recreational facilities. Badger went on to make ammo for the wars in Korea and Vietnam. Since then it has been gradually deactivated and the site cleaned up in preparation for new uses.

Devil's Lake: West Bluff

This is one of the tougher hikes in the book. It takes in two paths, including the West Bluff Trail, in one of Wisconsin's showcase state parks, which features two bluffs rising over an oval lake that covers over 350 acres. The park has a fascinating geologic history, with quartzite boulders piled up at the bottom of two bluffs that rise some 500 feet over the lake, providing fantastic views.

The descent on this hike is more treacherous than the climb up to the top of one of the bluffs, taking you down a very steep stone staircase through thick forest. The rocks can get slippery so make sure you have good hiking shoes here. Devil's Lake is one of the most popular state parks in Wisconsin, and you can expect to see plenty of other hikers here. This isn't the spot for a quiet, solitary nature walk. Boating and camping are among the other popular activities in the park, as is swimming at the beach near the visitor center.

Start: Trailhead near visitor center and parking area
Distance: 2.7-mile loop
Hiking time: About 2 hours
Difficulty: More challenging; very steep climb and descent
Trail surface: Paved path
Best seasons: Spring through fall
Other trail users: None
Canine compatibility: Leashed dogs allowed; but only on roads, trail, and pathways
Land status: State park
Fees and permits: Vehicle admission sticker required to enter park; available for purchase at visitor center
Schedule: Daily, 6 a.m. to 11 p.m.; visitor center daily, 8 a.m. to 11 p.m. in summer; 8 a.m. to 4 p.m.

in fall, winter, and spring
Maps: USGS Baraboo, WI; trails map available at visitor center
Trail contact: Devil's Lake State Park, S5975 Park Rd., Baraboo, WI 53913; (608) 356-8301; http://dnr .wi.gov/org/land/parks/specific/ devilslake/; www.devilslake wisconsin.com
Other: Restrooms available near trailhead; bicycles not allowed on path

23

THE HIKE

From the trailhead this well-established path snakes through fields of boulders along the shore of the lake. Many of the boulders are Baraboo quartzite, a colorful pink-and-lavender rock created by extreme geologic processes that began over a billion years ago, when ancient rivers drained quartz sand into shallow seas. The sand bonded into huge chunks of sandstone, which were converted by heat and pressure into massive forms of quartzite. Frost and ice eventually cracked the quartzite into smaller boulders, which tumbled down the hill to the edge of the lake. Look closely and you can still see ripple marks from the ancient sea on some of the boulders.

This stretch of path is also a nice spot to watch for raptors soaring over the crystalline blue waters. Eventually, the path ducks through some tall pine trees. Take a look back at the diminishing snack bar and beach.

Exiting the woods, you're hemmed in even tighter by the boulders as you walk single file along the path close to the water. Canoeists and kayakers take advantage of the smooth, placid waters while fishermen cast away. The lake's maximum depth is close to 50 feet.

Passing some more impressive rock formations on the bluff above the path, you soon walk past a few houses and a small pond, then reach a road that runs along the edge of the park. Turning right, you pick up the West Bluff Trail, which here runs concurrent with the Ice Age Trail as you begin your ascent of the bluff at a trailside shoe scraper.

It's a strenuous climb with a steep, stone staircase near the start, with the path then ascending through thick tree cover. It briefly levels off as it passes some nice maple trees with brilliant leaf colors in the fall, then hits another steep stretch, at one point climbing what feels like 45 degrees uphill.

Finally, you reach the top of the bluff, with a spur trail leading to a scenic overlook. There is a bench to provide a welcome resting spot after the climb. *Caution:* There are no guardrails here.

As you move along the top of the bluff, you're in an even better position to watch for raptors. Every October, massive flocks of turkey vultures fill the skies above the lake as they migrate southward for the winter. You may spot hundreds of the red-headed, broad-wingspan birds as they soar overhead. They can fly for hours without flapping their wings. You can also spot large groups of the vultures roosting in the treetops. Blue and gray jays hop through the branches as well.

The snack bar building between the parking area and the lake, along the paved path that runs to the trailhead, was a popular dancehall during Devil's Lake's heyday as a vacation destination from the late 1800s through much of the twentieth century. You can still see the remains of the bandstand at the north end of the building where there are still occasional music performances

Quartzsite boulders pile up along the lakeshore.

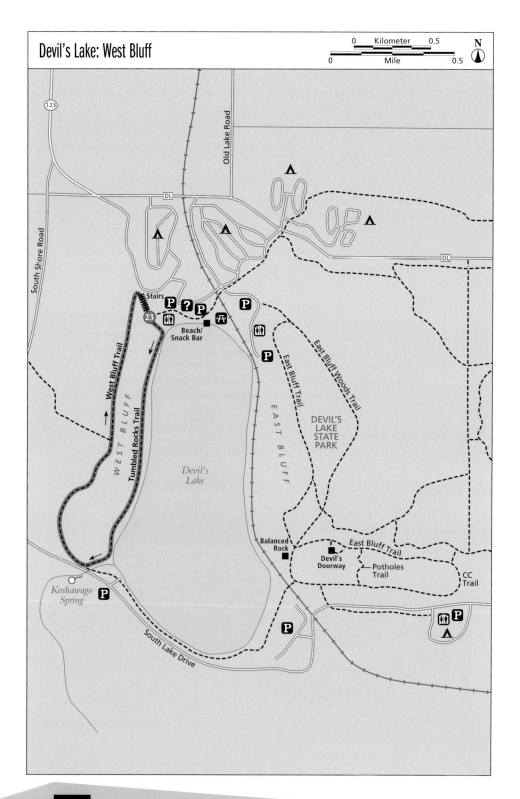

Devil's Lake: West Bluff

0   Kilometer   0.5

0   Mile   0.5

N

123

Old Lake Road

South Shore Road

DL

Stairs

23

West Bluff Trail

Tumbled Rocks Trail

W E S T   B L U F F

Beach/
Snack Bar

Devil's
Lake

Koshawago
Spring

South Lake Drive

East Bluff Trail

East Bluff Woods Trail

E A S T   B L U F F

DEVIL'S
LAKE
STATE
PARK

DL

Balanced
Rock

Devil's
Doorway

East Bluff Trail

Potholes
Trail

CC
Trail

Walking along the top of the bluff, you pass a fire road running off to the left. The hike gives you excellent views of the lake. The formation of Devil's Lake began when the ancient seas receded and an uplift formed the quartzite bluffs into a canoe-shaped ellipse of a gorge. A river cut slowly through the gorge, which deepened further as softer sandstone and limestone eroded away.

About 18,000 years ago a glacier rolled into the area and impounded the river between the massive quartzite bluffs. Devil's Lake has no natural drainage outlet and is supplied completely by local drainage and springs. The glacier also left behind rocky debris, which formed into terminal moraines, or small hills, which can still be seen around the park, including the spot where the nature center sits.

Devil's Lake was known by different names by the various Native American tribes that lived in the area, including Spirit Lake, Holy Lake, Mystery Lake, or Sacred Lake. Just prior to the arrival of the railroad in the mid-1800s, a map referred to it as Lake of the Hills. Once the railroad was up and running, entrepreneurs looking to develop the area as a tourist destination settled on Devil's Lake as an ideal name for drawing publicity (and pleasure seekers) to the area.

The park's boathouse and snack bar stand in the distance.

Reaching the end of the trail atop the bluff, you begin your descent down another stone staircase. The descent begins gradually, but soon turns into a strenuous scramble down the staircase, which is even longer than the one you took earlier up the bluff. Take it easy and pause as often as you need to sturdy your footing and get your bearings. Coming down to the bottom, you come to Park Road and follow a path to the trailhead.

MILES AND DIRECTIONS

0.0   Begin at the trailhead, following the path as it skirts boulders with the lake on the left.

0.4   Enter a wooded area with trees blocking the view of the boulders and the lake still on the left.

0.9   Reach the end of the trail and continue walking straight on a road as it passes the far end of the bottom of the bluff.

1.2   Follow the road as it curves right and passes a pond on the left before reaching South Lake Drive. Veer right onto a paved path that runs parallel to the road before veering right into the woods and beginning to run uphill—you are now on the West Bluff Trail, which here runs concurrent with the Ice Age Trail.

1.6   Make the steep climb up the bluff. When you reach the top, a spur trail runs to the right. Follow it to a nice scenic overlook. *Caution:* There are no guardrails here. Return to the main path and walk along near the edge of the bluff.

1.8   Pass into a clearing and reach a forest road running off to the left along the bluff. Continue walking on the path with the edge of the bluff to the right.

2.5   Descend a steep staircase at the north end of the bluff. At the bottom of the staircase, you will come to Park Road where you'll follow a path that turns to the right of the road.

2.7   Arrive back at the trailhead.

HIKE INFORMATION

Local information: Baraboo Area Chamber of Commerce, 600 West Chestnut St., Baraboo; (800) BARABOO (800-227-2266) or (608) 356-8333; www.baraboo.com
Local attraction: International Crane Foundation, E11376 Shady Lane Rd., Baraboo; (608) 356-9462; www.savingcranes.org

Devil's Lake: East Bluff

Believe it or not, this hike is even more challenging than the hike up the west bluff, with one section that is quite treacherous. **Caution:** *Don't attempt the CCC Trail part of the hike, which drops through a boulder field in a remote, isolated area of the park, unless you are looking for an extremely difficult hike that takes a great deal of agility and concentration along a twisting and rocky path.*

While very challenging, the hike also goes through some of the most breathtakingly beautiful scenery in the state, with paths winding past the park's most stunning rock formations, like Devil's Doorway and Balanced Rock. In addition to the bluff, the hike also runs through a bucolic stretch of woods down at ground level.

Start: Trailhead by parking area

Distance: 4.6-mile double loop

Hiking time: About 3 to 3.5 hours

Difficulty: More challenging; there is a very steep and rocky descent and ascent as you move down and then up the bluff

Trail surface: Gravel, dirt, paved path

Best seasons: Spring through fall

Other trail users: None

Canine compatibility: Leashed dogs permitted

Land status: State park

Fees and permits: Vehicle admission sticker required; available for purchase at visitor center

Schedule: Daily, 6 a.m. to 11 p.m.; visitor center daily, 8 a.m. to 11 p.m. in summer; 8 a.m. to 4 p.m. in fall, winter, and spring

Maps: USGS Baraboo, WI; trails map available at visitor center

Trail contact: Devil's Lake State Park, S5975 Park Rd., Baraboo, WI 53913; (608) 356-8301; http://dnr.wi.gov/org/land/parks/specific/devilslake/; www.devilslakewisconsin.com

Special considerations: Good hiking shoes and clothes are an absolute must

Other: Restrooms available near trailhead; bicycles not allowed on paths

Finding the trailhead: From Madison, take the Beltline Highway west to US 12, where you head north toward Baraboo, about 35 miles. About 1 mile before you reach the Baraboo limits, turn right onto WI 59 and follow it about 1 mile to where it becomes WI 123. Follow WI 123 as it turns right, then drive past an alternate turnoff to Devil's Lake on the right as you continue to follow the road past the park entrance. You are now on Park Road, which you will follow as it winds downhill, passing the park's nature center off to the left, and turning right on the road as it runs down to the visitor center and park headquarters.

After paying for your vehicle admission sticker, drive into the park, passing the parking area by the lake and snack bar as you continue on Park Road over the railroad tracks and then veer right into a parking area where the road dead-ends. Start the hike on the East Bluff Woods Trail, at the far end of the parking area, past the restrooms, on the left.
GPS: N43 25.708' / W89 43.602'

THE HIKE

From the trailhead, you walk to a fork and bear left to the East Bluff Woods Trail, one of several paths that make up this hike, and start heading uphill. As with the hike on the West Bluff, there are lots of nice maples as you walk through the woods, with beautiful leaf colors in fall.

Not far past the trailhead, the path passes a rocky creek bed on the left. Moving away from the creek, you make a more gradual ascent on the gravel path than the path makes on the West Bluff. Soon enough the climb gets steep and unlike the West Bluff, there's no staircase here to help you uphill.

Coming to the top of the bluff, you pass through thick stands of oak and maple, then turn right onto a paved path that goes to the edge of the bluff. Turning left, you are now on the East Bluff Trail, which here runs concurrent with the Ice Age Trail. *Caution:* Walk carefully here; there are no guardrails.

There's a nice view of the lake below as you walk past picturesque pine trees and purple aster. An even more striking sight is just ahead, where you take a spur trail off to the right, stepping down below the top of the bluff. Walk carefully as you move along this stretch and step onto a narrow rock ledge.

Smack in the middle of this spur is Devil's Doorway, a stunning formation of rocks balanced on top of each other and sticking out from the edge of the bluff. It's perhaps the most jaw-dropping sight you'll see on this hike or any other in Wisconsin. The huge monolith of rocks is balanced so precipitously it looks like it could collapse at any moment. (Relax, it's been around for many thousands of years.)

Back on the main path, you walk past some more impressive overlooks, then a stone staircase descends and brings you in front of an impressive rock wall. You'll notice far fewer hikers as you move along this section, and you might want to catch your breath before you tackle the CCC Trail, which goes off to the right and begins heading down the bluff. *Caution:* This is where the hike gets especially difficult as it descends the bluff through a boulder field. Not only must you navigate between the rocks, you have to keep your eye on the path, as it grows very faint.

The descent begins with another jaw-dropping view, this one of a sheer cliff face not far from the path itself. There's not much of a path here, so pay close attention as you move farther down the bluff. At the same time, you're clambering over boulders that come up to and on the path, until a sharp right turn brings you to a true hiking challenge: a nearly vertical descent just above a humongous boulder field with an endless number of the large rocks running halfway up the bluff. Take your time and make sure you have sturdy handholds and footholds. The reward for this tough section are some up-close views of rock formations that rival Devil's Doorway.

After a few more precipitous twists and turns amidst the boulders, you find yourself back on a dirt trail with a more moderate descent, which zigzags through a few switchbacks until you reach the bottom of the bluff, where you are standing on a forest floor amidst a thick tree canopy.

A view of the lake from the bluff.

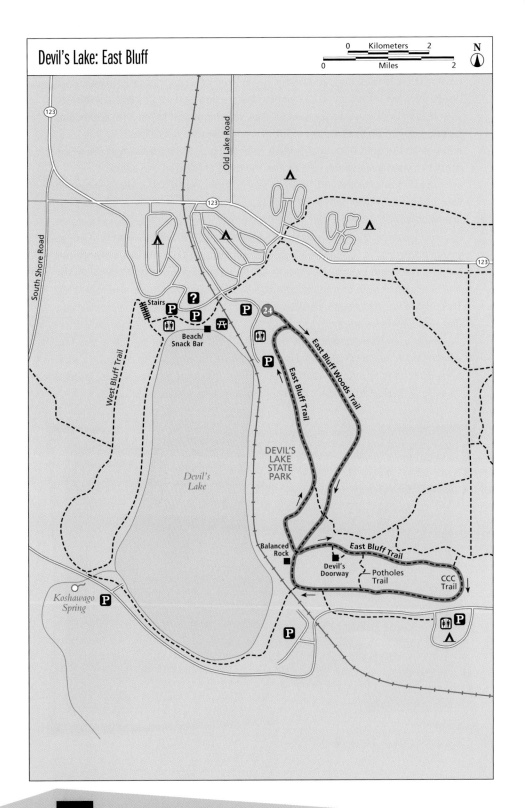

Devil's Lake: East Bluff

0   Kilometers   2

0   Miles   2

N

123

Old Lake Road

123

South Shore Road

123

Stairs

Beach/Snack Bar

24

East Bluff Woods Trail

East Bluff Trail

West Bluff Trail

DEVIL'S LAKE STATE PARK

Devil's Lake

Koshawago Spring

Balanced Rock

Devil's Doorway

Potholes Trail

East Bluff Trail

CCC Trail

A walk through the woods on the Grottos Trail gives you another chance to catch your breath, as you swing by the boulder pile you just descended past on the CCC Trail. In fact, you definitely want to catch your breath, as after a short distance (and a quick glimpse of the lake), you head up a steep rocky path up the face of the bluff on the Balanced Rock Trail.

While not quite as steep and rugged as the earlier descent, this climb is just as strenuous, as you move up through open rock. (You may have to step out of the way of descending hikers who use this more popular trail.) The viewing spot for Balanced Rock is about halfway up the bluff. Balanced Rock is not as large as other formations in the park, but it's just as impressive, if not more so.

After completing the climb to the top (the result of an incredibly tough descent and ascent), the final mile or so of the hike seems like a milk run, as you turn left and walk on the bluff above the lake, eventually swinging past a small cave, then taking a gradual descent back to the trailhead, where you may be tempted to go for a dip at the park's swimming beach.

MILES AND DIRECTIONS

0.0   From the trailhead walk into the woods on the path. Reach a fork in the path and bear left onto the East Bluff Woods Trail.

Rock outcroppings along the path.

1.0 Follow the path as it begins a steep uphill climb toward the top of the bluff.

1.4 Pass a path coming in from the right and continue walking to the top of the bluff, where you reach a fork in the path and go right onto the paved path. Walk to near the edge of the cliff and veer left, following the path along the top of the south face of the bluff, passing by trails including the East Bluff Woods Trail, Potholes Trail, and Hawk's Nest Trail, as well as a short loop that goes down to Devil's Doorway.

2.1 Descend a stone staircase and walk past a large rock wall. Continue walking straight, splitting off from the Ice Age Trail as it runs off to the left, then following the path as it veers right and becomes the CCC Trail. *Caution:* This is where the hike gets especially difficult as it descends the bluff through a boulder field. Not only must you navigate between the rocks, you have to keep your eye on the path, as it grows very faint.

2.5 Complete the CCC Trail and reach the forest floor, where you turn right by a parking area and walk onto the Grottos Trail, walking along at the base of the bluff and passing by the Potholes Trail on the right, an unmarked trail on the left, and the Group Camp Trail

3.2 Veer right onto the Balanced Rock Trail and begin climbing a stone staircase up the face of the bluff. You eventually reach a viewing spot for Balanced Rock, making it a good spot to rest as you make the climb.

3.5 Past the viewing spot, climb a stone staircase on the left and reach a three-way junction (you passed this way before). Take the path farthest on the left (East Bluff Trail), heading the opposite direction that you walked earlier along the top of the bluff.

3.8 Reach a junction in the path and go left.

4.5 Reach a junction and turn left.

4.6 Arrive back at the trailhead.

HIKE INFORMATION

Local information: Baraboo Area Chamber of Commerce, 600 West Chestnut St., Baraboo; (800) BARABOO (227-2266) or (608) 356-8333; www.baraboo.com
Local attraction: Leopold Center/Leopold Shack & Farm, E13701 Levee Rd., Baraboo; (608) 355-0279; www.aldoleopold.org

Pewit's Nest

Even though it's a rather short hike, this trek to a picturesque sandstone gorge along Skillet Creek has a wealth of opportunities for exploration: You might pick your way through the underbrush on the creek's banks to try to spot wildlife, or just stop and admire the sandstone formations that arch overhead (however, in order to help preserve the formations, please don't climb on the rocks).

Also known as Peewee's Nest, this 36-acre site along a rural road west of Baraboo was once the abode of a hermit who constructed a dwelling in one of the sandstone caves above the creek that resembled the nest of a phoebe, a bird also called a peewit, or pewit. It was designated a State Natural Area in 1985.

Start: Trailhead by parking area

Distance: 1 mile out and back

Hiking time: About 30 minutes

Difficulty: Moderate; path can get slippery, including on a descent at the halfway point and then an ascent on the turnaround

Trail surface: Dirt

Best seasons: Spring through fall

Other trail users: None

Canine compatibility: Leashed dogs permitted

Fees and permits: None

Schedule: Daily, 6 a.m. to 8 p.m.

Land status: State natural area

Maps: USGS North Freedom, WI; basic map available from trail contact

Trail contact: Devil's Lake State Park, S5975 Park Rd., Baraboo, WI 53913; (608) 356-8301; http://dnr.wi.gov/org/land/er/sna/index.asp?SNA=200; www.devilslakewisconsin.com/information-center/other-natural-areas/pewits-nest/

Other: No restrooms at trailhead; climbing on rock faces not permitted

Finding the trailhead: Take the Beltline Highway west from Madison and pick up US 12 north, driving about 35 miles north to Baraboo. As you reach the Baraboo city limits, turn left onto County Road W and drive 1.5 miles to an unmarked parking area on the left, where the trail begins.

GPS: N43 27.157' / W89 47.366'

THE HIKE

The hard dirt path begins right at the small parking area and immediately plunges into thick stands of trees. Coming to a fork in the trail, stop to check out the box elder alongside the path, then take the right fork and move along the path. The path is often muddy as it moves through tallgrass and crosses a few open areas among the thick tree cover.

Reaching Skillet Creek brings you to an amazing sight. The sandstone bluffs that tower overhead have many interesting formations, including the narrow gorge and a grotto with a waterfall at the back of it. The creek cuts through the gorge, which was formed when a glacier receded during the Cambrian period some 500 million years ago and waters from a drained glacial lake flowed through the creek and shaped the sandstone.

The creek now flows at a more moderate pace as it tumbles over a few modest waterfalls. There are also some deep pools along the creek, but there are several shallow spots as well, which give you the opportunity to hop on rocks and take in the bucolic scene from the opposite bank. Vegetation grows thick along the creek, with downed trees scattered along the banks. Living trees providing habitat for a variety of birds, while squirrels and chipmunks skitter through the ground cover.

The terrain soon grows rather rugged as you move along the bank, so turn around, cross back to the other side, and retrace your route back to the junction

Sandstone bluffs create a scenic gorge.

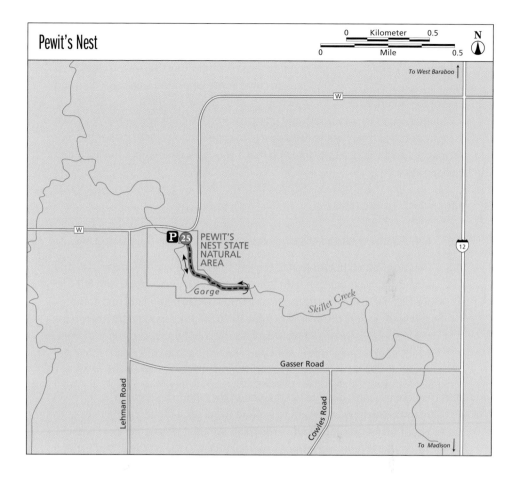

0   Kilometer   0.5

0   Mile   0.5

N

To West Baraboo

W

P 25 PEWIT'S
NEST STATE
NATURAL
AREA

Gorge

Skillet Creek

Gasser Road

Lehman Road

Cowles Road

12

To Madison

where a path leads up one of the bluffs overlooking the gorge. The climb is a little steep, but it's not that long or difficult.

The view is just as spectacular over the gorge, which is about 35 feet across and about just as deep. The narrow space between the gorge walls makes it easy to check out the rippling rock formations. *Caution:* Don't get too close to the edge, as there are no guardrails here. Birdcalls echo above the sound of water rushing below.

Trees sprout from the rock formations, arching over the creek and waterfalls. The hermit who once lived here constructed a waterwheel that used the creek's waters to power lathes, although no trace remains today.

Eventually the path drops down a jagged descent to reach creek level. Take it slow and steady here, as the muddy and rocky path can become quite slippery. Walking along the path by the creek, it's just a few steps to a dead end at a cornfield. You may want to stop here for a breather. It's a good spot to wait and watch for wildlife, with deer sometimes moving through the nearby fields. Plenty of birds are here as well, including crows and robins.

Before you head back up to the top of the bluff, keep your eyes peeled for a narrow rock ledge that creeps along the face of the bluff, just above the creek. It's a bit of a tricky walk, but worth it, as you come right alongside a small rock dam and one of the waterfalls.

Returning to the main path and going back up the bluff, you eventually reach the junction. You may want to head over to the creek for one more look at the rock formations and the grotto before you make your way back to the trailhead and parking area.

MILES AND DIRECTIONS

0.0 Begin at the trailhead, walking on the path away from the parking area.

0.2 Pass a spur trail that runs off to the left, then come to a fork in the path and bear right. Next, reach a path junction at a creek, where you turn left and walk closer to the nearby grotto and the waterfall behind it. Cross the creek and walk a short distance down the bank to look around a bit, then cross back over the creek and walk back to the junction where you turn right, heading up a small ridge. After you reach the top of the ridge, above the gorge, go left at a path junction and walk with the gorge on the right.

0.5 Follow the path downhill at the end of the ridge, descending to the level of the creek (you may want to explore the creek a bit here). The path goes about 50 feet past the end of the ridge, where it dead-ends in a cornfield. Turn around here and retrace your route back to the trailhead and parking area.

1.0 Arrive back at the trailhead.

HIKE INFORMATION

Local information: Baraboo Area Chamber of Commerce, 600 West Chestnut St., Baraboo; (800) BARABOO (227-2266) or (608) 356-8333; www.baraboo.com
Local attractions: The Mid-Continent Railway Museum, E8948 Museum Rd., North Freedom; (608) 522-4261; www.mcrwy.com; Circus World Museum, 550 Water St., Baraboo; (608) 356-8341; http://circusworld.wisconsinhistory.org

Black Hawk Unit

Named after a Native American chief who led a group of followers in an unsuccessful war against federal troops in the 1830s, the Black Hawk Unit of the Lower Wisconsin State Riverway is a stretch of woods and grassland that lies just east of the Wisconsin River where it flows by the twin river towns of Prairie Du Sac and Sauk City.

The hike starts out with a climb up a steep ridge that takes in the view of the surrounding rolling countryside, then moves through woodland before looping up into lowland territory, with wildflowers clustered along several stretches. Plenty of wildlife inhabit the unit, and the trails see relatively little use, so it's not difficult to spot deer and other forest creatures.

Start: Trailhead by parking area
Distance: 5-mile double loop
Hiking time: About 3 hours
Difficulty: Moderate; some hills and a bit lengthy
Trail surface: Dirt, paved road, gravel
Best seasons: Spring through fall
Canine compatibility: Leashed dogs permitted
Land status: State wildlife area
Other trail users: Cross-country skiers and horseback riders in some sections
Fees and permits: None

Schedule: Daily, 6 a.m. to 11 p.m.
Maps: USGS Black Earth, WI; map available from trail contact
Trail contact: Wisconsin Department of Natural Resources, 1500 North Johns St., Dodgeville, WI 53533; (608) 935-1914; http://dnr .wi.gov/org/land/wildlife/ wildlife_areas/blackhawk.htm
Other: No restrooms at trailhead; restrooms are available near the pavilion and picnic shelter on top of the ridge at the end of Wachter Road

Finding the trailhead: From Madison, head north on US 12. After driving about 16 miles, come to the intersection with WI 78, just before the bridge over the Wisconsin River to Sauk City. Turn left onto WI 78 and drive 2 miles, passing a cemetery and historic plaque on your left, to reach the parking area and trailhead on the left.
GPS: N43 14.372' / W89 43.643'

From the trailhead, the sound of traffic from the road alongside the parking area soon fades as you walk into a forest of maples and oaks, taking a small entry path to a junction, where you turn right. The path is a bit sandy at first, and carpeted with a colorful assortment of leaves if you make the hike in the fall.

The path grows more sandy as you move deeper into the woods, turning right and taking a short path to a blacktopped road. Stepping onto the road and going left, you begin heading uphill on a moderately steep climb.

The road winds gradually up the middle of a ridge, with a steep dropoff to the right. Once at the top of the hill, you turn left onto a path and pass a complex of structures used for special events, including a barn, pavilion, and picnic shelter. A cabin with an outdoor water pump to the left of the path serves as a warming house for cross-country skiers. Clumps of pine trees near the path provide cooling shade in the summer.

This area was once the Wachter family farm, with eleven family members living in an even older cabin, built in the later nineteenth century, that stands at the far end of the parking area alongside the road. The farm site and the rest of the unit were purchased by the state of Wisconsin in 1990.

Following the path past the structures, you are soon walking through grasslands lined with wildflowers, including white fleabane, atop the ridge. The view is

The top of the ridge is thickly forested.

great up here, as you can see into several adjoining valleys and are nearly 300 feet above the valley floor.

To the west, and largely obscured from view, is the Wisconsin River. The river valley and surrounding landscape were shaped by a glacier that poured huge amounts of sand and rubble during the Cambrian period some 500 million years ago. The sand and rubble eventually formed into the sandstone bedrock beneath the ridge on which you are standing.

Entering the woods, the air immediately becomes much cooler, and much more pleasant on hot days. Following the path, you swing past some large oaks, with acorns crunching underfoot. Elm, hickory, maple, and basswood are also found in the woods here, while wildflowers may include anemone, bloodroot, hepaticia, trillium, and wood violet.

As you move downhill along the gradually winding path, you should see plenty of tall maples and pine trees. Turning onto a narrower path, you find yourself on a much steeper descent, with the sound of highway traffic growing nearer.

Down, down, down you walk along the path, passing under more birches and oaks, then coming alongside a thick stand of pines on your right. Swinging back near the starting point of the hike, you go up and over some small hills, with a rock face looming on the right.

Robins hop in the trees as you move into the northern section of the unit as you crest another ridge just over the highway. A quick descent brings you to a spur trail that leads rightward to a cluster of Native American effigy mounds. The mounds were constructed between AD 600 and 1300 and are found only in an area bounded by southwest Wisconsin, southeast Minnesota, eastern Iowa, and northwest Illinois. Though they may be burial mounds, their real function is still unknown and a source of continuing research and study by archeologists.

Retracing your steps back to the main path, you walk through another open area reminiscent of the prairie that once dominated the landscape, then descend to where the path moves near a bubbling brook. This area feels almost swamplike, with soggy ground underfoot and dragonflies buzzing in the air.

Passing by a farmer's field, you hike right along the unit's boundary and then climb a small ridge, at the top passing a spur trail to the left. With another descent (the last one on the hike), you're back in the swampy area, coming closer to the sound of traffic as you walk along the soggy path.

After crossing the brook, you soon reach the highway, where a historic plaque provides information about the Battle of Wisconsin Heights, fought here in 1832. Under the command of Chief Black Hawk, a band of warriors from the Sac (or Sauk) and Fox tribes lay in ambush along the ridges and faced off against militia who had been engaged in conflict with Black Hawk and his followers in the Black Hawk War.

While Black Hawk and his men were badly defeated in the battle, their stand allowed a large group of women and children to escape across the nearby Wisconsin

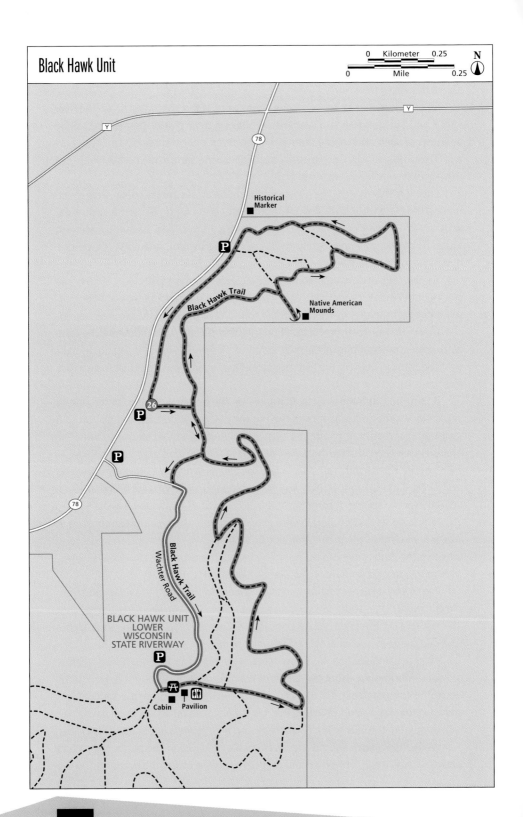

Black Hawk Unit

0 Kilometer 0.25
0 Mile 0.25
N

Historical Marker

Black Hawk Trail

Native American Mounds

26

Black Hawk Trail
Wachter Road

BLACK HAWK UNIT
LOWER
WISCONSIN
STATE RIVERWAY

Cabin Pavilion

River. Black Hawk's band lost the war a few months later, in what became an early and significant instance of Indian removal by the United States government.

Continuing, the homestretch of the hike brings you down the path as it moves parallel to the highway, moving along a small ridge just above the road and back to the parking area.

MILES AND DIRECTIONS

0.0 Follow the path into the woods as it heads uphill. Come to a trail junction and turn right.

0.2 Reach a fork in the path. Go right and walk along the path until you reach Wachter Road cutting through the forest. Turn left and walk along road.

1.1 Reach the top of a hill and come to a path junction. Turn left onto path and walk past a cabin on the right. Pass an open pavilion on the right and come to a junction just past the pavilion, where you go right onto a path.

1.3 Come to a four-way path junction and continue walking straight, following the path into a field.

1.5 Reach a T-junction and turn left onto a path.

2.2 Follow the path as it moves downhill and banks sharply to the left.

2.5 Pass a spur trail running off to the left and keep walking straight. Soon after, you reach a path splitting off to the right. Turn onto this path and follow it as it plunges down a steep descent. Continue following the path as it curves to the left and passes an overgrown path running off to the right.

3.2 After reaching a sign marked Waypoint #2, you turn right, retracing the path you walked on earlier. Shortly after, pass by the path to the left that heads back to the trailhead as you continue walking straight. **Option:** If you want a shorter hike, head back to the trailhead from here.

Green Tip:
If you're toting food, leave the packaging at home. Repack your provisions in zip-lock bags that you can reuse and that can double as garbage bags on the way out of the woods.

3.7 Reach a path junction and turn right. Walk a short distance to view Native American mounds, then retrace the route back to the main path, where you turn onto the path farthest to the right. Follow this path as it moves out of the woods and heads toward a hill.

3.9 Climb a hill to reach a junction, where you go right. Follow the path as it loops past a field to the right, then climbs a hill and passes a spur trail on the left. Next, cross a brook and come to a junction, turning right.

4.5 Reach a T-junction overlooking WI 78. Go left and follow path as it parallels the road to the right.

5.0 Arrive back at the trailhead.

HIKE INFORMATION

Local information: Sauk Prairie Area Chamber of Commerce, 421 Water St., Suite 105, Prairie du Sac; (800) 68-EAGLE (683-2453) or (608) 643-4168; www.sauk prairie.com

Local attraction: Wollersheim Winery, 7876 Highway 188, Prairie du Sac; (608) 643-6515 ; www.wollersheim.com

The Driftless Area: Southwestern Wisconsin

A view of Twin Valley Lake.

Sprinkled among towns and farm fields, these hikes offer a pastiche of topography, including streams and hills, that make for a pleasant day on the trail. Earthen mounds provide some of the highest points in southern Wisconsin and give a nice view of the jagged hills and other features of topography unaffected by the glaciers that stopped just west of Madison.

While largely a rural area, there is also the occasional and in some cases interesting spot of civilization, including New Glarus, settled by Swiss immigrants and with a distinctive Old World charm. It's a nice place to have a snack or cold beverage after hiking in the nearby state park. A more extensive set of trails is found at Governor Dodge State Park, appropriately located just outside Dodgeville, where the paths meander through woods and prairie and pass by an impressive waterfall.

So while it's a bit of a drive to get to some of these hikes, it's well worth it: You'll have the path virtually to yourself. Sometimes hiking is about going a little off the beaten path, and plenty of these hikes allow you to do just that.

Donald Park

Located in the area where rolling hills shaped by glaciers meet the more rugged terrain of the Driftless Area, Donald Park sits amidst the picturesque fields and barns of the former Donald/Woodburn farm. The Donald/Woodburn family donated the original 105 acres for the park. It has since grown to nearly 700 acres of oak woods marked by scenic vistas, rock outcroppings, and long stretches of restored prairie and savanna.

Three trout streams meander through the sprawling park, with Deer Creek and Fryes Feeder joining to form Mount Vernon Creek, and provide a nice spot for local anglers. Pop's Knoll is a popular picnic area by the trailhead.

Start: Trailhead by parking area
Distance: 2-mile lollipop
Hiking time: About 1 hour
Difficulty: Moderate; there is one steep hill along the path
Trail surface: Dirt
Best seasons: Spring through fall
Other trail users: Cross-country skiers, snowshoers, and horseback riders
Canine compatibility: Leashed dogs permitted; a dog permit is required, and is available for purchase from a self-pay kiosk in the park or from Dane County Parks at www.reservedane.com/permits

Fees and permits: None for hikers
Schedule: Daily, 5 a.m. to 10 p.m.
Land status: County park
Maps: USGS Mt. Vernon, WI; trail map available from trail contact
Trail contact: Dane County Parks, 1 Fen Oak Court, Room 208, Madison, WI 53718; (608) 224-3730; www.countyofdane.com/lwrd/parks/donald.aspx
Special considerations: Bicycles not permitted. Parts of the park are used for hunting; check with the trail contact for more information.
Other: Pit toilets available at trailhead

Finding the trailhead: From Madison, take the West Beltline Highway to exit 258/Verona Road/US 18/151 and drive west on US 18/151 about 10 miles to exit 75/County Road G, heading southwest. Follow County Road G for 3.5 miles to Messerschmidt Road and turn right. Follow Messerschmidt Road for 1.9 miles and turn right on WI 92. The park entrance is just after the turn, on the left. Follow the park road to the parking area, then walk down the gravel track to the picnic area where the trail begins.
GPS: N42 57.587' / W89 40.454'

THE HIKE

As you begin walking from the trailhead on this well-marked path, you pass some impressive large oaks with birds hopping noisily in the branches. The bluebird is especially prevalent here, although there are numerous other species you can spot if you are patient.

The path moves past a large cornfield on the right as Fryes Feeder Creek flows lazily by on the left. Soon after, there's a bridge to the left with a massive oak beside it. The bridge leads to a public hunting and fishing area, but you want to keep walking straight until you reach another bridge that crosses just upstream from the confluence of Frye Feeder and Deer Creeks into Mount Vernon Creek.

After crossing the creek, follow the path as it moves up a small ridge on the edge of a forest, giving you a nice look over the prairie landscape to the right.

Early morning sunshine comes through trees.

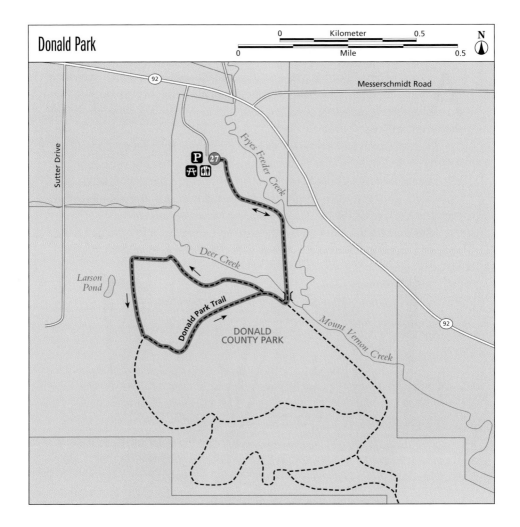

Turning right and following the path through the woods and above Deer Creek, you pass some nice cottonwoods, then some interesting rock formations on the left.

Exiting the woods, you are looking out on a beautiful, pristine swath of prairie to the right. A path junction is notable for the large number of wildflowers in bloom. At the junction, the path continues straight toward Hitchcock Ridge, but you want to turn left, going past Larson Pond, which is sunken very low in the ground; you may have to strain a bit to see it.

More wildflowers mark the path as you continue walking south, then you spot a huge grove of pine trees on the right, marching up a hill. Soon, you're back in the woods, walking on rather sandy soil. This is where you hit an unexpected tough stretch, with the path suddenly heading up a very steep hill, and then an even steeper descent.

The walk downhill tapers off and becomes more gradual as you reach ground level, then makes its way through more woods before coming back to the bridge over the creek and heading back to the trailhead.

MILES AND DIRECTIONS

0.0   Walk from trailhead and follow the path past a cornfield on the right.

0.4   Cross a bridge over Mount Vernon Creek, then reach a trail junction and turn right. Pass a path that goes off to the left as you continue walking straight along the path, moving through the woods.

0.8   Reach a trail junction and turn left, following the path another 0.15 mile to a junction where you turn left and follow the path, passing a spur trail on the right.

1.4   Arrive back at bridge, cross over creek, and continue back toward trailhead.

2.0   Arrive back at the trailhead.

HIKE INFORMATION

Local information: Mount Horeb Chamber of Commerce, 300 East Main St., Mt. Horeb, WI 53572; (608) 437-5914 or (888) 765-5929; www.trollway.com.

Friends of Donald Park, PO Box 235, Mt. Horeb, WI 53572; www.donaldpark .org/history.html, is a group of volunteers who have worked with local officials to preserve and document the park's history. The group also organizes numerous hikes and other activities in the park.

Local attractions: Cave of the Mounds, 2975 Cave of the Mounds Rd., Blue Mounds; (608) 437-3038; www.caveofthemounds.com; Little Norway, Blue Mounds; (608) 437-8211; www.littlenorway.com; features include a replica Norwegian homestead and stave church.

> 🐾 Green Tip:
> *Stay on the trail. Cutting through one part of a switchback to another can destroy fragile plant life.*

Located in the heart of the Driftless Area just north of the Illinois-Wisconsin border, the Browntown–Cadiz Springs State Recreation Area nestles in a landscape of rolling hills untouched by the glaciers that rolled over much of the rest of the state.

Overseen by the Wisconsin Department of Natural Resources, the area features two lakes formed by an impounded creek. Beckman Lake, the larger of the two lakes, is very popular for recreation and features a beach, boat launch, and fishing pier.

After cutting between the two lakes, the hike crosses Allen Road, through forest festooned with red, white, and black oaks. It's a nice hike if you want to spot local wildlife, with plenty of birding opportunities and glimpses of reptiles in the marshes. Waterfowl and raptors use both lakes as a stopover during seasonal migrations.

Start: Trailhead by parking area
Distance: 4-mile double loop
Hiking time: About 2 to 2.5 hours
Difficulty: Easy; one short muddy stretch, but largely flat and steady terrain
Trail surface: Paved path, dirt
Best seasons: Spring through fall
Canine compatibility: Leashed dogs permitted
Land status: State recreation area
Other trail users: Cross-country skiers
Fees and permits: Permit required; available from self-service kiosk at park entrance

Schedule: Daily, 6 a.m. to 11 p.m.
Maps: USGS Browntown, WI/IL; trail map available at park entrance
Trail contact: Green County DNR Parks Office, W5450 CTH NN, PO Box 805, New Glarus, WI 53574; (608) 527-2335; http://dnr.wi.gov/org/land/parks/specific/browntown/
Special considerations: Parts of the area are open for hunting on dates from Sept through Jan; check with trail contact for more information
Other: Restrooms near trailhead

Finding the trailhead: From Madison, follow Beltline Highway west to exit 258 and continue driving west on US 151. Drive 7 miles west to exit 77/WI 69 and head south.. Drive 34 miles on WI 69 to Monroe and turn right at the turn-off for WI 11, heading west. Drive 7.5 miles to Cadiz Springs Road, turn left, and drive 0.6 mile to the park entrance on the right. Turn right and enter the park, picking up a permit at the entrance booth. Past the entrance booth, go right to reach the parking area. The hike begins at the far end of the parking area, with a paved path starting at a map board and running between two lakes.
GPS: N42 35.009' / W89 46.177'

THE HIKE

This hike has one of the more scenic beginnings. From the trailhead you are immediately walking on a narrow spit of land between Zander and Beckman Lakes. A short distance from the trailhead, there's a viewing platform on the left that provides a nice spot to watch the clear water, lily pads sprinkled across its smooth surface. Herons, wrens, and kingfishers all reside in the marshes surrounding the lake a little farther down the path, and you may see one or more of them flit out of the tall grasses if you are patient.

The area is chock-full of wildlife, including a full roster of snakes. Garter, red-bellied, fox, bull, hognose, and northern brown water snakes all call this place home. Fortunately, they're non-poisonous. Other animals found in the area include frogs, muskrat, and several types of turtles, including the snapping, painted, and endangered Blandints species.

As you continue to move past the lakes, the landscape grows more marshy with submerged trees, grasses, and other plant life sprouting up from the waters. The path then takes a short jog through a thin forest of sun-dappled tree trunks before arriving at Allen Road.

Veering left and heading uphill, you soon turn off the road and walk on a path that runs between a farm field and forest. The path swings north and runs parallel to Allen Road as you reach the area boundary, then turn right and head east along

The path opens up as it moves along Beckman Lake.

Browntown–Cadiz Springs

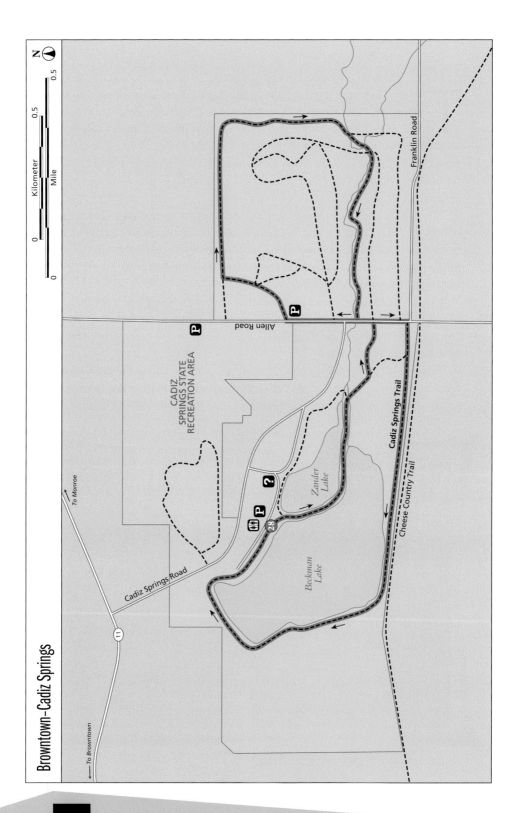

a row of electric poles. Before you go too far down this path, turn around and take in the view of rolling hills, with farmhouses and silos dotting the horizon. It's a perfect Midwestern tableau and an ideal shot if you've brought your camera.

Moving on down the path, keep your ears open for birdcalls. There are plenty of robins and blue and gray jays. While there are a few trees and woods just down the path, you have to walk through a long stretch of open field to reach the trees, and it can get windy! Wispy tops of pussytoes blow away in the breeze while the tall grasses wave vigorously.

Following the path as it turns to the right, note the massive pine trees. A huge wall of them looms up ahead as you go right and head west. Walking through the woods, you pass a confluence of two small creeks on your left, which flow from here to the lakes. The path winds through the woods and comes back to Allen Road, where you head in the opposite direction you went before and cut back toward the lakes just before you reach an overpass spanning the road.

After stepping off the road, you may feel as though you're bushwhacking your way along the path. It is very soggy with water and mud and so overgrown it's difficult to see at times, so stay alert. Fortunately, it's just a short walk along this path before you step onto a wider and much better maintained path through the marshy area.

Walking past some large trees, you spot the lakes off to the right as the path comes along the shoreline of Beckman Lake. The path turns sandy and you get a great view of the waters stretching to the horizon from a pathside bench that makes a nice rest stop.

Circling Beckman Lake, keep an eye out for diving ducks and herons gliding over the water. As you come around the far end of the lake, you reach the park's beach and playground as well as a small fishing pier. Anglers cast on the lakes for largemouth bass as well as brown and rainbow trout, pike, and catfish. From here, you've pretty much completed the loop back to the trailhead.

MILES AND DIRECTIONS

0.0 From the trailhead walk down the path between the two lakes. Continue walking on the path as it turns to dirt.

0.5 Turn right on the path and cross a bridge over a small brook. Follow the path about 330 feet and turn left onto another path.

0.7 Reach Allen Road, turn left, and walk along the road. Pass Cadiz Springs Road on the left as you continue to walk uphill on Allen Road.

0.9 Come to an opening with a dirt track running off to the right of the road. Follow the track to a small parking area, then walk on a path that forks to the left. Walk along the path with a farm field to the left as the path bends leftward and runs parallel to Allen Road.

1.1 Reach a T-junction and go right. Walk along a path that runs past electric poles on the left.

1.5 Follow the path as it curves to the right and enters the woods. Walk about 0.1 mile, reach a fork in the path, and turn onto the path on the right. Pass a path that runs to the right and keep walking straight. The path then goes to the left; keep following it.

1.8 Reach a path junction and veer to the right. Walk about 0.2 mile and pass a path running to the left. Keep walking straight along the path.

2.2 Reach a three-way path junction just before a shed on the side of the path. Take the far-left path and follow it toward Allen Road. Just before reaching the gate, which you passed earlier in the hike, take the path that turns to the left, then turn left again onto Allen Road and walk toward an overpass, passing Cadiz Springs Road and the path you took earlier from the trailhead. A few steps past Franklin Road, just before you reach the overpass, there is an overgrown path leading to the right. Take this path, heading back the direction you came earlier. *Caution:* This path is very muddy and overgrown. Stay alert as you are walking this section. (One way you might stay on track is to walk parallel to the elevated road to the left.)

2.5 Reach the end of the narrow path at a T-junction and go left.

3.2 Pass a bench on the left side of the path and follow the path as it turns to the right. Continue following the path around the lake and walk through the beach area to reach the end of the park road, which leads back to the parking area.

4.0 Arrive back at the trailhead.

HIKE INFORMATION

Local information: Green County Tourism, 1016 16th Ave., Monroe; (608) 328-1838; www.greencounty.org

Local attraction: National Historic Cheesemaking Center, 2108 6th Ave., Monroe; (608) 325-4636; www.nationalhistoriccheesemakingcenter.org

New Glarus Woods State Park

A pleasant hike along a path that runs over modest hills and through a thick swath of woods, New Glarus Woods State Park sits amidst rolling farmland south of Madison. The park, which lies on the boundary between the Driftless Area with its steep hills and the rolling prairie to the east, is also a popular spot for camping and picnics.

The Havenridge Trail, which makes up most of the hike, is marked with numbered signs that correspond to entries in the Havenridge Trail Companion Booklet, which is available at the park office. The park also has Discovery Backpacks full of activities perfect for kids who want to hike and explore the park.

The hike also swings by an access trail for the Sugar River Trail, which runs for over 20 miles on an abandoned railroad bed, following the Sugar River and its tribu-

taries.

Start: Trailhead by parking area

Distance: 4-mile loop

Hiking time: About 2 hours

Difficulty: Easy; some hills, but not steep ones

Trail surface: Dirt, gravel

Best seasons: Spring through fall; especially nice in fall for leaf colors

Canine compatibility: Leashed dogs permitted

Land status: State park

Other trail users: Cross-country skiers

Fees and permits: Permit required; available for purchase at

park entrance

Schedule: Daily, 6 a.m. to 11 p.m.

Maps: USGS New Glarus, WI; trail map available from trail contact

Trail contact: Green County DNR Parks Office, W5450 CTH NN, PO Box 805, New Glarus, WI 53574; (608) 527-2335; http://dnr.wi.gov/org/land/parks/specific/ngwoods/

Special considerations: Parts of the park are open for hunting on dates from Sept through Jan; check with the trail contact for more information

Other: Water and toilets available by the picnic

area near the trailhead

Finding the trailhead: From Madison, follow Beltline Highway west to exit 258/US 151. Follow US 151 7 miles to exit 77/WI 69 and take WI 39/69 20 miles south, passing through the town of New Glarus and reaching the turnoff to the park on the right. After purchasing a permit at the park entrance, park by the playground and picnic shelter. The trailhead is across the road from the parking area.

GPS: N42 47.214' / W89 37.867'

THE HIKE

Following the Havenridge Trail you get a good look at the park's topography of woods and prairie, moving along hills through a forest studded with oaks, maples, and black walnut trees before emerging into an open field with a largely denuded hillside sloping downhill to WI 69. Traffic runs along the road toward the town of New Glarus to the north. Purple aster bloom in the open space, while other prairie plants in the area include bluestem, prairie smoke, prairie clover, and spiderwort. There's a bench here if you want to sit and take an extended view.

The path soon veers to the right, circling the top of a hill and re-entering the woods, where you may spot a deer or two. There's plenty of other wildlife here as well, including some of the rarer bird species for this area, so bring your binoculars. This is the wilder section of the park, where there's virtually no recreational

The path moves through woods atop rolling hills.

development. It's very quiet and peaceful, and another good spot to watch for birds and wildlife.

After a short walk through the woods, you again emerge into an open field with a view of the surrounding farms. The landscape is very spare here, with little vegetation besides grasses along the path, which soon turns right and again heads uphill. Along this stretch, you may kick aside a corn cob or husk from the farmer's field just to the left of the barbed wire fence that marks the park boundary.

You're also coming back into the woods here, with lots of leaves crunching underfoot. The hill you are going up is the one vigorous climb on the hike and it's a bit of a workout. Reaching County Road NN, you cross the road and are back in a more developed area with campsites past the path to the right.

Moving down a hill and then up another one, you skirt the northern edge of the park, looking out on more prairie, and then come to a paved path. Turning left will take you to the Sugar River Trail, but the hike goes right as it moves onto the last section of the loop through the park.

Walking along the path parallel to WI 69, you go uphill again, passing a restroom and several campsites right along the path. After passing campsite No. 19 on the left, you walk through a long gravel parking area that leads all the way back to the park office along County Road NN.

The road has an interesting history. Built along the length of an old Native American trail, it became known as the Old Lead Road and, beginning in 1828, was used to haul lead from mines in the area and eventually extended all the way to Mineral Point and Galena, Illinois. It was also utilized by General Henry Dodge as he pursued Black Hawk and his followers during the Black Hawk War in 1832. Eventually, the road became part of an early passage that connected the Mississippi River with Lake Michigan and an important trading route.

MILES AND DIRECTIONS

0.0 Walk from trailhead into woods on path. Follow path through a field and then turn right as it re-enters forest. Next, follow the path downhill and then uphill.

0.9 Reach a junction with a path that veers off to the right. Continue walking on the path as it turns to the left and curves around the southern end of the park, with farm fields visible to the south.

1.7 Follow the path as it completes the circle around the southern end of the park, curves to the right and heads north. Here the path starts going uphill with a cornfield to the left of the woods.

2.5 Reach a T-junction with a gravel track and turn left onto it. Reach County Road NN, cross it, and continue walking through the woods on a dirt and

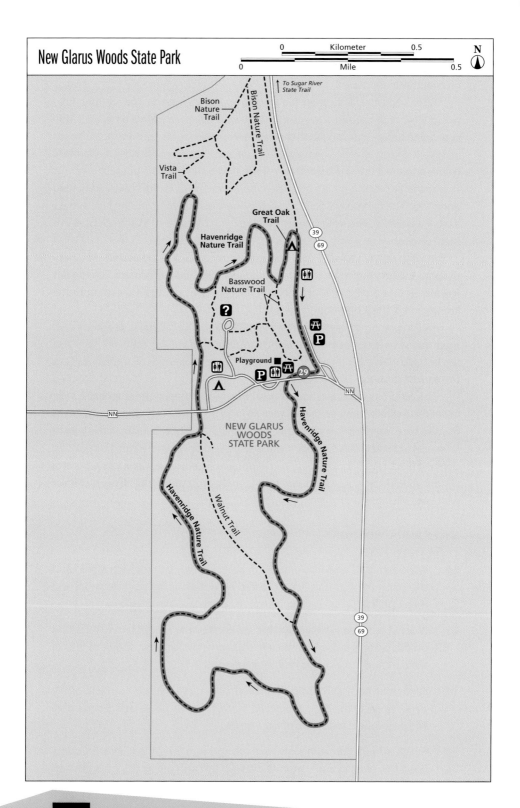

New Glarus Woods State Park

Kilometer
0   0.5
0   Mile   0.5

N

To Sugar River
State Trail

Bison Nature Trail

Bison
Nature
Trail

Vista
Trail

Great Oak
Trail

Havenridge
Nature Trail

Basswood
Nature Trail

39
69

Playground

P

P

29

NN

NN

NEW GLARUS
WOODS
STATE PARK

Havenridge Nature Trail

Walnut Trail

Havenridge Nature Trail

39
69

grass path (NOT the gravel track that runs off to the left). Walk about 0.2 mile and pass a path running to the right as you continue walking straight.

3.0   Come to a spur trail that runs off to the left. Go right and follow the path as it goes uphill. Come to a bench by an opening in the tree line on the left. Continue walking straight on the path.

3.3   Reach a trail junction and turn left. Walk a little over 0.1 mile to another junction and go left again. You are now walking on the Great Oak Trail.

3.7   Reach a paved path, turn right, and follow it, with WI 69 off to the left. You are walking south on a path that to the north connects with the Sugar River Trail. Continue walking south, passing by campsites and a restroom.

3.8   Reach a parking area past the campsites. Walk through parking area on the way back to the park office.

4.0   Arrive back at the trailhead.

HIKE INFORMATION

Local information: New Glarus Chamber of Commerce, 418 Railroad St., New Glarus, WI 53574; (608) 527-2095 or (800) 527-6838; www.swisstown.com
Local attraction: New Glarus Brewing Company, 2400 WI 69, New Glarus; (608) 527-5850, www.newglarusbrewing.com

The path moves past native grassland before entering the woods.

This hike, a rails-to-trails conversion that runs from open countryside north to the suburban fringe of Madison, is a bit different than others in this book. The popular cycling path along an old railroad bed shoots straight alongside a highway, giving two-wheelers plenty of room to pick up speed. Still, it also makes for a nice country stroll, at one point joining up with the Ice Age Trail as it moves along through the rural landscape.

While the trail goes through a well-known old railroad tunnel south of Belleville, this hike runs north from Belleville to Paoli, passing by long stretches of farm fields as the trail heads to the outskirts of Madison, crossing numerous small bridges and moving through a shaded corridor of trees that is a nice respite from the surrounding farmland. Thick stalks of corn sprout from the black earth, growing to impressive heights in the late summer and fall when you'll spot combine harvesters chugging up and down the rows of plants. It's a great hike to take at sunrise or sunset, when you can watch the sun paint the fields a rich palette stretching to the horizon.

Start: Trailhead by parking area

Distance: 11 miles out and back

Hiking time: About 4 hours

Difficulty: Moderate; very flat and straight but also a very long hike

Trail surface: Paved, crushed limestone

Best seasons: Spring through fall; fall provides a chance to see a harvest up close

Canine compatibility: Leashed dogs permitted

Land status: State trail

Other trail users: Cyclists, cross-country skiers, and snowmobilers

Fees and permits: Permit required; available for purchase at self-pay kiosk at trailhead; more information available from the Wisconsin Department of Natural Resources; http://dnr.wi.gov/org/land/parks/fees/trailpass.html

Schedule: Daily, 6 a.m. to 11 p.m.

Maps: USGS Belleville, WI; USGS Verona, WI; trail map available from library next to post office at trailhead; look on rack inside front door

Trail contact: Green County DNR Parks Office, W5450 CTH NN, PO Box 805, New Glarus, WI 53574; (608) 527-2335; http://dnr.wi.gov/org/land/parks/specific/badger/

Other: Porta-potty available at trailhead; but no water

Finding the trailhead: From Madison, take Beltline Highway west to exit 258/ US 151. Follow US 151 7 miles to exit 77/WI 69, and drive south on WI 69 10 miles to Belleville. Turn left onto East Main Street, then take the first right onto South Park Street, then turn right onto West Pearl Street. The parking area and trail are on the left, in front of the old depot and behind the post office. **GPS:** N42 51.507' / W89 31.999'

THE HIKE

Before starting out, you may want to stroll around Belleville, a pleasant little town with a nice main street of shops and restaurants. Heading north from the trailhead, you leave behind Belleville's modest town green and cross over the Sugar River on the first of many numbered bridges along the path. After passing by a small manufacturing facility on the left, you soon catch sight of the first farms, with barns and silos standing off in the distance.

You're not quite out of town yet, though, as the path moves past the residential outskirts of Belleville. Check out the backyard gardens just off the path, especially in the fall, as squash and other vegetables are ready for harvest.

Fall leaf colors are nice along this section as well, with maple branches drooping over the path. Soon, you come to a mill humming along on the left. This is

The trail runs up a bluff through forest and grassland.

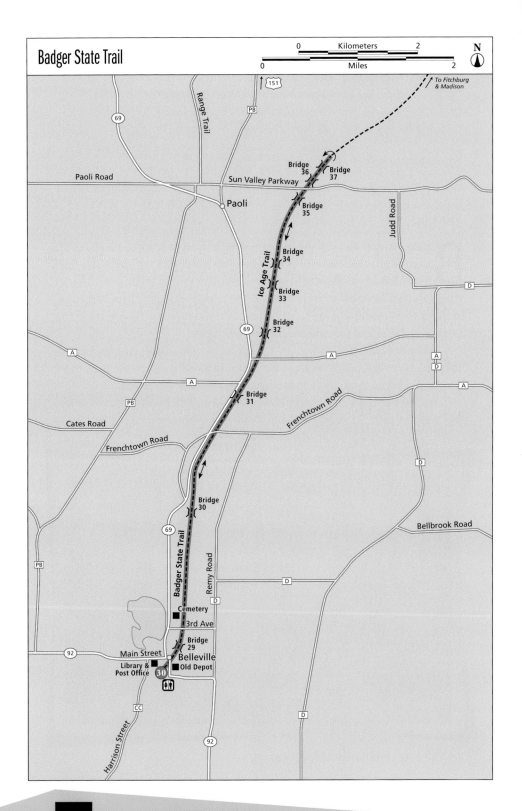

0   Kilometers   2

0   Miles   2

N

151

To Fitchburg
& Madison

69

PB

Range Trail

Paoli Road

Sun Valley Parkway

Bridge
36

Bridge
37

Paoli

Bridge
35

Judd Road

Ice Age Trail

Bridge
34

Bridge
33

69

Bridge
32

A

A

A

A

D

D

A

A

PB

Bridge
31

Frenchtown Road

Cates Road

Frenchtown Road

D

Bridge
30

69

Bellbrook Road

Badger State Trail

Remy Road

D

D

PB

Cemetery

3rd Ave

92

Bridge
29

Main Street

Belleville

Library &
Post Office

69

Old Depot

CC

D

Harrison Street

92

another sight worth seeing in the fall, as farmers bring in their corn crop from the fields. Adding to the agricultural theme is the huge field of corn to your right past the mill. You're surrounded here by open countryside, with tractors or combines moving down the long rows of crops. They will be especially busy during fall harvest, and you may even have to wait at road crossings as a tractor pulls a cart full of corn to the mill.

There's other foliage here as well, with the occasional Queen Anne's lace cropping up alongside the path and a stand of aspen off to the left. Birds flit out of the scattered trees, including flocks of sparrows. The wide-open space alongside the path gives you the opportunity to look for tracks and you may spot raccoon or badger as well as deer.

As the path comes alongside WI 69, note the large stand of pine trees across the road. From here on out, it's nothing but farmland, with only a sparse row of trees separating the path from the highway.

The path picks up the Ice Age Trail as it cuts in from a farm field on the right, marked with yellow blazes, and runs concurrent with the Badger State Trail past Paoli. The point where the Ice Age Trail merges has a bench and it's a nice spot to stop and rest.

After you've walked about 3.5 miles, the path enters a shaded corridor flanked by berms on both sides, with a canopy of trees arching overhead. These provide a nice baffle for the traffic noise on the highway, as well as relief from the sun if you're hiking in the summer.

As you continue down the path, it diverges from the road, gradually moving farther and farther away and into a quiet stretch of trees and farm fields. Crossing Bridge 33, listen closely for the bubbling brook underneath, then keep walking on the path, which comes into more tree canopy. It's very quiet and peaceful, and another ideal resting spot.

Unfortunately, the path cuts to the right and thus does not allow you to visit the charming little town of Paoli on this hike. After reaching Bridge 37, it's time to turn around and head back to Belleville.

If it's the harvest, the mill will probably still be busy with farmers bringing in corn. It's really quite a sight when there's a long line of tractors and trucks waiting to pull in their load. Back in Belleville if you didn't check out the town before setting out on the hike, you definitely should now. It's one of the nicer towns in southern Wisconsin.

MILES AND DIRECTIONS

0.0   From the trailhead, go left and walk along the path, passing the old train depot on the right, crossing Pearl Street, and following the path as it crosses Bridge 29 over the Sugar River.

0.4 Cross County Road D/3rd Avenue at the intersection with McCormick Street and continue walking on the path.

1.6 Cross Bridge 30 over a creek and continue walking on the path.

2.4 Walk along path parallel to WI 69, reach Frenchtown Road and cross it, continuing to walk on path. Walk about 0.3 mile and cross Bridge 31.

3.0 Reach the intersection with the Ice Age Trail, which runs off into a field on the right. From here, the Ice Age Trail runs congruent with the Badger State Trail. Walk 0.3 mile and cross County Road A, then cross Bridge 32.

3.8 Reach and cross Henry Road and continue on path. Walk about 0.2 mile and cross Bridge 33 and then cross Bridge 34.

4.5 Reach an intersection with an unmarked farm road, by a bluff to the left. Continue walking straight on path.

4.8 Reach another intersection with another unmarked farm road, marked Dane County Intersection 14. Continue walking straight on path. From here you are walking on Corridor 38E. Walk 0.3 mile and cross Bridge 35, then walk under an overpass. Just past the overpass, cross Bridge 36.

5.5 Reach Bridge 37. This is the turnaround point, where you begin to retrace your route back to the trailhead. *Option:* If you keep walking on the path, it leads another few miles to the outskirts of Madison and a connection with the Capital City and Military Ridge Trails and the Southwest Commuter Path.

11.0 Arrive back at the trailhead.

HIKE INFORMATION

Local information: Verona Area Chamber of Commerce, 205 South Main St., Verona; (608) 845-5777; www.veronawi.com

Local event: Hometown USA Days, Verona; www.veronahometowndays.org

Pine Cliff and Lakeview Trails

Breathtaking views atop steep ridges mark this hike at Governor Dodge State Park north of Dodgeville, in the heart of the Driftless Area. The park's sharp, steep bluffs with stone ledges overlooking Cox Hollow Lake are perfect examples of terrain untouched by the glaciers which shaped much of the rest of Wisconsin into rolling hills and prairie.

This hike takes you first along the rugged Pine Cliff Trail as it winds up some of those forested bluffs above the lake, then along the easier Lakeview Trail. About three-quarters through, the hike includes a picnic area and a concession stand open in the summer, which makes a nice spot for a break during a day spent at the park.

Start: Trailhead at Enee Point Picnic Area by parking area
Distance: 5-mile loop
Hiking time: About 3 hours
Difficulty: More challenging; some steep climbs and rugged terrain
Trail surface: Dirt, paved path
Best seasons: Spring through fall; summer is optimum for boating and swimming on the park's two lakes
Canine compatibility: Leashed dogs permitted
Land status: State park
Other trail users: Cross-country skiers; only on Lakeview section
Fees and permits: Permit required; available for purchase at park entrance
Schedule: Daily, 6 a.m. to 11 p.m.
Maps: USGS Pleasant Ridge, WI; trail map available from trail contact
Trail contact: Governor Dodge State Park, 4175 Hwy. 23 North, Dodgeville, WI 53533; (608) 935-2315; http://dnr.wi.gov/org/land/parks/specific/govdodge/
Other: Restrooms available at trailhead

Finding the trailhead: From Madison, take Beltline Highway west to exit 258/Verona Road/US 151. Follow US 151 for 38 miles to exit 47/US 18 and follow US 18 into Dodgeville. Drive west 1.5 miles on US 18 and turn right onto WI 23, heading north. Drive 3 miles to park entrance on the right. Enter park, purchasing permit if needed, then drive into park and take the right fork of the road toward Cox Hollow Lake. Drive 1.5 miles to Enee Point Picnic Area, on the right. Pull into parking area, park by picnic shelter. The trail starts just beyond the picnic shelter where a bridge crosses over a creek.
GPS: N43 00.655' / W90 07.345'

THE HIKE

Right from the trailhead this is a scenic hike, with a rocky bluff rising to the right, trees sprouting precariously from it. Ferns grow along the dirt path as you begin the ascent up a steep, forested ridge, a good example of the drift-less terrain, with the jagged rise having none of the rounded, smooth surfaces of areas to the east that were formed by glaciers moving across the land.

A log staircase provides some assistance up near the end of the climb, as you pass an impressive sandstone arch, formed out of sands deposited by ancient seas that washed over what is now Wisconsin some 355 to 600 million years ago.

After reaching the top, you walk through a forest of shagbark hickory, sugar maple, white oak, basswood, and hophornbeam. As the ridge narrows a bit, you have a nice view through the trees of U-shaped Cox Hollow Lake below, off both sides of the path.

Pine trees jut dramatically over the edge of the bluff.

Just after you begin a descent of the ridge, the path veers sharply to the right, passing by a stand of pine trees. This is one of the few places in southern Wisconsin where pine trees grow naturally. They do grow naturally farther north, but started growing here after the glaciers moved in nearby, bringing cooler temperatures which allowed the trees to thrive. When the glaciers receded to the north, most of the pine trees in this part of the state died out but these ones stayed, due to the cooler temperatures in the park as well as the acidic, well-drained soil in the area.

As the path winds down toward the lake it grows very narrow. Stop and listen for birds in the trees, which include red cardinal, black-capped chickadee, and white-breasted nuthatch. The sun warms this side of the ridge, which is protected from the north winds that blow up against the side you climbed over at the start of the hike.

The path continues along Cox Hollow Lake, formed in 1958 when a dam was built across Mill Creek. Walleye, panfish, and bass all live in the lake. There are no natural lakes in this area, due to the fact that the glaciers halted east of here, thus allowing streams and creeks in the area to drain freely.

Once you reach ground level, look off into the distance to the left to see the dam that forms the lake. Continuing along the path, you come to a plaque with information on area lead mining. In the 1820s and 30s, numerous diggings were set up throughout the area to mine for lead, which was fairly easy to extract from the earth since the glaciers never buried the area under debris and rock.

Continuing on, turn left at a junction where a path to the right leads back to the trailhead, and skirt a marsh at the southern end of the lake (the path may be marked White Oak Trail along this section, but follow the directions around the lake). Moving up the east side of the lake, note the small creek feeding into it.

Just past the creek you begin a climb up an even steeper ridge. There's no stairway to help you out this time. Take this climb slowly if you need to. Before long the lake fades away to the left, as the path moves through thick forest. Reaching a junction near the top of the ridge, you may want to take a little side hike to head out to an overlook where the rock ledges strike out over the lake. *Caution:* The ledges are very jagged and narrow. The view is truly spectacular, with pine trees jutting out from the ledges.

If you went out to the ledges, you'll turn around, head back to the trail junction, and turn left to follow the path. You then follow the path as it begins winding down the ridge, with the lake becoming more visible through the trees. There are also plenty of impressive rock formations and pine trees.

Coming once again to ground level, you follow the path as it curves around a small inlet. Soon after, you step onto the Lakeview Trail, which actually moves away from the lake as it tops a much more modest ridge before returning to the path you were on before. Eventually, you reach a paved road that leads off to the Military Ridge Trail, about 2.2 miles to the right, but you want to turn to the left. Walk past

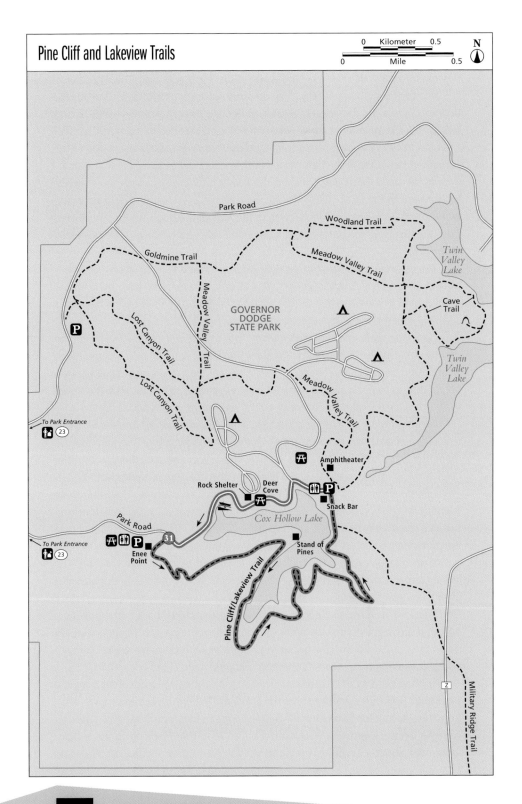

Pine Cliff and Lakeview Trails

0   Kilometer   0.5
0   Mile   0.5
N

Park Road

Woodland Trail

Goldmine Trail

Meadow Valley Trail

Twin Valley Lake

Meadow Valley Trail

GOVERNOR DODGE STATE PARK

Cave Trail

Lost Canyon Trail

Twin Valley Lake

Lost Canyon Trail

Meadow Valley Trail

P

To Park Entrance
23

Amphitheater

Rock Shelter   Deer Cove

P

Snack Bar

Park Road

Cox Hollow Lake

To Park Entrance
23

31

Enee Point

Stand of Pines

Pine Cliff/Lakeview Trail

Z

Military Ridge Trail

the dam and a nice series of small waterfalls before you head uphill to the concession building. Canoes, kayaks, and rowboats are also available for rent nearby.

The final leg of the hike takes you along a park road back to the parking area by the trailhead. On the way, you pass by Deer Cove picnic area on the right, where a short path leads to a small rock shelter, used at least as early as 500 BC by Paleo-Indians and today by the park's deer population.

MILES AND DIRECTIONS

0.0   Cross the bridge over a small creek and turn left onto the dirt path, walking into the woods, as you begin the hike.

0.4   Reach a trail junction and turn onto the left fork, which is marked Pine Cliff Nature Trail. Continue to walk on path through forest.

0.8   Follow the path as it turns sharply to the right, then descends a ridge as it runs past the shore of Cox Hollow Lake.

1.2   Reach a trail junction and go left onto a trail marked White Oak Trail to Cox Hollow Beach. (There's also a trail marked Pine Cliff Trail to the right, which runs back to the trailhead.) Walk about 0.1 mile, reach a trail junction, go left, and walk along path.

A small creek crossing.

1.5 Reach a trail junction and turn left, continuing on Pine Cliff Trail.

2.0 After climbing a high ridge, reach a trail junction and make a hard right. *Caution:* This junction is not well marked. If you come to a rock outcrop looking out over the lake, you have missed the junction. After making the hard right, follow the path as it swings left and runs parallel to the lake.

2.8 Reach a trail junction and go left, staying on the Pine Cliff Trail. Walk 0.2 mile and turn right onto the Lakeview Trail, which makes a short loop back to the Pine Cliff Trail, where you go right again and walk along the Pine Cliff Trail until you reach a paved path. Make a left onto the paved path, walk along a dam, and then follow the paved path uphill toward the parking area at the concession building.

3.7 Arrive at the concession building. Walk away from the building across the parking area and go left onto the road. Walk along the road as it heads downhill, with the lake off to the left. Walk 0.2 mile and pass a sign on the road that runs off to the right toward Twin Valley Lake, Twin Valley Campground, Cox Hollow Campground, and amphitheater, continuing to follow the road as it turns to the left. Pass the Deer Cove picnic area on the right and Cox Hollow Lake boat landing on the left as you continue walking along the road.

5.0 Arrive back at trailhead.

HIKE INFORMATION

Local information: Spring Green Area Chamber of Commerce, 259 East Jefferson St., Spring Green; (800) 588-2042; www.springgreen.com

Local attractions: Taliesin and Frank Lloyd Wright Visitor Center, 5607 County Rd. C, Spring Green; (877) 588-7900; www.taliesinpreservation.org; House on the Rock, 5754 State Rd. 23, Spring Green; (608) 935-3639; www.thehouseontherock .com

Meadow Valley and Cave Trails

Like the other hike in Governor Dodge Park, this one takes in several trails as it runs up and over several ridges. The climbs can be challenging, including a vigorous ascent to some hollow caves in bluffs overlooking a remote leg of Twin Valley Lake.

This hike mainly follows the park's Meadow Valley Trail, while also incorporating several shorter paths through hardwood forest. It also swings by the park's concession area where you can stop for a rest and fuel up before heading out on this challenging hike, which includes the climb to the caves.

Start: Trailhead by roadside parking area

Distance: 8.5-mile loop

Hiking time: About 4 hours

Difficulty: More challenging; a lengthy hike with lots of hills and a somewhat tricky series of paths

Trail surface: Paved path, crushed limestone

Best seasons: Spring through fall; summer is nicest

Canine compatibility: Leashed dogs permitted

Other trail users: Cyclists, horseback riders, and cross-country skiers in some sections

Fees and permits: Permit required; available for purchase at park entrance

Schedule: Daily, 6 a.m. to 11 p.m.

Maps: USGS Pleasant Ridge, WI; trail map available from trail contact

Trail contact: Governor Dodge State Park, 4175 Hwy. 23 North, Dodgeville, WI 53533; (608) 935-2315; http://dnr.wi.gov/org/land/parks/specific/govdodge/

Other: No restrooms at trailhead

Finding the trailhead: From Madison, take Beltline Highway west to exit 258/Verona Road/US 151. Follow US 151 for 38 miles to exit 47/US 18 and follow US 18 into Dodgeville. Drive west 1.5 miles on US 18 and turn right onto WI 23, heading north. Drive 3 miles to park entrance on the right. Enter park, purchasing permit if needed, then drive into park and take the left fork of the road toward Twin Valley Lake and Hickory Ridge Group Camp Area. Follow the road for 1 mile, passing the parking area for the Uplands Trail, then park on the right side of the road by the sign for Stephens Falls. The hike begins on the paved path.

GPS: N43 01.628' / W90 07.871'

A s you set off from the trailhead you pass near a rock springhouse hidden off to the left of the path. Located at the junction with the Lost Canyon Trail, this natural refrigerator dates to the 1850s, and was used to keep milk and food cool in the springwaters. The house also contains the remains of an old hydraulic pump system, which brought water uphill to a homestead.

The path runs a short distance above the falls, and you then descend a stone staircase to get even closer to the rushing water. After stopping to take in the falls, you walk past a large sandstone formation jutting out of a ridge on the left. More formations appear as you continue down the path, which passes through boulders along the banks of a creek.

Stephens Falls is a lovely sight at all times of the year.

Cross the creek and walk with the creek on your left. Making your way through the woods, you eventually head up a steep ridge. It's quite a climb, but once you make it to the top there's a great view of the forested valley below.

Moving along the ridge, you eventually cut away from the edge and come to a multi-path junction just as you are exiting the woods. Heading east on the Meadow Valley Trail, you cross a wide open field and then back into the woods, with plenty of oaks and a stand of aspen. You then take a short detour along a road before you pick up the Meadow Valley Trail again, eventually coming to a steep descent that brings you past a woodland amphitheater, then down a steep drop to the park's concession building. (The amphitheater is not exactly where it appears on the park map.)

Take a break here as you take in the placid waters of Cox Hollow Lake. You'll need to gather your strength for the tough stretch just ahead.

Slipping into the woods not far from the southern end of Twin Valley Lake, the path soon moves into a more rugged and isolated part of the park, moving over some modest hills. After one of the hills, you are greeted with an open view of the lake, which stretches a long distance with several small inlets. Circling the lake keep a lookout to the right for large rock outcrop on top of a hill; you'll be up there soon.

Turning right onto the Cave Trail, you skirt right by the shore of the lake, surprising flocks of geese and ducks. Heading uphill on another very steep climb, you eventually come to a spur trail leading to the left, moving through thick woods to the massive rock formations at the top. Explore the rocks, which are just as interesting as the caves highlighted on the park maps, and look out over the lake below.

Returning to the main path, you eventually come down the hill on the Cave Trail, then pick up the Woodland Trail which takes you onto a small plateau over the north end of the lake. After a pleasant stroll past fields and through corridors of oaks, you make another steep ascent. Relax, it's the last one on the hike.

Once you've made it to the top of this climb, you swing back onto the Meadow Valley Trail and move along a long ridge. There are plenty of birds in the trees here, especially jays and chickadees.

The final stretch of the hike takes you down a moderate descent with a sweeping view of the meadows that give this trail its name. You make quick turns onto the Goldmine and then finally the Lost Canyon Trail, which may not appear on park maps. The Lost Canyon Trail then brings you back to the springhouse where you can take the paved path to the right to the trailhead.

MILES AND DIRECTIONS

0.0 From the trailhead follow the paved path as it moves away from the road. Walk about 0.1 mile and cross Lost Canyon Trail where an old springhouse is off to the left. Continue on the path and then descend to the falls. Go

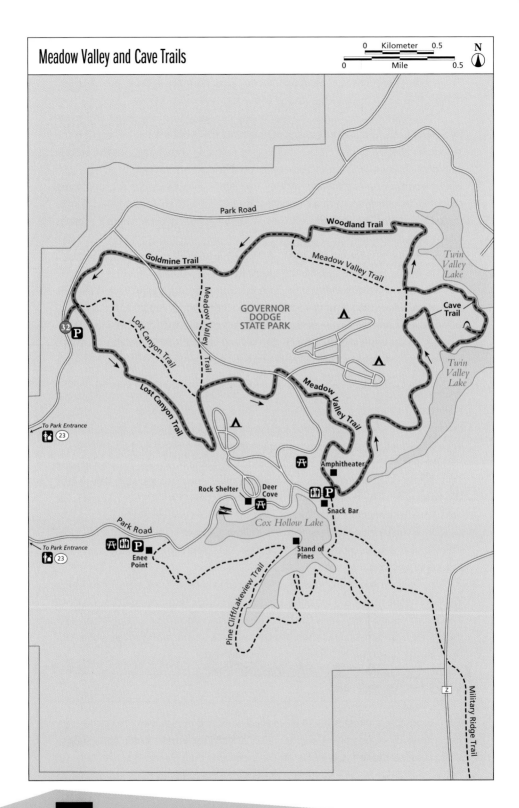

Meadow Valley and Cave Trails

Woodland Trail

Goldmine Trail

Park Road

Meadow Valley Trail

Twin Valley Lake

Cave Trail

Meadow Valley Trail

GOVERNOR DODGE STATE PARK

Lost Canyon Trail

Lost Canyon Trail

Twin Valley Lake

Meadow Valley Trail

To Park Entrance
23

Amphitheater

Rock Shelter

Deer Cove

Snack Bar

Cox Hollow Lake

Park Road

To Park Entrance
23

Enee Point

Stand of Pines

Pine Cliff/Lakeview Trail

Military Ridge Trail

Z

right onto a dirt path and walk with a creek on your left. Cross the creek on a small bridge and walk with the creek on the right.

0.4 Reach a junction with the Lost Canyon Trail and go left onto it. You're moving from the Stephens Falls Trail onto the Lost Canyon Trail as it heads toward the Meadow Valley Trail. Follow the path as it makes a 180-degree turn and ascends a ridge.

1.2 Just as you reach the top of the ridge, reach a trail junction. Turn left onto the wider path and walk along the ridge.

1.5 Reach a multi-trail junction with a gravel road off to the right. Walk to the road, cross it, and continue walking on the same path. You are on the Meadow Valley Trail, heading east.

2.0 Reach a trail junction and take the left fork. Walk 0.1 mile and reach a road. Turn right onto the road, then cross another road that leads to the Twin Valley Campground. Continue another 0.1 mile to where a trail intersects the road, and turn left, heading east. This is the Meadow Valley Trail again.

2.5 Come to a four-way trail junction. Turn right onto path that leads away from Twin Valley Campground, moving along the Meadow Valley Trail.

A creek meanders along the trail.

3.1 The path dovetails with a paved road coming in from the right. Walk straight along the road, passing an amphitheater on the left and a parking area off to the right, up a few steps. The path turns to dirt as you follow it down a steep, twisting descent to the parking area at the park's concession building. Pick up the Meadow Valley Trail at the edge of the parking area to the left of the concession building.

4.6 Pass a spur trail on the left and continue walking straight. Walk about 0.2 mile and take a path that forks to the right. This is the Cave Trail, and it runs to a junction where you will go right and follow the path as it runs along the lake, then begins a very steep climb, eventually reaching a spur trail that runs to the left, climbing to the top of the bluff and the caves in the rocks. After checking out the caves, head back to the main path, turn left, and continue along the Cave Trail, heading back toward the Meadow Valley Trail.

6.0 Complete the Cave Trail loop and reach a junction. Take a right onto a path. This takes you onto the Woodland Trail. (The Meadow Valley Trail is straight ahead from the junction where you complete the Cave Trail.)

6.6 Reach a trail junction and go left, staying on Woodland Trail.

7.2 A path merges with the path you are on. Follow it. You are now back on the Meadow Valley Trail.

7.8 Come to a trail junction and continue walking straight onto the Goldmine Trail.

8.2 Cross a road as you follow the path down a hill. You reach another trail junction, where you continue walking straight, which brings you onto a short section of the Lost Canyon Trail.

8.4 Return to the trail junction by the old springhouse. Trailhead is down the path.

8.5 Arrive back at the trailhead.

HIKE INFORMATION

Local information: Spring Green Area Chamber of Commerce, 259 East Jefferson St., Spring Green; (800) 588-2042; www.springgreen.com
Local attractions: Taliesin and Frank Lloyd Wright Visitor Center, 5607 County Rd. C, Spring Green; (877) 588-7900; www.taliesinpreservation.org
House on the Rock, 5754 State Rd. 23, Spring Green; (608) 935-3639; www.thehouseontherock.com

Stewart County Park

This shorter hike winds its way through a series of loops that take you past a lake and through wooded hills bounded by residential development on the outskirts of Mount Horeb.

Just a short drive from Madison, Stewart County Park, which opened in 1935, is Dane County's oldest park. Fishing is popular on the lake, which also has a beach and nearby playground area.

Start: Trailhead by parking area
Distance: 3.5-mile loop
Hiking time: About 2 hours
Difficulty: Moderate; some steep climbs
Trail surface: Crushed limestone
Best seasons: Spring through fall
Canine compatibility: Leashed dogs permitted; a dog permit is required, and is available for purchase from Dane County Parks at www.reservedane.com/permits/
Land status: County park
Other trail users: Cross-country skiers
Fees and permits: None

Schedule: Daily, 5 a.m. to 10 p.m.
Maps: USGS Cross Plains, WI; trail map available from trail contact
Trail contact: Dane County Parks, 1 Fen Oak Court, Room 208, Madison, WI 53718; (608) 224-3730; www.countyofdane.com/lwrd/parks/stewart.aspx
Special considerations: Good hiking shoes are essential for the portion of the hike that goes around and across Moen Creek
Other: There are restrooms available at the parking area, but they close in the early fall and reopen again in spring

Finding the trailhead: From Madison, follow Beltline Highway west to exit 258 to US 151 and continue driving west on US 151. Drive 16 miles to exit 69/US Business 151 at Mount Horeb and exit. Follow the road as it merges with County Road ID/Springdale Street, and drive 2 miles to a roundabout at 8th Street. Follow the roundabout around to its other side, where you are driving on Main Street. Drive 1 mile into the center of Mount Horeb and turn left onto County Road JG/North Washington Street. Drive 1 long block and turn left onto Wilson Street. Drive 1 block and turn right onto Lake Street. Drive 0.7 mile to the parking area for the park on the left. Start the hike at the trailhead, walking toward the lake.
GPS: N43 01.093' / W89 44.675'

THE HIKE

Soon after setting out from the trailhead, you reach the lake and pass by the park's small beach, which is claimed by Canada geese in cooler months. Off to the left, you can see the dam that created the lake. With patience, you may spot one of the lake's snapping turtles.

Moving down the path, you pass a small pump house that can get rather loud. Soon, however, you swing past a marsh thick with cattail and then step onto the yellow loop trail. The path takes you through the woods as you walk up a steep hill. There are shagbark hickory trees growing amid the oaks and maples, with robins flitting throughout the woods.

Coming to a trail junction just outside the woods, you turn onto the red loop, which takes you past some houses and then over bare hills. Head west as you walk right along the tree line. This is the easiest way to stay on the red loop.

Tall pines arch overhead.

Passing under the limbs of a large maple, you move back into a stretch of woods. A large clump of black-eyed Susans sits trailside, and a little farther down the path there's a grove of pine trees.

Leaving the woods once again, the sky opens up over a hilltop free of trees. The view here stretches to take in several farms, as well as a nearby water tower and the surrounding countryside. Passing by a few more houses, you step back onto the yellow loop.

Soon, you reach a trail junction in a clearing where there's a map board to mark your spot. Here, you pick up the long yellow loop trail to the left. Following the path, you walk past a long, curving berm that forms a bowl then move through some more woods. There's a modest climb up a hill before you head back down to the junction with the map board.

Back on the yellow loop, you turn off the path and cross Moen Creek as it descends through a gentle waterfall. Right after the crossing the ground gets very muddy. Be prepared for a soggy length of path.

Picking up the green loop you find yourself on another workout of a climb, with the path shooting uphill. Coming out of the woods, you walk through a field atop the hill, with houses just beyond the path. There's a bench along this section where you can stop and rest.

Heading back down the steep slope, you pass under some towering oaks and maples. Slogging through the mud and crossing the creek you complete the green loop and then veer left back onto the yellow loop.

From here it's one last short, uphill trek to the junction back at the pump house, and then the beach and the trailhead.

MILES AND DIRECTIONS

0.0 Walk from the trailhead toward the lake, where you'll move onto a crushed limestone path that runs to the right of the lake.

0.3 Reach a trail junction and take the path to the left onto the yellow loop trail. Follow the path through the woods and up a hill. Exit the woods and reach a T-junction, which is difficult to see if the grass has not been mowed. Look for a sign that indicates different loops. Step onto the red loop by following the path that runs to the left. Pass some houses and then walk past the edge of the woods. Follow the path through some trees before emerging again onto the bare hilltop.

1.2 Complete the red loop and reach a trail junction, where you turn left onto the yellow loop.

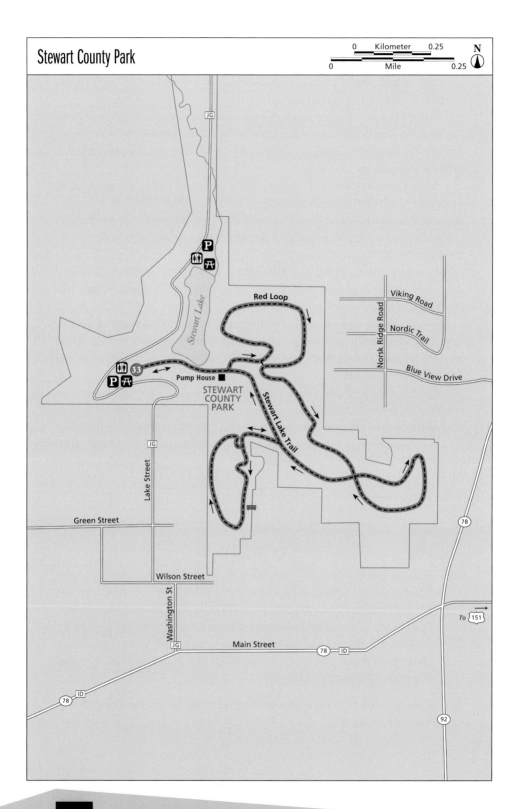

Stewart County Park

0 — Kilometer — 0.25
0 — Mile — 0.25
N

JG

P

Stewart Lake

Red Loop

Viking Road

Norsk Ridge Road

Nordic Trail

Blue View Drive

33

Pump House

STEWART
COUNTY
PARK

Stewart Lake Trail

Lake Street

JG

Green Street

Wilson Street

Washington St

78

To 151

JG   Main Street   78   ID

ID   78

92

1.5 Reach a multi-trail junction with a map board. Go left and begin to follow the long yellow loop (the path to the right heads back toward the trailhead).

2.2 After completing the long yellow loop back to the multi-trail junction, walk straight and downhill on the yellow loop trail. Take the first path off to the left and cross over Moen Creek. It can get rather muddy along this section. Continuing along the path, reach a trail junction and turn left. Follow the path as it heads uphill.

3.0 After completing the climb and then coming downhill on the green loop, recross Moen Creek and veer left back onto the yellow loop. Turn left as you ascend a small ridge and walk along the ridgeline. Walk 0.1 mile back to an earlier trail junction and veer left, following the path back to the trailhead.

3.5 Arrive back at the trailhead.

HIKE INFORMATION

Local information: Mount Horeb Area Chamber of Commerce, 300 East Main St., Mount Horeb; (608) 437-5914; www.trollway.com

Organization: Discover Stewart Park, www.discoverstewartpark.com; information on the park's history, geology, and plant and animal life, as well as a calendar of events

Local attractions: Cave of the Mounds, 2975 Cave of the Mounds Rd., Blue Mounds; (608) 437-3038; www.caveofthemounds.com; Little Norway, Blue Mounds; (608) 437-8211; www.littlenorway.com; features a replica Norwegian homestead and stave church

> 🌱 **Green Tip:**
> *Keep your dog on a leash unless you are certain it can follow your voice and sight commands. Even then, keep the leash handy and your dog in sight. Do not let it approach other people and their pets unless invited to do so.*

Blue Mound State Park

Yet another fine example of driftless topography, this hike takes you around a steep hill, or mound, that is the highest point in this part of the state. Sprawling Blue Mound State Park has a large network of trails popular with both hikers and cyclists. This hike takes in several of the trails, giving visitors some challenging hikes through woods and prairie, with plenty of ascents and descents.

Numerous birds and wildlife roost in the park, including wild turkeys and deer. The park also has a swimming pool and two observation towers with fine views over the sweeping countryside. The weather is a little easier to take in the summer, as cooler winds blow across the mound in the fall. However, if you do come in the cooler months, you may very well have the trails largely to yourself.

Start: Trailhead by west observation tower

Distance: 5.6-mile loop

Hiking time: About 3 hours

Difficulty: More challenging; a lengthy hike with some steep climbs

Trail surface: Dirt, crushed limestone

Best seasons: Spring through fall; especially nice in fall for leaf colors

Canine compatibility: Leashed dogs permitted on some trails in the park, although not on the Flint Rock Nature Trail, which makes up the beginning part of this hike

Other trail users: Cyclists and cross-country skiers; limited to certain trails

Fees and permits: Permit required, available for purchase at park entrance

Schedule: Daily, 6 a.m. to 11 p.m.

Land status: State park

Maps: USGS Blue Mounds, WI; trail map available at park entrance or from trail contact

Trail contact: Blue Mound State Park, 4350 Mounds Park Rd., PO Box 98, Blue Mounds, WI 53517-0098; (608) 437-5711; http://dnr.wi.gov/org/land/parks/specific/bluemound/

Other: Toilets located near trailhead

Finding the trailhead: From Madison, follow Beltline Highway west to exit 258 to US 151 and continue driving west on US 151. Drive 23 miles and exit at County Road F. Turn right onto County Road F, heading toward the village of Blue Mounds. Drive 0.5 mile and turn left onto County Road ID. Drive 0.5 mile and turn right onto Mounds Road. Follow Mounds Road as it turns left and then enters the park. Past the park entrance, where you can pick up a permit, drive 0.5 mile along the park road as it passes the swimming pool and then circles the top of the mound. Go right into the parking area by west observation tower. The trailhead is to the left of the tower, on a path marked Flint Rock Nature Trail.
GPS: N43 01.588' / W89 51.362'

THE HIKE

Before you set off from the trailhead, take a climb up the tower for a look at surrounding farmland and the nearby town of Barneveld. The tower sits atop the mound that gives the park its name. At 1,716 feet, it is the highest point in southern Wisconsin. The mound is part of a chain of mounds in the Driftless Area, untouched by the glaciers that flattened much of Wisconsin and northern Illinois into prairie. The mounds extend south and include the highest point in Illinois, Charles Mound, at 1,236 feet.

Starting off on the Flint Rock Nature Trail, you immediately descend a hill, including one section that goes down a log staircase. You also pass by a boulder on the right with fossils embedded in it from a shallow sea that covered southern Wisconsin over 400 million years ago. Look for quartz crystals sparkling in this and other rocks on sunny days. The crevices in the rocks provide homes and food storage spots for mice, squirrels, and chipmunks.

The path then moves through thick woods, passing trees including white and red oak and shagbark hickory. After continuing along the path through the woods, you step onto the Willow Springs Trail and make a short descent. There are some particularly nice oaks along this stretch as well as the occasional birch.

As you move onto the John Minix Trail, check out the small sinkhole to the left of the path. Soon after, you cross Mounds Park Road not far from the park entrance and then pass thick clumps of pine trees. There's a bench here just before you move onto the Pleasure Valley Trail, and it's worth taking a rest before you tackle the descent into the valley and then the trail back up.

The Pleasure Valley Trail is the most challenging and scenic portion of the hike. Just after stepping onto the hiking-only path from another path designated for cyclists, you pass a deep depression off to the left, just steps away. The descent through maple forest is steep and rocky, while the path narrows and in autumn can be buried under fallen leaves. Make sure you're still on the trail (there is the occasional trail marker).

The reward for descending into the valley is the plethora of wildflowers. Trillium and Dutchman's breeches are found among the forest section in the spring, while asters, goldenrods, and black-eyed Susans provide splashes of color when you briefly pass out of the trees and into an open area.

Climbing a steep hill out of the valley, you pass a larger prairie landscape sweeping into the distance. Flowers you see here may include goldenrod, prairie clove, and purple coneflower. Once on the Walnut Hollow Trail, you get a glimpse of neighboring farms. Onto the Ridgeview Trail, you can spot the Military Ridge Trail running parallel along the border of the park, as it moves from Madison to the east farther west across the fields and hills of the Driftless Area.

Impressive evergreens along the path.

The last part of the hike is actually one of the toughest climbs yet, as you make your way through forest, then pass near a campground where it's not a bad idea to take a break. Continuing up the side of the mound, you pass near the park's amphitheater. Shortly after, you finally break through the tree line to emerge on the wide open expanse atop the mound. You have done a near-complete circumnavigation of the mound, with the observation tower just a little ways off to the left.

Note: The park's nature center is located near the amphitheater and has several interesting displays. Stop in on your way up the mound near the end of the hike, or on your way out of the park.

MILES AND DIRECTIONS

0.0   Walk on the path as it moves down a slope. Walk 0.1 mile and reach a trail junction. Turn right and walk along path.

0.5   Walk past a spur trail running to the right as you continue walking to the left. (The spur rejoins the path you are on several feet down the path.)

1.0   Reach a trail junction and go left onto a wider path closed to cyclists. You are now on the Willow Springs Trail.

1.4   Reach a trail junction and veer left. You are now on the John Minix Trail.

1.8   Come to a trail that leads to a park road on the left. Keep walking straight, staying parallel to a single-track bike trail on the left.

2.1   Reach a trail junction and go left. You are still on the John Minix Trail.

2.4   Cross a bike trail and reach Mounds Park Road. Cross the road and turn left onto a path. You are now on the Pleasure Valley Trail, which is shared with cyclists. Walk about 0.1 mile and go left onto a path closed to cyclists.

2.9   Reach a trail junction on the bottom of the valley and turn right.

3.2   Cross a bike trail as you reach the top of the ridge over the valley and turn right onto a path. Walk about 250 feet to another trail junction and go left.

3.6   Reach a trail junction and veer left onto path. Walk a short distance and cross Mounds Park Road, near the park entrance. Continue walking on the path and pass a cycling turnoff on the right. Reach a trail junction and proceed left onto Walnut Hollow Trail.

4.2   Complete the loop of the Walnut Hollow Trail as you come to the Ridgeview Trail and go left onto it. Follow the path as it runs parallel to the Military Ridge Trail to the left. Walk about 0.4 mile and follow the path as it goes to the right.

Blue Mound State Park

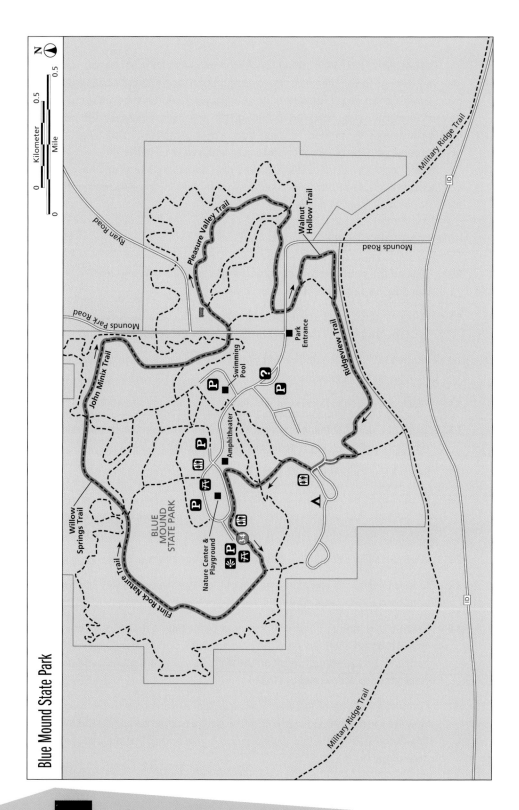

4.8   Reach a trail junction and go to the right. Begin an ascent and come to paved road. Follow the road as it continues uphill and bends to the left. Reach a junction with a park road and turn left onto it. Pick up the trail that leads to the amphitheater, beginning just to the right of the campground restrooms.

5.2   Reach a trail junction and go left. Walk 0.3 mile to the park road atop the mound. Turn left onto the road and follow it toward the west observation tower.

5.6   Arrive back at the trailhead.

HIKE INFORMATION

Local information: Mount Horeb Area Chamber of Commerce, 300 East Main St., Mount Horeb; (608) 437-5914; www.trollway.com

Local attractions: Cave of the Mounds, 2975 Cave of the Mounds Rd., Blue Mounds; (608) 437-3038; www.caveofthemounds.com; Little Norway, Blue Mounds; (608) 437-8211; www.littlenorway.com; features a replica Norwegian homestead and stave church

A creek crossing in the maple forest along the Pleasure Valley trail.

Kettles and Cornfields: Southeastern Wisconsin

A bridge crosses the Crawfish River.

From the distinctive (and eponymous) geological features at Kettle Moraine State Forest, to the well-preserved Native American Aztalan settlement on the Crawfish River, a wealth of natural and human history is found on these hikes in the natural wonderland between Madison and Milwaukee. You can also cross the river on a hiking and biking trail that runs through farmland and woods, where there are some great spots for bird watching.

The long shadow of the glaciers that carved the landscape loom over this region, in sharp contrast to the Driftless Area to the west. In addition to kettles and moraines, you'll spot small hills known as glacial drumlins and a general rolling landscape. Especially for the Kettle Moraine hikes, you'll want to make a day trip and explore at least a few of the trails in the forest. The hikes that meander on and around the Crawfish River are also worth a daylong excursion, or at least a stop along the way to Milwaukee or Wisconsin Dells, just a short detour off several main highways.

Cam-Rock Park

Woods, prairie, and wetlands are highlights of this short hike in a county park on the eastern edge of Dane County. This hike follows a curvy path through several switchbacks in woods marked with oaks and maples before circling a wide prairie and then coming close to a wetland through which flows Koshkonong Creek.

The creek once flowed into a dam, but the dam was removed in 2000, allowing the creek to meander through the marshy landscape at the edge of the woods. It's a peaceful spot with opportunities to see frogs and other wildlife.

The path of the hike runs past several cutoffs that will cut your time and distance, but this is such a short hike you'll want to follow the whole route. This hike takes place in Section 2 of the park. While there are also trails in the other two sections, this is the best hike.

Start: Trailhead by parking area
Distance: 2-mile loop
Hiking time: About 1 hour
Difficulty: Easy; short distance with a few small hills
Trail surface: Dirt
Best seasons: Spring through fall
Canine compatibility: Leashed dogs permitted; a dog permit is required, and is available for purchase at a self-pay kiosk at the trailhead; more information available from Dane County Parks; www.reservedane.com/permits/
Land status: County park
Other trail users: Cyclists and cross-county skiers
Fees and permits: None for hikers
Schedule: Daily, 5 a.m. to 10 p.m.
Maps: UGSS Rockdale, WI; trail map available from trail contact
Trail contact: Dane County Parks, 1 Fen Oak Court, Room 234, Madison, WI 53718; (608) 224-3758; www.countyofdane.com/lwrd/parks/cam-rock.aspx
Other: Porta-potty at trailhead but no water source; trails open to bikes May 1 through Oct 31

Finding the trailhead: From Madison, take I-94 east to exit 250/WI 73, about 18 miles from downtown. At the exit, go right onto WI 73, heading south. Drive 6 miles, passing through the town of Deerfield to the intersection with US 12/18. Turn left onto US 12/18 and drive 3 miles to the town of Cambridge. In downtown Cambridge, turn right onto County Road B and drive south 2 miles, passing the entrance to Cam-Rock County Park Area 1, and then turning right at the entrance to Area 2. Drive along the entrance road and park at the small parking area on the left, just across the road from the trailhead (if you drive all the way to the turnaround by the picnic shelter and playground, you've driven too far).
GPS: N42 58.683' / W89 01.376'

THE HIKE

From the trailhead the path runs near the park road before heading into woods marked by large oaks. After a short walk through the woods, you emerge from the trees and climb a small hill. Here you have a sweeping view of tallgrass prairie, part of 2 acres planted by the county parks department and volunteers. There are plenty of wildflowers along this section, including some nice black-eyed Susans.

Continuing along the path, you walk up another hill and come near the turnaround at the end of the park road, as well as pass some spur trails. Stay on the main path as you walk past a picnic shelter and restroom just to the left.

From here, the path heads back into the woods, with pine trees rising on both sides. Deer crash through the woods along this section as the path runs downhill and comes near County Road B to the left. There's a wide sea of tallgrass off to the right.

Following the path as it takes a sharp right turn, you pass some nice maple trees, then make a climb up a steep hill. At the top, you have an even better view of the prairie below. A descent and a sharp turn on the path to the left brings you around to the other side of the prairie you have been viewing.

Off to the left are cattail in the area where the millpond once stood before the dam was removed. The landscape away from the path is wetland, with Koshkonong Creek peeking through the trees. The terrain grows a little muddy as you move down the path.

A little farther down the path, the tree line on the left opens up to reveal the broad, flat creek. The water is muddy even as the current moves along. Take some time to look across the creek to other sections of the park.

The creek soon recedes from view, as you walk past some marshy bottomlands. You'll pass a couple spur trails to the right as the path comes near the area by the park road turnaround, off to the right through the woods.

Stay on the main path as you reach a turnoff to the right that leads onto a loop through a stretch of prairie, which was planted in 1974. Along this loop look for mounted poems about local flora and fauna, written by local students. There are also some large oaks, their branches drooping over the path, which you'll have to duck under as you walk along this section.

Completing the loop, you turn right onto the main path and are soon walking close to the wetlands, with the marshy landscape stretching toward the road in the distance. There's a bench a little farther down the path, which is a nice place to take a break. A little farther still there's a viewing platform looking out over both marsh and prairie. It's a good spot to look for birds and wildlife.

From here, the path follows one last short stretch along the marsh before it heads back into the woods, where another short stretch comes to a junction just to the left of the trailhead.

Stands of pine allow the sun to shine through.

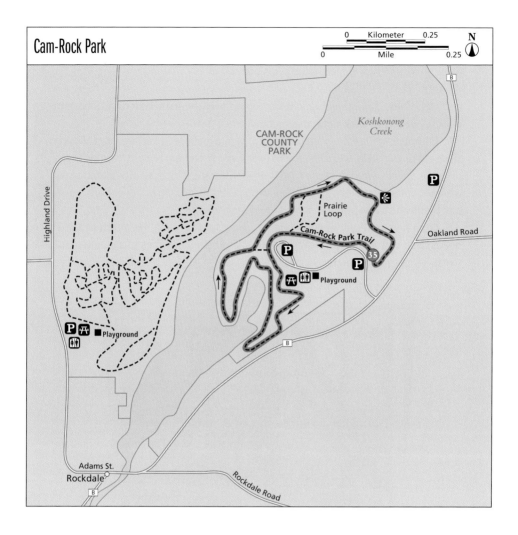

Cam-Rock Park

0   Kilometer   0.25   **N**

0   Mile   0.25

Koshkonong
Creek

CAM-ROCK
COUNTY
PARK

Prairie
Loop

Cam-Rock Park Trail

35

Oakland Road

Highland Drive

Playground

Playground

Adams St.
Rockdale

Rockdale Road

*While you pass through the town of Cambridge on
the way to the trailhead, the park is actually located
closer to Rockdale, one of the smallest villages in
the state with around 200 residents. The dam that
once crossed Koshkonong Creek was Rockdale dam.
It created a pond that powered a local mill.*

MILES AND DIRECTIONS

0.0 From the trailhead walk into woods along path. Turn left at junction and continue to follow the path through the woods.

0.2 Reach a trail junction with the park road just to the left. Continue walking straight and pass another trail junction. Pass a gate to the left. Beyond the gate is the park road.

0.4 Pass by a spur trail that branches off to the right as you continue walking straight. Follow the path as it curves right and passes by a playground off to the left.

0.6 Reach a junction and follow the path as it takes a sharp turn to the right, heading toward a wide prairie. Climb a hill so you are looking out over the prairie. Reach a fork in the path and go left onto a path. Follow path along pond to the left.

1.1 Reach a fork in the path and turn left, heading toward the water. Pass a spur trail off to the right as you move down the path.

1.3 Turn onto a path to the right as it runs into the nearby prairie. It makes a loop of about 0.2 mile through the tallgrass before returning to the main path. Turn right back onto the main path and follow it as it moves away from the water. Make a right onto a short path.

2.0 Arrive back at the trailhead.

HIKE INFORMATION

Local information: Greater Madison Convention & Visitors Bureau, 615 East Washington Ave., Madison; (608) 255-2537; www.visitmadison.com
Local attractions: Feed Mill, 159 West Main St., Cambridge; (608) 423-2100; Cambridge Wood-Fired Pottery, 10 Tranquil Lane, Cambridge; (608) 423-4507; www.cambridgepottery .com; Rowe Pottery Works, 214 Main St., Cambridge; (608) 423-3935; www .rowepottery.com/shop; Zen Gallery, 210 West Main St., Cambridge; (608) 423-2093

One of the shorter hikes in the book, this trip through the site of an ancient Native American village takes in a wide sweep of history in less than one and a half miles.

    Aztalan State Park is perhaps the most important archeological site in Wisconsin, located in a glacial drift region along the Crawfish River east of Madison. The area is believed to have been settled around AD 900. About AD 1000 people of the Mississippian culture built a fortified village at the site, notable for its many ceremonial mounds.

    Numerous archeological surveys and excavations in the park have provided a wealth of information on pre-Columbian Native American cultures, including the Woodland as well as the Mississippian. The stockade walls that once divided the town into different living and working areas have been restored, as have two mounds that supported a ceremonial temple and other important structures. There are also several conical mounds at the north end of the park.

    Researchers continue to study the site in an attempt to better understand these earlier civilizations, including the answer to an intriguing question: What happened to the people who lived here? Everything from dwindling resources to competition from other tribes has been suggested as to why the site was suddenly abandoned around AD 1200. Walking through the park you can imagine what it was like for the earlier residents, as well as enjoy the soft breezes off the river and opportunities to spot birds and wildlife.

Start: Trailhead by parking area

Distance: 1.3-mile loop

Hiking time: About 1 hour

Difficulty: Easy; rolling terrain with some moderate hills

Trail surface: Dirt

Best seasons: Spring through fall

Canine compatibility: Leashed dogs permitted in designated areas only

Land status: State park

Other trail users: Cross-country skiers

Fees and permits: Permit required; available for purchase at self-pay kiosk at park entrance

Schedule: Daily, 6 a.m. to 10 p.m.

Maps: USGS Jefferson, WI; trail map available at park entrance and from trail contact

Trail contact: Aztalan State Park, 1213 South Main St., Lake Mills, WI 53551; (920) 648-8774; http://dnr .wi.gov/org/land/parks/specific/ aztalan/

Other: Restrooms available at far end of park road

Finding the trailhead: From Madison, take I-94 east to exit 259/WI 89 (about 25 miles from downtown Madison). Turn right onto WI 89, enter the town of Lake Mills, and immediately turn left onto County Road V. Drive 2 miles and turn left onto County Road B. Drive about 1 mile and turn right onto County Road Q. Drive past the Aztalan Museum on the left and continue driving straight 0.3 mile to the park entrance on the left. Park just past the self-pay kiosk. The hike begins on the trailhead at the far end of the parking area, running toward the mounds on the left.
GPS: N43 04.139' / W88 51.760'

THE HIKE

From the trailhead at north end of the park, you see several marker mounds, which rise to the left of the path. When the site was first mapped in 1850, there were over 40 such mounds in the area. Now only a few remain. Their name comes from discoveries made when archeologists discovered a large post steadied inside each mound.

The posts would have been visible from several miles, and thus may have been used to mark the site for travelers in the area. They also may have been used to announce village events or calculate astronomical phenomena, which the village may have then incorporated into harvest ceremonies or other important moments.

Interestingly, archeologists discovered only one burial in these mounds, a young woman adorned with decorative shells. Although it was dubbed the "princess burial" the exact status of the body found in the mound or her significance remains unknown.

Continuing the hike, you walk along a tree line at the park's northern boundary, then circle around and down an open field until you are standing downhill from the parking area. This area was probably used by the inhabitants for growing corn, squash, gourds, and sunflowers.

Soon after, you reach the first of two reconstructed stockade walls, which divided the village into areas for different uses. The path moves along the outside of the wall and eventually moves along the river, where it enters an area dedicated to the inhabitants' residences. Homes were small bark structures covered with a clay made from plants to provide insulation. Archeologists have also discovered many artifacts like stone tools and fragments of ceramic bowls and plates, giving more insight into daily life in the village.

Moving along the path, you are walking parallel to the Crawfish River, which played an important role in the life of the inhabitants. In addition to fishing they also collected freshwater mussels from the waters, which were used as a food supply, with the shells used for making spoons, hoes, and other tools.

A cacophony of robins, sparrows, and other birds rings in the dense tree growth along the river. Following the path to the right as it exits the woods into an open field, walk near a natural gravel knoll off to the side of the path and near the second reconstructed stockade wall. Its use is still largely unknown, but it may have been a platform for an important structure like the park's larger mounds.

The first of these two mounds is just ahead; a pyramid-style reconstruction with steps leading to the top. The inside served as a sort of early silo, used to store corn. It may have thus been a central storehouse for the distribution of food to the village. The top of the mound, which was originally covered with a clay cap rather than the grass top you'll see here, may have also been utilized for ceremonies and rituals.

Continuing across the open field, you are heading toward the other side of the earlier stockade wall. This is also the spot for the second reconstructed mound, which once had an elaborate structure constructed of clay, willow branches,

> *Aztalan is just one of several sites throughout the Midwest that have preserved the mound-building Mississippian culture. Perhaps the largest and most well-know is Cahokia Mounds in Illinois, just east of St. Louis, which at its peak housed over 20,000 people and covered 5 square miles. Cahokia is home to Monks Mound, the largest prehistoric earthen construction in North America. At 14 acres, its base is larger than that of the Great Pyramid of Khufu, the largest pyramid in Egypt.*

The old stockade stands in the distance.

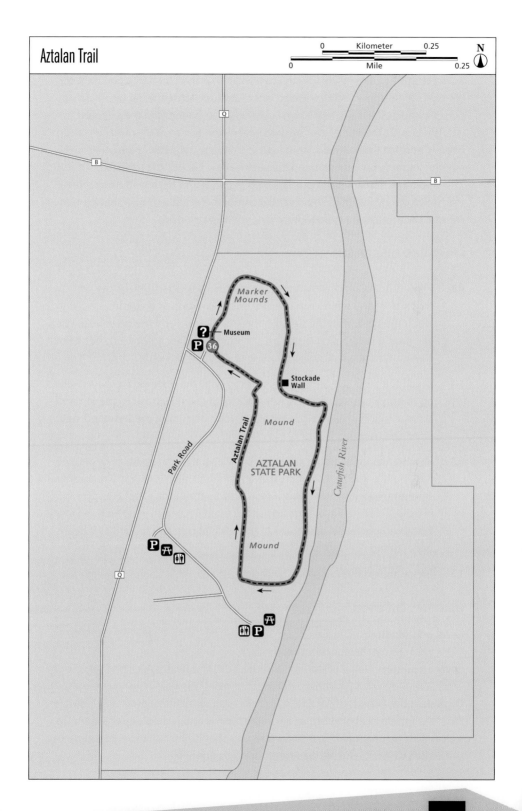

Aztalan Trail

0   Kilometer   0.25
0   Mile   0.25

N

Q

B   B

Marker
Mounds

? — Museum
P 36

Stockade
Wall

Aztalan Trail

Mound

AZTALAN
STATE PARK

Crawfish River

Park Road

Q

P ⛺ 🚻

Mound

🚻 P ⛺

grasses, and cattails that served as a burial and cremation site. After death, bodies were placed in groups inside the structure which was then burned, a common ceremony in Mississippian cultures. Excavations here have led to the discovery of many personal effects that have helped researchers further understand these rituals.

Walking to the left of the stockade, take care not to step into some deep depressions that line the field. From here you can see the parking area, with modern silos looming up behind it, and the path leading back to the trailhead.

Tidbit: The name Aztalan is a version of Aztec. It was bestowed upon the site after it was discovered in the nineteenth century, in a mistaken belief that the people who once lived here were somehow connected to Mexico.

MILES AND DIRECTIONS

0.0 From the trailhead walk along the path just to the right of the conical mounds on the left. Reach the tree line, turn right, and continue walking along the path, with the trees on the left. As you circle the open field, you will pass a path running toward the Crawfish River to the left, but keep walking straight, eventually heading toward the stockade.

0.4 Reach the stockade and go left, walking with the restored stockade walls on the right. As you approach the banks of the river, turn to the left and cross through a gap in the stockade wall, then take the left-hand path along the river.

0.7 Reach a fork in the trail and keep left, walking along the path closest to the river. Follow the path as it crosses a few spur trails. Turn right at another stockade wall and walk into a field and to the right of a large pyramid mound. From here continue across the open field until you reach the first stockade, where the path turns to the left and passes a mound as it heads back toward the trailhead.

1.3 Arrive back at the trailhead.

HIKE INFORMATION

Local information: Jefferson County Area Tourism Council, Jefferson; (920) 674-4511; www.enjoyjeffersoncounty.com

Local attraction: Hoard Historical Museum, 401 Whitewater Ave., Fort Atkinson; (920) 563-7769; www.hoardmuseum.org

Organization: Friends of Aztalan State Park; http://xyezsite.com/aztalan/aztalan.htm, has a great deal of information on the history and archeology of the site, as well as a listing of annual events and hours for the site's small museum/interpretive center, which is usually open from spring through fall.

Pelishek-Tiffany Nature Trail

This long hike on a path that runs through flat terrain largely along an interstate highway isn't the most scenic of walks, but it's good for exercise and at many points gives you almost uninterrupted views of surrounding farm fields. These are especially impressive at sunrise and sunset, when the sun's rays paint the sky over the country-side a rich palette of colors.

The trail for this hike runs along an old railway line that was used by several rail-roads before being abandoned in 1980. You can still spot relics of its earlier use, such as switchboxes and the remains of railroad ties.

Start: Trailhead by parking area
Distance: 11.1 miles out and back
Hiking time: About 4.5 hours
Difficulty: Moderate; flat terrain the entire length of the hike, but very long
Trail surface: Dirt, crushed lime-stone
Best seasons: Spring through fall
Canine compatibility: Leashed dogs permitted
Land status: County park
Other trail users: Cyclists, horse-back riders, and snowmobilers
Fees and permits: None
Schedule: Daily, sunrise to sunset
Maps: USGS Clinton, WI; trail map available at trailhead and from trail contact
Trail contact: Rock County Parks, 3715 Newville Rd., Janesville, WI 53545; (608) 757-5451; www.co .rock.wi.us/index.php/park-info-a-maps/pelishek-tiffany-trail
Other: Restrooms available at trailhead

Finding the trailhead: From Madison, drive south on I-39/90, about 42 miles to where you pick up I-43 heading east. Drive about 6 miles to exit 6/WI 140, where you head south toward the town of Clin-ton. Drive 1 mile on Church Street/WI 140 and turn left onto County Road X. Drive 3 blocks and turn right onto Mill Street/County Road J. Drive 3 blocks, passing the town library on your right, then cross front street and pass between the silos of an old feed mill. The park-ing area and trailhead are on the left, next to a covered bridge.
GPS: N42 33.193' / W88 51.668'

THE HIKE

S tarting out from the trailhead in a farmer's park, you follow the path as it moves under the looming forms of the old silos off to the left. The town of Clinton flows past as you move along the path and into the countryside.

At 0.25 mile, look for a small swath of prairie on the left side of the path. The grass and plants were planted by students at a local elementary school. Along this stretch through a grove of trees, a narrower path runs off to the left side of the wider trail, and is well worth taking to explore the wooded area. It joins back with the main path before you cross the first road.

Before you reach the road, however, there's a bench and small trail shelter, then a pair of benches sitting in a small glade. Just past here, the narrow path crosses over to the right side, where it runs past some old electric poles by a farm field before rejoining the main path and crossing South Kemmerer Road.

The long, straight path seems to move infinitely through a canopy of trees.

The path soon approaches a tunnel of trees, their branches arching overhead and disappearing far into the distance. The tree canopy is occasionally interrupted by an opening where milkweed often grows, and a look out into a vast cornfield (you'll step over some cobs along the path). The view to the horizon really does seem endless, especially in the fall, after the corn has been harvested and the fields are barren.

Moving down the path you reach a section marked by a variety of evergreen trees, which lends the path something of a Christmas feel. Another bench on the left side of the path and a small swath of prairie on the right soon give way to even more evergreens.

Next up on the left is the clubhouse of the Clinton Fencehoppers Snowmobiling Club. Local snowmobilers were instrumental in obtaining the land for the trail. You can see how the path is ideal for snowmobiling. It's quite wide right from the beginning and has an average width of 100 feet.

The next path-side shelter and resting spot marks the site of an 1845 homestead and a farm built on the same site a century later. Just up ahead a lone maple on the right is full of color in the fall, a nice change from the long stretches of brown dirt and green cornstalks in the surrounding fields.

Passing by some picturesque farms, the trees thin out and you soon come within waving distance of cars on I-43. Following the path behind a berm, there are a few more benches as well as a small planting of sunflowers. Afterward, the path moves even closer to the road.

Fortunately, it doesn't take long for the scenery to get a little more varied. There's a field of tallgrass off to the left, waving in the wind. The path also has a canal running alongside it for this section, its banks stained blue-green from fertilizer. One last prairie remnant crops up on the right, its golden grasses shoehorned in between the path and yet another farm field.

Just a little farther on, the path reaches the hamlet of Allen's Grove, which is the end of the maintained trail. It does continue across the road, but it's best to turn around here and head back toward the trailhead. Cattle graze contentedly less than 100 yards from traffic speeding down the highway. If you're on the trail in the late afternoon, keep your eyes on the farm fields for a memorable sunset as you head back.

Green Tip:
When hiking with your dog, stay in the center of the path and keep Fido close by. Dogs that run loose can harm fragile soils and spread pesky plants by carrying their seeds.

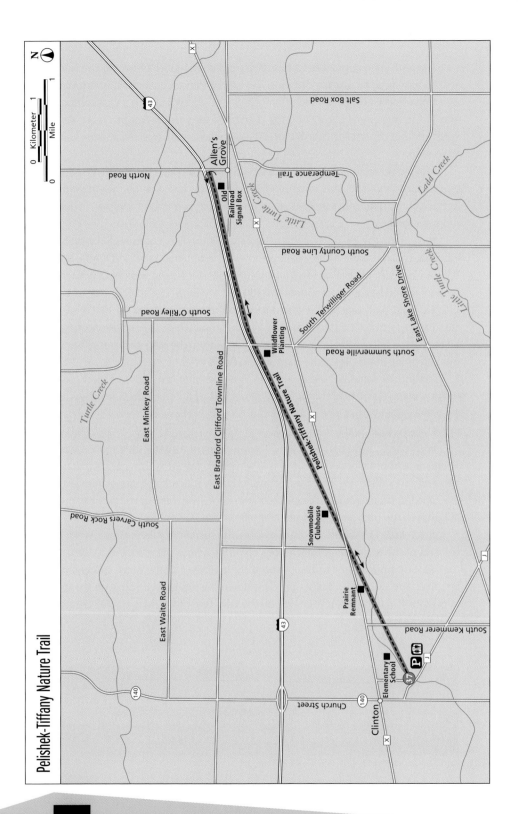

Pelishek-Tiffany Nature Trail

N

0 Kilometer 1

0 Mile 1

Allen's Grove

Old Railroad Signal Box

Little Turtle Creek

Temperance Trail

Ladd Creek

Salt Box Road

North Road

South County Line Road

South O'Riley Road

South Terwilliger Road

East Lake Shore Drive

Little Turtle Creek

Wildflower Planting

South Summerville Road

Turtle Creek

East Minkey Road

East Bradford Clifford Townline Road

Pelishek-Tiffany Nature Trail

South Carvers Rock Road

Snowmobile Clubhouse

East Waite Road

Prairie Remnant

South Kemmerer Road

Elementary School

P

Clinton

Church Street

MILES AND DIRECTIONS

0.0 From the trailhead, begin the hike on the path to the east, heading away from the road.

0.6 Cross South Kemmerer Road and continue walking on path.

1.5 Cross an intersection at South Carvers Rock Road leading to County Road X to the left. Continue walking straight on path.

1.8 Cross County Road X on path and continue walking, passing a farm driveway.

2.6 Cross another farm road, just to the right of I-43 and continue on the path.

3.8 Cross South Summerville Road and continue on path.

5.5 Reach North Road where it intersects with Hill Street. Turn around and retrace the route to the trailhead.

11.1 Arrive back at the trailhead.

HIKE INFORMATION

Local information: Rock County Tourism Council, Janesville; (920) 757-5587 or (866) 376-8767; www.rockcounty.org

Local attraction: Milton House Museum, 18 South Janesville St., Milton; (608) 868-7772; www.miltonhouse.org

With a path that clambers up a craggy sandstone bluff to a sweeping view over surrounding farmland, this scenic hike also offers some good exercise as you head up the steep slope. There are two overlooks, one at both the east and west ends of the bluff, with clear, unobstructed sight lines.

The park, less than an hour outside of Madison, is popular with horseback riders as well as hikers, with an equestrian-designated parking lot where the park road reaches the top of the bluff. The paths move through woods thick with trees that climb both sides of the bluff. There may not be many magnolia trees, but there are plenty of oaks and other species all along the hike.

Start: Trailhead by parking area

Distance: 2.8-mile loop

Hiking time: About 1.5 to 2 hours

Difficulty: Moderate; relatively short distance, but a steep bluff climb

Trail surface: Dirt

Best seasons: Spring through fall

Canine compatibility: Leashed dogs permitted

Land status: County park

Other trail users: Horseback riders and cross-country skiers

Fees and permits: None

Schedule: Daily, 5 a.m. to 10 p.m.

Maps: USGS Orfordville, WI; trail maps available from trail contact

Trail contact: Rock County Parks, 3715 Newville Rd., Janesville, WI 53545; (608) 757-5451; www.co.rock.wi.us/index.php/park-info-a-maps/magnolia-bluff

Special considerations: Hiking trails are shared with horse trails through some sections of the park

Other: Pit toilets available at trailhead

Finding the trailhead: From the Beltline Highway in Madison, take exit 261/US 14 east toward Oregon. Drive 16.5 miles and merge with WI 59. Drive 3 miles to the outskirts of Evansville and go right onto WI 59/WI 213 South. Drive 3.2 miles and turn right onto WI 59. Drive 3 miles and turn left onto Croak Road. Drive 0.5 mile to park entrance on the right and pull into the parking area. The trailhead is just past the parking area, by the map board.
GPS: N42 43.823' / W89 21.357'

THE HIKE

S tarting out from the trailhead, follow the path as it begins a gradual climb up the bluff. Note the craggy rocks of sandstone jutting out from the top as you move through woods along both slopes. Listen for birdcalls from the treetops.

After reaching the park road, you turn left and walk uphill a short distance before doubling back along another path through the woods. The path comes very close to the top of the bluff, and the views are striking as you pass oak, hickory, and black walnut trees.

Reaching the top, you are in a large open area with numerous picnic tables. Before setting out on the path, take a detour over to the west overlook marked by a log fence for erosion control. The views from here are even more striking, with an endless, clear sweep over surrounding farm fields, which stretch to the horizon. The wind rustles through gnarled tree trunks clinging to the edge of the bluff, and the sound of distant traffic doesn't interrupt your hearing birds chirping or wood-peckers clattering away on tree trunks.

You can also examine the honeycombed patterns in the rust-colored sand-stone surfaces before you head back onto the path. Walking with the open area on your right, there is thick forest on your left, defined by oaks and the occasional evergreen and large birch.

Reaching a junction where you turn right and head uphill, you can see more evergreens stretching off to the right and several birches tucked away on the slope to the left. Moving toward the eastern end of the bluff, you pass a deep ravine just off the path as it goes through some modest descents and climbs, passing by another open field. There's a thick stand of pine above the ravine as well.

Coming around the back of the bluff, you follow the path as it moves back into the woods, with plenty of birds hopping in the branches. A small thicket of aspen breaks up the many oaks as the path drops slightly downhill and moves along the edge of the bluff. Farms can be spotted in the distance as you reach the east over-look, which doesn't have as impressive a view as the west but is still a nice spot to take in the surrounding countryside.

Back on the path, you head west along the edge of the bluff back toward the trailhead. After just a few hundred feet, the path winds downhill in a sharp S-curve. Coming to ground level the oaks are noticeably larger, with many nests sitting high up in their branches. Continuing along, there are birch and pine in the shadow of the bluff off to the left.

The path curves slightly and comes closer to the steep forested slopes. Soon, you pass below near the west overlook, then follow the path past the edge of the bluff, where it turns left and runs past a pond on the right. From here, it's just a few hundred feet back to the parking area.

Magnolia Bluff County Park

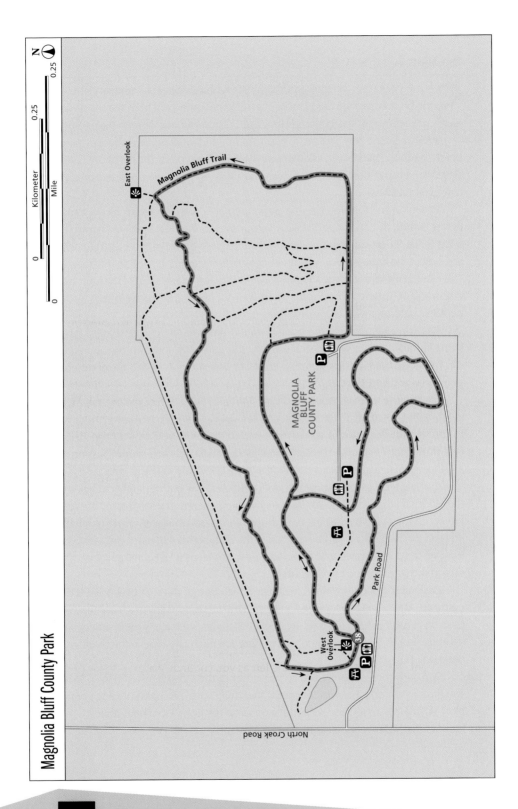

East Overlook

Magnolia Bluff Trail

MAGNOLIA BLUFF COUNTY PARK

Park Road

West Overlook

38

North Croak Road

N

Kilometer

0.25

0.25

0

Mile

0

0.25

Alternate route: At the start of the hike, rather than take the path that winds gradually up the bluff, you may want to go straight up the bluff to the west overlook from the parking area via the path to the left of the path at the trailhead. This is an interesting although challenging route, with a steep climb up a rocky trail line with numerous thorn bushes. Be careful when you reach the top that you do not step into the area marked by the erosion control fence.

MILES AND DIRECTIONS

0.0   Begin the hike at the trailhead as you move to the right and walk along the base of the bluff, following the path as it moves parallel to the park road to the right. The road turns to the right as you follow the path as it circles the end of the bluff and moves into deeper woods. The path goes left, then climbs slightly up the bluff before heading downhill and turning right, then heads uphill again and eventually reaches the park road. Go left onto the road, walk about 200 feet, and reach three boulders on the left. Step onto the path just past the boulders and follow the path as it goes to the right.

0.5   Reach a path that turns to the right toward the park road. Continue walking straight. Come to an open area at the top of the bluff, go right, and walk across the open area. Turn to the left of the latrine onto a narrow path. Walk to the last path at the edge of a bluff and turn to the right, following the path. (Before moving onto this path, you may want to walk to the far end of the open area to check out the west overlook.)

0.8   Walk about 500 feet on the path and reach a path turning to the left as you continue straight.

1.0   Reach a path junction, where you turn right and head uphill. Walk about 350 feet to a path junction with a parking area to the right. Walk straight and then go left onto a path, moving away from the road and past an open field on the right. Head slightly downhill and pass a path to the left as you continue walking straight. Follow the path uphill and pass another path to the left as you continue walking straight. Follow the path as it turns to the left.

1.7   Reach a path junction and go right. Walk a few steps to the east overlook, then return to the path and walk straight, passing a path turning to the right. Pass a path veering to the left as you continue walking straight. Follow the path as it moves downhill through an S-curve.

1.9   Reach a four-way trail junction and go straight. Walk past a path that turns to the left as you continue walking straight.

2.2 Reach a path branching off to the left. Keep walking straight.

2.5 At a path that turns to the left, keep walking straight. Come to a junction and go left.

2.8 Arrive back at the trailhead.

HIKE INFORMATION

Local information: Rock County Tourism Council, Janesville; (920) 757-5587 or (866) 376-8767; www.rockcounty.org

Local attraction: Logan Museum of Anthropology, 700 College St., Beloit; (608) 363-2305; www.beloit.edu/logan

Green Tip:
Be courteous of others. Many people visit natural areas for quiet, peace, and solitude, so avoid making loud noises and intruding on others' privacy.

Glacial Drumlin State Trail

Named for the low hills left behind by the glaciers that shaped the landscape in southeastern Wisconsin, this is one of the best hikes in the book for bird watching, with a plethora of species that roost in the trees that line the path as it moves through farm country.

This trail is very popular year-round, with snowshoers and snowmobilers taking advantage of its long, straight stretches. Spring brings cyclists who zip along the trail's 52 miles beginning on the eastern edge of Madison and running all the way to the town of Waukesha.

This hike takes in perhaps the most scenic section of the trail, beginning with a crossing over the Rock River and later crossing the Crawfish River just south of Aztalan State Park, which is another hiking spot worth exploring. While it's a long walk, you'll have plenty of opportunities to stop and watch the birds.

Start: Trailhead by parking area
Distance: 12 miles out and back
Hiking time: About 6 hours
Difficulty: Moderate; a long hike, but the path goes through largely flat terrain
Trail surface: Crushed limestone
Best seasons: Spring through fall
Canine compatibility: Leashed dogs permitted
Land status: State trail
Other trail users: Cyclists, in-line skaters, snowmobilers, snowshoers, and cross-country skiers

Fees and permits: None
Schedule: Daily, 6 a.m. to 11 p.m.
Maps: Trail map available at parking area and from trail contact
Trail contact: Glacial Drumlin Trail-West, 1213 South Main St., Lake Mills, WI 53551; (920) 648-8774; http://dnr.wi.gov/org/land/parks/specific/glacialdrumlin/index.html
Other: No restrooms at the trailhead

Finding the trailhead: From Madison take I-94 east to exit 267/WI 26, about 34 miles east of downtown Madison. Exit onto WI 26, heading south. Drive just under 4 miles and exit the highway to the right onto Schreiber Road, then turn right onto Felson Ridge Court to reach the parking area by the trail.
GPS: N43 02.202' / W88 48.408'

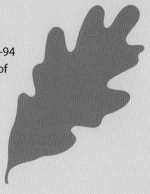

THE HIKE

tarting from the trailhead walk away from traffic on WI 26. The path crosses the Rock River and enters a long tunnel of trees, their branches arching high overhead. This crossing is on a old railroad trestle, and the river is impressively wide. The Rock River joins up with the Crawfish River a little to the south of here, and eventually flows into the Mississippi.

After the crossing follow the path as it enters a long tunnel of trees stretching far into the distance. All sorts of birds roost along this section, including the dark-eyed junco and red-headed woodpecker. There's a large stand of aspen on the left which is a favorite roosting ground of a huge flock of crows with their distinctive caw.

The scenery is very peaceful and pastoral, with farm fields lining both sides of the path and the occasional corn cob lying on the crushed limestone. Sumac and tallgrass are scattered among the tall oaks and other trees, as are clumps of wildflowers.

After crossing Popp Road, note the huge duo of weeping willows to the right. Another 0.5 mile or so brings you to the bridge over the Crawfish River, a wide stretch of river which has even more impressive willows along its banks, their drooping branches skimming the water. Birds swoop overhead and you can spot fish in the water below.

A bridge crosses a small creek.

Just upriver is Aztalan State Park, site of a village dating from around AD 1000 that is Wisconsin's preeminent archeological site. Ceremonial mounds in the park have been restored and researchers have discovered many artifacts that have given insight into Native American life in Wisconsin. The park is about 2 miles north of the path on County Road Q, which you'll cross about 0.5 mile after going over the bridge.

After crossing County Road Q there's another nice stand of aspen on the left and a cornfield on the right. The surrounding scenery fades gradually back into farmland after you cross the Crawfish River, and you may spot a tractor or combine harvester chugging along depending on the time of year.

Eventually tree cover falls away, and there's nothing but flat, open farmland as far as the eye can see. The first glacial drumlin along the trail rises off to the left. Note how long and slender it is. Typical of glacial drumlins, it resembles a hard-boiled egg cut lengthwise, with a steep front end and a tapering back that points in the direction of the glacial flow that created it. Glacial drumlins provided a challenge for farmers by forcing them to plow around them, although many drumlins were removed by settlers who quarried them to obtain gravel.

Soon another drumlin rises to the left, near a spot in the path where there's a bench on the right. It's a nice, peaceful spot to take a break and take in the view of the countryside. Just beyond here is a great stretch for bird watching. There are scattered trees standing in open countryside, which makes for less branch cover, and thus easier to see the birds, which may include sparrows, American redstart, and the dark-eyed junco, whose presence indicates the coming onset of winter.

Crossing a canal you spot the outskirts of Lake Mills off to the right. You finally reach the old Lake Mills train depot, a distinctive building across from a feed mill on the southern edge of town. The depot has restrooms and picnic tables as well as an intermittently open trail office with information and brochures.

Unfortunately, the center of Lake Mills is a mile or so up the road, so there isn't a whole lot to see around here. But you can at least stretch your legs and relax a bit at the depot before returning on the path back to the trailhead, taking advantage of the bird-watching opportunities along the way.

MILES AND DIRECTIONS

0.0 At the trailhead turn right onto the path and cross Schreiber Road, then cross a long wooden bridge over the Rock River. Continue walking and cross County Road N.

1.3 A mound rises on the left as you pass the 20-mile marker on the path.

2.0 Cross Popp Road and continue walking on path.

Glacial Drumlin State Trail

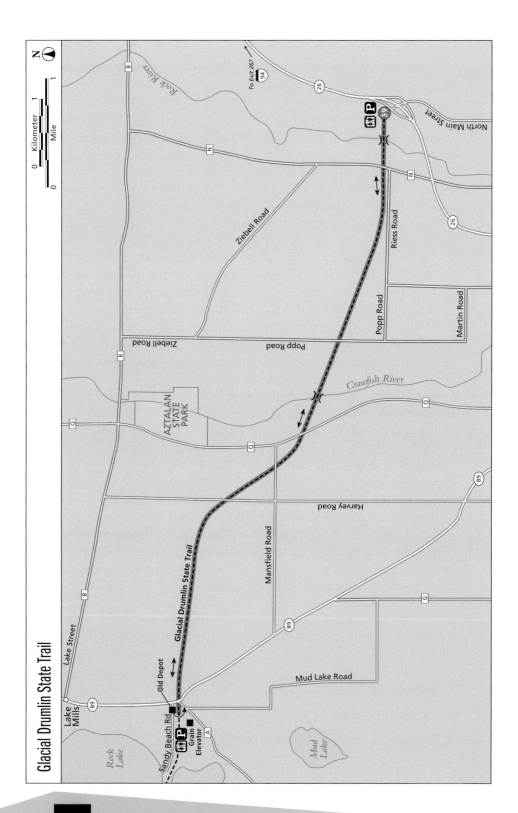

2.6   Take the bridge over the Crawfish River and continue walking.

3.0   Stay on the path as it crosses County Road Q and continue walking on path.

3.4   Follow the path as it crosses Mansfield Road. You are at mile marker 18; continue walking on the path.

4.0   Cross Harvey Road.

5.0   Cross a small bridge over a canal and continue walking.

5.5   Follow the path as it passes a snowmobiling trail that branches off to the right.

6.0   Arrive at the Old Lake Mills Depot, located on WI 89 just north of the intersection with County Road A. From here, turn around and retrace your steps back to the trailhead.

12.0   Arrive back at the trailhead.

HIKE INFORMATION

Local information: Jefferson County Area Tourism Council, Jefferson; (920) 674-4511; www.enjoyjeffersoncounty.com

Local attractions: Hoard Historical Museum, 401 Whitewater Ave., Fort Atkinson; (920) 563-7769; www.hoardmuseum.org.

Sandhill Station; http://dnr.wi.gov/org/land/parks/specific/glacialdrumlin/camping.html; a campground located about a mile from the depot, down County Road A in an oak savanna. It's conveniently located for a hike that would begin at the depot and follow the listed route in reverse.

Emma Carlin Trail

This hike along numerous interlocking trails in Kettle Moraine State Forest takes you over numerous hills formed 10,000 years ago by the Wisconsin Glacier Episode. The Kettle Moraine State Forest is a showcase of largely unspoiled glacial landscapes, which extends for some 30 miles across southeast Wisconsin between Milwaukee and Madison. There are over 150 miles of trails, including the 33-mile Moraine Ridge Trail. The Ice Age Trail comes through the forest as well.

The landscape of this hike is hardwood forest with some huge pine trees clustered near the trailhead and along the path, plus, of course, kettles and moraines, small hills and depressions, respectively, which were left behind by the glaciers.

At about the hike's halfway point, there's a scenic overlook with some nice views of the surrounding countryside and nearby Spring Lake. The trail is very popular with mountain bikers, so stay alert as you hike through the woods. Hikers and cyclists move in opposite directions along the paths.

Start: Trailhead by parking area
Distance: 4.4-mile loop
Hiking time: About 2 hours
Difficulty: Moderate; a few steep climbs and descents
Trail surface: Dirt/crushed limestone
Best seasons: Spring through fall
Canine compatibility: Leashed dogs permitted
Land status: State forest
Other trail users: Cyclists and cross-country skiers
Fees and permits: Permit required; available for purchase at the forest headquarters and visitor center
Schedule: Daily, 6 a.m. to 11 p.m.
Maps: USGS Little Prairie, WI; trail maps available at forest office and from trail contact
Trail contact: Southern Unit Kettle Moraine State Forest Headquarters, S91 W39091 Hwy. 59, Eagle, WI 53119; (262) 594-6200; http://dnr.wi.gov/org/land/parks/specific/kms/
Special considerations: Open for hunting on designated dates from Sept through May; contact the forest office for details. It's advisable to wear bright orange during hunting seasons. Hikers must follow the paths clockwise, while cyclists follow them counterclockwise.
Other: Restroom available at trailhead

Finding the trailhead: From Madison, drive east on I-39/90 to exit 160/WI 73, about a 24-mile drive from downtown. Exit I-39/90 and take a left on WI 73. Drive 1 mile and turn right on WI 106. Drive 29 miles, passing through the town of Fort Atkinson, to the town of Palmyra. Turn left onto WI 59 and drive 2.5 miles, entering Kettle Moraine State Forest. Turn right onto County Road Z and drive 0.5 mile to parking area and trailhead (if you need to stop at the forest office to buy a permit before beginning the hike, it's on WI 59, 1 mile east of the intersection with County Road Z).
GPS: N42 52.224' / W88 32.639'

THE HIKE

The hike, which follows the green loop of the Emma Carlin Trail, begins at the trailhead in a stand of pines so thick you can smell the pine sap as you move down a path carpeted with needles. Swinging past a small pond, you head uphill past some impressive towering oaks.

The path ambles up to the top of a ridge, where it moves through some small dips and rises. It then takes a long, steep descent through a thicket of trees before immediately heading back uphill. (Feel those leg muscles work!)

This climb is even steeper than the earlier ones, and takes you to a vista with breathtaking views of the nearby hills. The descent from this hill snakes down to the emerald-green forest floor. Keep your eyes peeled for a kettle pond off to the left.

The path continues about midway to the top of a ridge as it heads into deeper woods. You'll crunch over some acorns as you move past ravines off to the side of the path and some smaller hills.

Next, the path levels off as it comes by some sumac plants and cedar trees. Stop for a moment and take a deep breath of the crisp air scented with cedar. There is a large grove of aspens just before you reach a scenic overlook that opens up over the valley below. This is an even more breathtaking view looking out over Lower Spring Lake and Palmyra, as well as surrounding farms and countryside. You may also spot raptors taking advantage of the drafts to soar over the valley.

Take a moment to look around, but remain alert for cyclists. Back on the path, hike along the continued level stretch as you move through a meadow and then back into the woods. The flat route is a nice change of pace from the constant climbs and descents leading up to the overlook.

Continue walking along the top of the ridge. Eventually you'll pass a pair of kettle lakes, then cross a wooden walkway as you move into a marshy landscape. You have a chance to spot waterfowl here, and it's rather different than the forest that has dominated the landscape of this hike.

The final stretch of hike takes you once again through a forest of sweet-smelling pine before turning off to come back to the trailhead. (The final few turns are a bit tricky, as numerous spur trails braid across the main path—make sure you know where you're going.)

MILES AND DIRECTIONS

0.0 From the trailhead begin on the left-hand path, walking clockwise on the trail. Proceed about 0.2 mile and come to a trail junction, where you turn left.

0.8 As you begin a descent, an overgrown path goes off to the left. Keep walking straight as the path becomes crushed limestone. After another descent and a climb uphill, the path becomes dirt again, while a limestone path turns off to the left. Stay on the dirt path, which soon makes a hairpin turn to the left.

A small stand of pines along the trail.

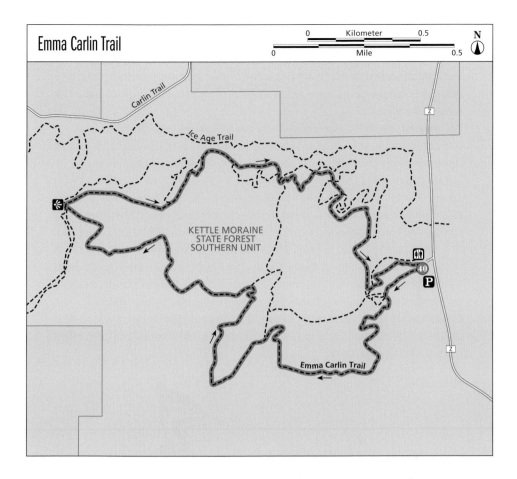

0   Kilometer   0.5

0   Mile   0.5

N

Carlin Trail

Ice Age Trail

KETTLE MORAINE
STATE FOREST
SOUTHERN UNIT

Emma Carlin Trail

1.0   Reach a junction with a path going off to the right. Keep straight, staying on the green loop (the Do Not Enter sign is for cyclists).

1.5   Pass a path that turns off to the right as you continue walking straight.

2.4   Reach a scenic overlook. From the overlook, veer right onto the wider path before a bench. Walk about 0.3 mile and pass a smaller path coming in from the left as you continue walking straight.

3.0   Come to a fork in the trail and take the left path.

3.2   Come to a junction in the path and go left. Walk about 500 feet, reach a fork in the path, and bear right. Walk along path, passing two paths that cross it.

3.8   Reach a fork in the path and go right. Descend to a junction in the path and take the path on the right.

4.1   Reach a trail junction and continue walking straight toward the trailhead.

4.4   Arrive back at the trailhead

40

HIKE INFORMATION

Local information: Waukesha & Pewaukee Convention and Visitors Bureau, N14 W23755 Stone Ridge Dr., Suite 225, Waukesha; (262) 542-0330 or (800) 366-8474; www.visitwaukesha.org

Local event: The Fall Color Festival, held every September or October, is a series of mountain bike races. Held on the nearby John Muir Trail, it raises funds for trail repairs and improvements throughout the park; www.fallcolorfestival.org.

Local attractions: The forest office on WI 59, 1 mile east of the intersection with County Road Z, has a small, informative, well-done museum with exhibits on glacial ecology, local plant and animal life including several stuffed specimens, and Native American and pioneer history. Old World Wisconsin, W372 S9727 State Rd. 67 Eagle; (262) 594-6300 or (866) 944-7483; http://oldworldwisconsin.wisconsin history.org; a showcase of living history, including a re-created nineteenth-century farming village with teams of oxen and horses and costumed interpreters demonstrating daily work and domestic life of pioneer settlers. There are also trails through native habitats including wetlands, oak woodlands, savanna, and prairie and the opportunity to see sandhill cranes, black terns, and pied-billed grebes, among other birds.

Nordic Trail

Like other hiking areas in Kettle Moraine State Forest, this trail has several paths that braid and crisscross each other as they move through the woods and up and down glacial hills. This hike follows the green loop, which also incorporates some of the other colored loops for parts of the hike. Cross-country skiers find this trail challenging due to the many hills and descents, which make it a workout for hikers as well.

There's a shelter at the trailhead equipped with heaters, which can be a real benefit if you're hiking on colder days. The trailhead is just north of the village of La Grange, which makes it a good jumping-off spot for adventures in the forest.

Start: Trailhead by parking area
Distance: 3.6-mile loop
Hiking time: About 2 hours
Difficulty: Moderate; plenty of short climbs and descents
Trail surface: Dirt
Best seasons: Spring through fall
Canine compatibility: Leashed dogs permitted; but not when trails are groomed for skiing
Land status: State forest
Other trail users: Cross-country skiers
Schedule: Daily, 6 a.m. to 11 p.m.
Maps: USGS Little Prairie, WI; trail map available at trailhead and forest office
Fees and permits: Permit required; available for purchase at a self-pay kiosk at the trailhead or at the forest headquarters and visitor center
Trail contact: Southern Unit Kettle Moraine State Forest Headquarters, S91 W39091 Hwy. 59, Eagle, WI 53119; (262) 594-6200; http://

dnr.wi.gov/org/land/parks/specific/kms/
Special considerations: No hiking permitted when trail is groomed for skiing. Trail is open for hunting on designated dates from Sept through May; contact the forest office for details. It's advisable to wear some bright orange during hunting seasons.
Other: Bicycles not permitted on trail. Restrooms are available at the trailhead and water is available inside the adjacent shelter building.

Finding the trailhead: From Madison, drive east on I-39/90 to exit 163/WI 59, about a 27-mile drive from downtown. Exit I-39/90 and turn right onto WI 59, heading east. Drive 2.8 miles on WI 59 to intersection with County Road N, and turn left. Drive 10.8 miles to Whitewater and intersection with US 12, and turn right onto US 12. Drive 9.2 miles to La Grange and intersection with County Road H, and turn left onto County Road H. Drive 1.5 miles to the turn-off for the Nordic Trail on the right. Turn right and drive into the parking area for the trail. The trailhead is at the far end of the parking lot by the map board and restrooms.
GPS: N42 49.303' / W88 36.024'

In addition to its numerous hiking and skiing options, the Nordic Trail also features a nice steep sledding hill a short walk from the trailhead. Follow the signs or just fall in with the sledders who come out on winter days.

The path moves atop a ridge.

THE HIKE

From the trailhead the hike begins with the path moving over some short, rolling hills, typical of the forest, as it moves into woodland marked by tall pine trees. Endless rows of the tall trunks march off toward the horizon.

As you move along the path, you eventually reach a nice stand of aspen just about where you turn right and head uphill. There are plenty of moraines along this section, their long, low forms marking the landscape. Birds hop in the treetops. Stop and wait to see if you can spot the gray-and-white body of the black-capped chickadee.

After about a mile, you walk briefly atop a ridge with a nice view of a ravine below. Continuing along the path you soon pass a massive, gnarled oak tree and walk along a ridge above a kettle pond. The distinctive small, shallow depressions at times resemble sinkholes; formed by glaciers as they receded north from southern Wisconsin. Some are ponds with water, but many have no water at all.

Moving over some more rolling hills, you can see why this trail is so popular with skiers. The path takes you higher, until you come to an overlook with impressive views, including a view of the kettle pond you passed earlier. There's also a bench here if you want to take a rest and soak up some of the peace and quiet of the forest.

The hills just keep coming, giving your legs and lungs a real workout. The path continues to move through thick oaks and pines, with leaves and acorns strewn across the forest floor and the sweet smell of pine sap in the air.

Winding your way around the last portion of the hike, you should be able to spot some raptors overhead. Listen for their piercing call, which should help you zero in on them as they soar through the sky.

MILES AND DIRECTIONS

0.0 From the trailhead, begin on the path to the left, following the green loop to the north.

0.3 Pass an overgrown track that leads off to the left. Continue walking on the main path as it widens a bit.

0.6 Reach a four-way trail junction and turn right as you continue hiking on the green loop. Walk about 500 feet and begin a descent on the path. You then reach a fork in the path and go right, continuing to hike on the green loop.

0.8 Reach a trail junction atop a hill and turn left, continuing to hike on the green loop.

1.1 Reach a four-way trail junction and go straight on green loop.

1.4   Pass a trail that merges onto the path from the left. Walk about 0.1 mile and reach a fork in the path, where you bear right. Come to another fork and go right again.

2.1   Reach an overlook. Beginning a descent along the path, pass an overgrown spur trail running off to the right. Continue walking on the green loop.

2.4   Pass a path that merges with your path from the left. Continue following the path uphill. Come to a fork and bear right. Walk about 0.2 mile and go left at the fork.

2.8   Pass a path running off to the left, then another path turning off to the right. Reach a trail junction and turn left.

3.3   Follow the path as it turns to the right.

3.6   Arrive back at the trailhead.

HIKE INFORMATION

Local information: Waukesha & Pewaukee Convention and Visitors Bureau, N14 W23755 Stone Ridge Dr., Suite 225, Waukesha; (262) 542-0330 or (800) 366-8474; www.visitwaukesha.org

Local outdoor store: LaGrange General Store, W6098 Highway 12, Whitewater; (608) 495-8600; www.backyardbikes.com; located just south of the forest, at the intersection of US 12 and County Road H (the last turnoff before the parking area for the trail, as noted in Finding the Trailhead). This is a classic outdoor store and cafe with bikes, skis, and snowshoes stacked and ready to be rented, while inside tattooed employees serve up some tasty fresh soups and sandwiches (try the smoked trout!), including several interesting vegetarian options, as well as a full line of coffees to get you energized for your hike. You can also get your bike repaired or tuned up, and there are all sorts of outdoor gear for sale. Staff members are a good source of information and advice on local trails and outdoor recreation spots. The store is a popular gathering spot for hikers, cyclists, and skiers, and definitely not to be missed.

Nordic Trail

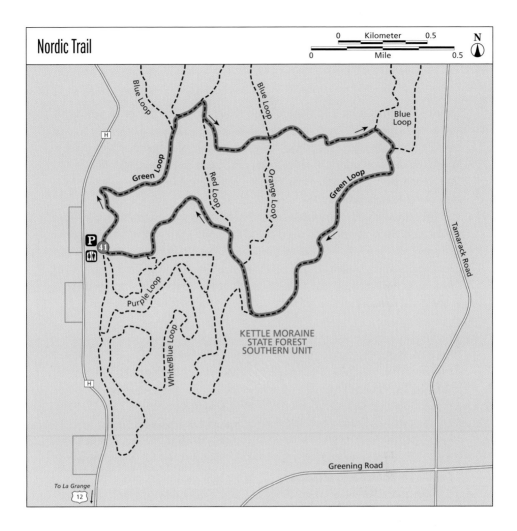

Blue Loop

Blue Loop

Blue Loop

Green Loop

Red Loop

Orange Loop

Green Loop

P

41

Purple Loop

White/Blue Loop

KETTLE MORAINE
STATE FOREST
SOUTHERN UNIT

Tamarack Road

Greening Road

To La Grange

12

H

H

0   Kilometer   0.5

0   Mile   0.5

N

Some of the most scenic and peaceful stretches of woodland can be found on this hike in Kettle Moraine State Forest, with lots of massive pines and other trees along the path. The hiking area, like others in the forest, consists of interlocking paths designated by different colors. The hike follows the trail's green loop, with the Ice Age Trail cutting across its northeast section. An observation loop takes you to a long view over the surrounding valley.

The southern unit of the forest covers 20,000 acres and stretches 30 miles from the village of Dousman at its northern end to the larger town of Whitewater near the southern end. The forest headquarters, which includes a visitor center with maps and a small museum, is located just west of the town of Eagle. This trail is to the north of Eagle, so it's easiest to self-pay for your permit at the trailhead. If you pick up your permit at the headquarters, you'll have to double back to reach the trailhead.

Start: Trailhead by parking area

Distance: 5.4-mile loop

Hiking time: About 3 hours

Difficulty: Moderate; several uphill climbs and descents

Trail surface: Dirt

Best seasons: Spring through fall

Canine compatibility: Leashed dogs permitted; but not when trails are groomed for skiing

Land status: State forest

Other trail users: Cross-country skiers, runners

Fees and permits: Permit required; available for purchase at a self-pay kiosk at the parking area by the trailhead or at the forest headquarters and visitor center

Schedule: Daily, 6 a.m. to 11 p.m.

Maps: USGS Eagle, WI; trail map available from trail contact

Trail contact: Southern Unit Kettle Moraine State Forest Headquarters, S91 W39091 Hwy. 59, Eagle, WI 53119; (262) 594-6200; http://dnr.wi.gov/org/land/parks/specific/kms/

Special considerations: No hiking permitted when trail is groomed for skiing. Trail is open for hunting on designated dates Sept through May; contact the forest office for details. It's advisable to wear some bright orange during hunting seasons.

Other: Restrooms are available at the trailhead; but water availability is sporadic.

Finding the trailhead: From Madison, drive east on I-94 to exit 282/WI 67, about 50 miles from downtown. Exit I-94 and turn right onto WI 67. Drive 9.5 miles on WI 67, passing County Road ZZ on the right, and turn left onto County Road ZZ. Drive 0.5 mile to the entrance to the Scuppernong Trail on the left. The trailhead is to the left of the restroom building and map board. **GPS:** N42 56.454' / W88 27.705'

THE HIKE

From the trailhead, the hike starts out with some awe-inspiring scenery as you walk down a corridor of towering red pines. The trees seem to be in almost perfect symmetry as you walk past. The path grows sandy, with pinecones scuttling across it. Other trees begin to crop up, including some nice black spruce. Squirrels scamper up and down the trunks.

A short climb takes you past a bench and through a large stand of white pine. The stillness along the path is broken only by the occasional birdcall and the thudding sound of runners who utilize this trail.

Soon, maples and northern pin oaks, with their reddish-brown acorns, take the place of the evergreens and bur oaks. But the pine trees soon return, from young saplings to majestic, their high trunks arching overhead.

The pines again thin out as you follow the path as it makes a small climb and walk along a ridge. Along the path is the first crossing of the Ice Age Trail, which cuts across the Scuppernong Trail as it moves through the forest. There are plenty of oaks along this section, with acorns all over the path.

Coming off the ridge the path swings north as you get a quick glimpse of civilization. There's a house or two on the edge of the forest here. You then head up another ridge.

The sky is gorgeous on clear days, with the sun's rays piercing through the treetops. A gradual descent brings you to another stand of pine trees. Then a walk along a flat stretch of path takes you through perhaps the most impressive stand of pines yet; a cathedral of trees, with ferns nipping at the bases of their trunks.

The path continues through more pines as it takes a hard left. There are also some impressive large oaks. Crossing the Ice Age Trail once again, you come to a bench where you can take a rest.

Continuing down the path, you see some smaller red pines, which have large bunches of needles hanging over the path. To the right is a turnoff for the observation loop, where the path goes by some red cedar trees alongside the more prevalent evergreens. Blue and gray jays shoot across the treetops as you come to the overlook, which looks out for miles over the small lakes that dot the surrounding valley.

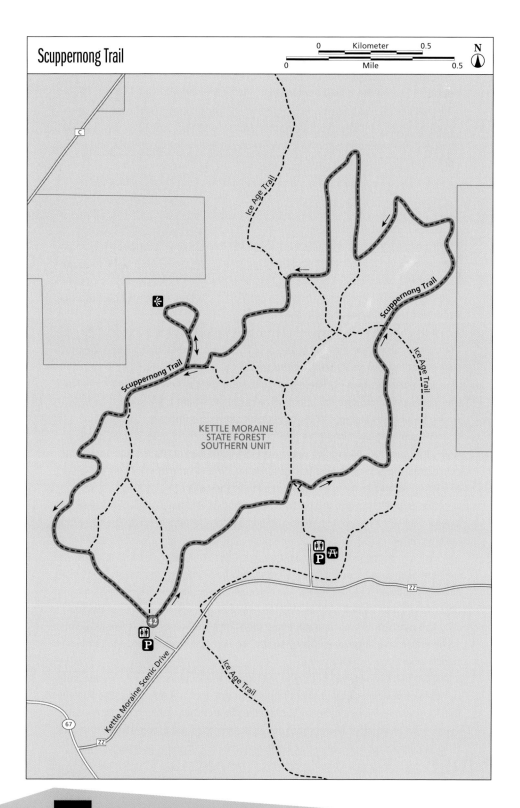

Completing the observation loop, you swing to the right back onto the main path, where there are more cedar trees. The path passes some more overlooks, including a view of a kettle you passed earlier. Then a hard left turn begins the descent, as the path moves over some true roller-coaster hills (just imagine if you were trying to negotiate them on skis!).

The path finally evens out, but not for long, before you hit some more roller-coaster terrain, as you follow steep climbs and drops past balsam firs. Take some time to catch your breath on the final stretch, which will give you the chance to watch for the broad-winged and Cooper's hawks soaring over nearby fields.

MILES AND DIRECTIONS

0.0 From the trailhead follow the path to a three-way junction. Take the path farthest to the right.

A cathedral of pines along the trail.

0.7 Reach another three-way trail junction and take the middle path, as you continue walking on the green loop.

1.5 Cross a path that turns off to the left as you continue walking straight. Just past the crossing, the Ice Age Trail merges in from the left. Walk on the main path as you continue following the green loop.

2.2 Follow the path as it passes by a road that leads to Pinewoods campground. Reach a trail junction and go right. Walk through a corridor of pine trees and reach a fork in the trail. Turn left as you walk past another path veering off to the right.

3.1 Reach the intersection with the Ice Age Trail. Continue walking straight on the path.

3.5 Reach a trail junction. Turn to the right and follow the path. Walk about 300 feet and go right onto a spur trail. This is the observation loop. Walk about 200 feet to a junction and turn right. Come to a scenic overlook, then loop around and head back to the main path, where you veer right back onto the path.

4.3 Reach a trail junction and go to the right, following the path.

5.0 Reach a trail junction and turn to the left. Come to a fork and go to the right. Continue to follow the path.

5.4 Arrive back at the trailhead.

HIKE INFORMATION

Local information: Waukesha & Pewaukee Convention and Visitors Bureau, N14 W23755 Stone Ridge Dr., Suite 225, Waukesha; (262) 542-0330 or (800) 366-8474; www.visitwaukesha.org

Local attraction: The Scuppernong Springs Nature Trail is a 1.5-mile loop that runs through scenic lowlands not far from both the Scuppernong Hiking Trail and Ottawa Lake. The nature trail features a boardwalk running along the Scuppernong River as it runs into Scuppernong Marsh. There are opportunities along the trail to spot great blue herons, kingfishers, and sandhill cranes. The trail begins alongside County Road ZZ to the west of WI 67. It's the opposite turnoff onto County Road ZZ from where you turn to reach the trailhead for the hiking trail.

Kettle View Trail

Lapham Peak, named for a local scientist and naturalist, is the highest point in Waukesha County. At 1,233 feet, it is a typical hill found in the glacier-formed landscape of southeast Wisconsin. Like the rest of Kettle Moraine State Forest and the surrounding terrain, it also features the shallow depressions and long, low hills that give the forest its name.

This hike takes in several color-coded paths that move around the peak and through the surrounding forest, doubling back on the original route and crisscrossing each other several times. On its way back, the path stops by an observation tower atop the hill.

As with other trails in the forest, the Ice Age Trail runs through the area. There are plenty of warblers and thrushes along the paths, and spring and fall bring large numbers of hawks on their annual migrations.

Start: Trailhead at parking area
Distance: 5.6-mile loop
Hiking time: About 3 hours
Difficulty: Moderate; some steep climbs and descents
Trail surface: Dirt
Best seasons: Spring through fall
Canine compatibility: Leashed dogs permitted; but not when trail is groomed for skiing
Land status: State forest
Other trail users: Cross-country skiers
Fees and permits: Permit required; available for purchase at a self-pay kiosk at the entrance
Schedule: Daily, 7 a.m. to 9 p.m. spring through fall; daily, 7 a.m. to 10 p.m. in winter
Maps: USGS Oconomowoc East, WI; trail map available from trail contact
Trail contact: Kettle Moraine State Forest, Lapham Peak Unit, W329 N846 County Road C, Delafield, WI 53018; (262) 646-3025; http://dnr.wi.gov/org/land/parks/specific/lapham/
Special considerations: Hiking not permitted when trail is groomed for cross-country skiing
Other: There is a very nice shelter at the parking area with restrooms, water sources, and a wood-burning stove.

Finding the trailhead: From Madison, drive east on I-94 to exit 285/County Road C, about 53 miles from downtown. Exit the highway and turn right onto County Road C, heading south. Drive 0.8 mile and turn left onto the road into Lapham Peak Unit of Kettle Moraine State Forest. After paying for a permit at the self-pay kiosk, follow the road into the park. Take the first right and drive to Evergreen Grove parking area. The hike begins behind the map board to the left as you pull into the parking area (the shelter is on the other side of the parking area).

GPS: N43 02.425' / W88 24.162'

THE HIKE

From the trailhead there is a small pond to the left behind a cluster of evergreens, including some nice red pines. Climbing a small rise, you pass a small amphitheater on the left, then make a right turn. Evergreens, primarily hemlock, stretch alongside the path into the distance.

A trio of pine trees stand at the edge of an open field, and the path is soon moving through a prairie landscape studded with huge oaks. The largely open skies along this section make for prime viewing spots for red-tailed hawks, who build nests high up in the oak trees. Cooper's hawk, great horned owl, and screech owl also compete for hunting in this area, swooping down over the wide open spaces.

There's a stand of aspen to the left of the path, while off to the right are makeshift stone walls, the result of efforts by early farmers to remove glacial stones, which were deposited on the landscape by freezing and thawing and then left behind when glaciers receded.

Continuing down the path, there's a thick row of cedar trees that blocks the sight, if not the sound, of traffic on County Road C. Then a left turn brings you past some sweet-smelling pines and hemlocks.

The climb that begins up the hill on the south side of the trail is known as the Gut Buster, and it's aptly named. Fortunately there's a bench near the top where you can stop and rest. It's also a nice spot to look for blue jays hopping from tree to tree. Once at the top of the hill, take a moment to watch for hawks, then begin the descent known as the Big Valley. There are some nice fall leaf colors as you head downhill.

As you come up on the stretch of path known as Pete's Pass, note the deep depression to the right. It's probably the most complete and perfectly formed kettle you'll see on any hike in the forest. Moving on there are red pines on the left and aspen on the right as the path levels out, then takes a small dip through an area known as Subdivision Hill (though there are no houses to be seen, save one or two well in the distance).

There are some black spruce along the path as you pass a hole to the left big enough to hold a large boulder. It's the remains of a root cellar, part of a pioneer's cabin from the 1830s. On the opposite side of the path is a pond that served as a watering hole for cattle, and today is home to ducks, frogs, and red-winged blackbirds.

Another kettle looms on the right, set amidst many oak trees. You soon come to Homestead Hollow, just off the park road. Here there is a 1.5-mile stretch of nature trail, along the path, that runs through a microcosm of local landscapes, including a meadow, pine, and spruce plantation and prairie, as well as a small butterfly garden.

Moving back roughly parallel to the route you followed earlier, you hit some roller-coaster-type hills, eventually arriving at the observation tower. Climb up it to get a good view of the surrounding countryside. The descent just past the tower is known as the Big Slide. Make sure you have steady footing before you head down it!

Look for crows as you move along the path. They're easy to spot in the stand of aspen on the right. The pileated woodpecker and Cooper's hawk can be seen as well. A short climb and sharp left turn brings you to what's known as the Magic Carpet Ride, a modest hill for the final half mile of the hike.

Fall colors along the trail.

Kettle View Trail

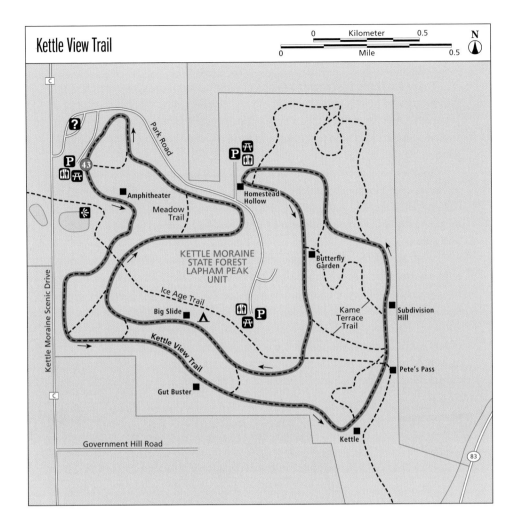

Alternate route: The main road through the park leads to the observation tower, so you can drive there if you don't feel like doing a hike but would still like to climb the tower. There is also an extensive mountain bike trail on the west side of County Road C.

MILES AND DIRECTIONS

0.0   From the trailhead turn right onto the path.

0.3   Reach a trail junction and go right. Walk about 0.1 mile and cross the Ice Age Trail. Continue walking straight on the path.

0.9 Walk past a path that branches off to the left as you continue walking straight. Walk about 0.2 mile and pass another path branching off to the left. Continue walking straight as the path begins to head uphill.

1.4 At the top of a hill, reach a four-way trail junction and continue walking straight. Walk about 0.1 mile and pass a path running off to the left. Continue walking straight, following the path downhill.

1.9 Reach a path that turns off to the left and continue to walk straight. Walk about 0.2 mile and come to a five-way trail junction and continue walking straight. Less than 0.1 mile farther, the path dovetails with a path from the left. Follow this conjoined path as it goes to the right.

2.3 Reach a fork in the trail and bear right. As you begin a descent, you pass a break in the tree line to the left. After about 0.1 mile, pass a spur trail leading to the right. Continue walking straight and pass a spur trail running off to the right.

2.6 Reach a fork in the path and bear left. Just past the fork, walk past two paths turning to the right. Stay on the path as it turns to the right.

3.0 Reach a trail junction just before you arrive at the area known as Homestead Hollow. There are restrooms and a shelter here. Turn left and then left again. Walk along a dirt and grass path. After about 0.2 mile, you climb a hill. At the top of the hill, the path dovetails with a path coming in from the right.

3.3 Reach a trail intersection with the trail's butterfly garden on the left. Continue walking straight on the path. Walk 0.2 mile and reach a four-way trail junction. Continue walking straight.

3.6 Reach a junction with the Ice Age Trail. Continue walking straight.

3.9 Reach the peak's observation tower. After climbing the tower, return to the path. Come to a fork in the trail and take the right fork. Just past the fork is a trail junction. Continue walking straight, heading downhill.

4.3 Pass a path leading off to the left. It goes to the path you walked earlier on the hike. Continue walking straight. Walk about 0.2 mile and reach a trail junction. Turn right.

4.7 Follow the path as it turns right and merges with a path coming in from the left. Walk about 500 feet and pass a path running to the left. Continue walking straight.

5.1 Follow the path up a hill. Reach a fork in the trail and bear left. Immediately past this fork, reach another fork and bear left again.

5.3 Reach a trail junction and veer right, then walk the final 0.3 mile toward the trailhead, passing by two paths to the left along the way. Turn left within sight of the trailhead and parking area.

5.6 Arrive back at the trailhead.

HIKE INFORMATION

Local information: Waukesha & Pewaukee Convention and Visitors Bureau, N14 W23755 Stone Ridge Dr., Suite 225, Waukesha; (262) 542-0330 or (800) 366-8474; www.visitwaukesha.org

Organization: Friends of Lapham Peak; www.laphampeakfriends.org; lots of information about trails and activities in the park

An autumnal scene along the trail.

Honorable Mentions

Ice Age National Scenic Trail

Stretching across Wisconsin in a lazy backward S-curve that roughly parallels the extent of the last glaciation in Wisconsin, the Ice Age Trail also skirts past many of the hikes in the book, and is worth hiking in its own right. Like the Appalachian and Pacific Coast Trails, the Ice Age is a national scenic trail, and takes in the wide variety of landscapes across the state.

Currently, only about 600 of the trail's planned 1,200 miles have been completed, with the path following yellow blazes along farm fields and through wilderness. The trail winds past Devil's Lake and Kettle Moraine, where it takes in some good views of the glacial features that can be seen throughout the forest. The section through Kettle Moraine also has backpacking shelters for hikers who wish to make a multi-day hike along the trail. Accommodations are available for hikers on the trail in other parts of the state as well.

The Ice Age Trail intersects trails including the Badger State Trail and the junction of the Capital City State Trail and Military Ridge Trail, and runs congruent with the Sugar River Trail (see below). You can also find some nice stretches near Portage in Columbia County, where the trail runs through some marshy lowland landscapes.

The trail is overseen by both the National Park Service and Wisconsin Department of Natural Resources. A good deal of trail maintenance is done by volunteers. The Ice Age Trail Alliance serves as a clearinghouse of information about the trail, including providing maps and guides for sale. With so much of the trail not yet completed, it's important to have a good idea of the route you wish to follow, and thus a good map is essential.

Ice Age Trail Alliance, 2110 Main St., Cross Plains, WI 53528; (800) 227-0046; www.iceagetrail.org.

Military Ridge Trail

This 40-mile hiking-and-cycling trail runs 40 miles between Dodgeville and Fitchburg, following an old railroad bed. The eastern terminus of the trail is near the western end of the Capital City State Trail (hike 9), and can be reached by following the directions to the parking area for that hike, then walking to the west on the Capital City State Trail to the self-pay kiosk at Verona Road/US 18/151.

The trail begins as a paved path, but then switches over to crushed limestone as it moves away from Madison and into the countryside. The trail meanders through the Sugar River Valley and passes through several towns in the Driftless Area, including Mount Horeb and Blue Mounds, and comes near Governor Dodge State Park as it winds through Dodgeville.

Military Ridge State Trail, 4350 Mounds Park Rd., PO Box 98, Blue Mounds, WI 53517; (608) 437-7393; http://dnr.wi.gov/org/land/parks/specific/militaryridge.

Friends of the Military Ridge Trail, PO Box 373, Mt. Horeb, WI 53572; www.militaryridge-trail.org.

Sugar River State Trail

This trail, which for part of its length is part of the Ice Age Trail, can be picked up by walking north away from the path at the north end of New Glarus Woods State Park. An easier starting point is the trail headquarters at the restored train depot in the town of New Glarus. From here, the trail runs 23 miles along Ward Creek, the Little Sugar River and, eventually, the Sugar River. It passes through the towns of Monticello and Albany before finally reaching its southern terminus at Brodhead.

This is another rails-to-trails conversion, and includes fourteen trestle bridges, including a replica covered bridge. Along the way, it takes in landscapes that include prairie, meadow, woods, and farmland.

Wisconsin Department of Natural Resources, Green County Work Unit, PO Box 805, W540 CTH NN, New Glarus, WI 53574-0805; (608) 527-2334; http://dnr.wi.gov/org/land/parks/specific/sugarriver.

Clubs and Trail Groups

Badger Trails, PO Box 210615, Milwaukee, WI 53221; (414) 777-3920; www
.badgertrails.org

Ice Age Trail Alliance, 2110 Main St., Cross Plains, WI 53528; (608) 798-4453 or
(800) 227-0046; www.iceagetrail.org

Wisconsin Go Hiking Club, (414) 299-9285; http://wisconsingohiking
.homestead.com/

Wisconsin Hoofers Outing Club, 800 Langdon St., Madison, WI 53706; (608)
262-1630; www.hooferouting.org

In addition, many individual hikes in the book list trail groups composed of volunteers who are involved with maintaining and promoting trails.

Further Reading

As one of America's great hiking states, there is no shortage of information on Wisconsin's hiking opportunities and natural environment.

Ecology and Conservation

Birmingham, Robert A. *Spirits of Earth: The Effigy Mound Landscape of Madison and the Four Lakes*. Madison: University of Wisconsin Press, 2009.

Buchholz, James. *Wild Wisconsin Notebook*. Black Earth, WI: Prairie Oak Press, 2001.

Leopold, Aldo. *A Sand County Almanac and Sketches Here and There*. New York/Oxford: Oxford University Press, 1949.

Hiking and Travel Guides

Brown, Harriet, and Young, Jamie. *Madison Walks*. Madison: Jones Books, 2003.

Crawford, Robert F. *Walking Trails of Southern Wisconsin*. Madison: University of Wisconsin Press, 2000.

Dillon, Pat, and Diebel, Lynne. *Green Travel Guide to Southern Wisconsin*. Madison: University of Wisconsin Press, 2010.

Hansen, Eric. *Hiking Wisconsin*. Guilford, CT: Globe Pequot Press, 2002.

Morgan, John and Ellen. *50 Hikes in Wisconsin*. Woodstock, VT: Back Country Guides, 2004.

Revolinski, Kevin. *60 Hikes Within 60 Miles: Madison*. Birmingham, AL: Menasha Ridge Press, 2008.

Local History

Levitan, Stuart D. *Madison: The Illustrated Sesquicentennial History, Volume 1, 1856–1931*. Madison: University of Wisconsin Press, 2006.

Mollenhoff, David V. *Madison: A History of the Formative Years*. Madison: University of Wisconsin Press, 2003.

Hike Index

Wisconsin provides wonderful hiking opportunities with plenty of varied terrain, perfect for all skill levels.

About the Author

Michael Ream is a travel writer and a lifelong avid hiker. Since his parents first took him onto a trail in California at the age of two, he has hiked throughout the United States as well as in Africa and South America, where he trekked through the Sahara Desert and the Bolivian Andes, respectively. He is the author of *Best Easy Day Hikes: Lincoln and Omaha* and *Best Easy Day Hikes: Des Moines,* both available from FalconGuides, and has contributed to publications including South *American Explorer, Saveur,* and *Southern Traveler.* He has also written guidebooks about Iowa, the Smoky Mountains, the Arkansas and Missouri Ozarks, Texas, and Mississippi, and for newspapers in Illinois, Mississippi, and Arkansas. A native of Chicago, he earned a master's degree in journalism from the Medill School of Journalism at Northwestern University. He lives in Des Moines, Iowa, with his family.

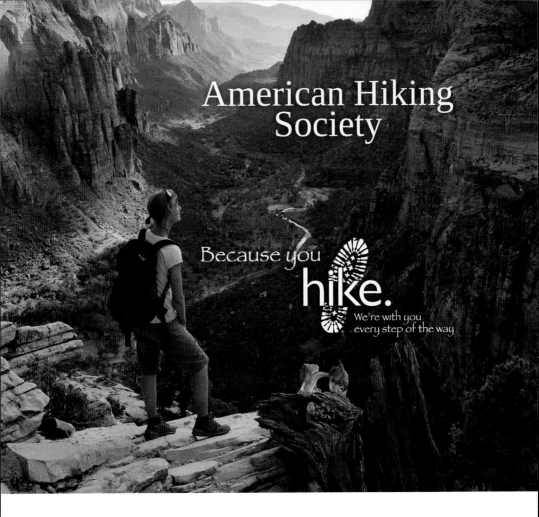

American Hiking Society

Because you **hike.**

We're with you every step of the way

As a national voice for hikers, **American Hiking Society** works every day:

- Building and maintaining hiking trails
- Educating and supporting hikers by providing information and resources
- Supporting hiking and trail organizations nationwide
- Speaking for hikers in the halls of Congress and with federal land managers

Whether you're a casual hiker or a seasoned backpacker, become a member of American Hiking Society and join the national hiking community! You'll enjoy great member benefits and help preserve the nation's hiking trails, so tomorrow's hike is even better than today's. We invite you to join us now!

American Hiking Society

www.AmericanHiking.org • info@AmericanHiking.org